N & W: Giant of Steam

I dedicate this book to my father

MELVILLE LEWIS JEFFRIES

whose journalistic touch enabled this work to come alive. I offer my heartfelt gratitude for his unselfish editing of the complete text.

N & W:

Giant of Steam

By

Major Lewis Ingles Jeffries

PRUETT **P** PUBLISHING COMPANY
Boulder, Colorado

Library of Congress Cataloging in Publication Data

Jeffries, Lewis I.   1942-
   Norfolk and Western.

   Bibliography: p.
   1. Norfolk and Western Railway. I. Title.
TF25.N77J43   385'.0975   79-23925
ISBN 0-87108-547-0

First Edition

2 3 4 5 6 7 8 9

Printed in the United States of America

ISBN 0-87108-547-X

Acknowledgements

The author felt that this story should be told while the information was available and while he was close enough to the source of information to research the topic adequately.

When the author was a young boy growing up in Radford, Virginia, he spent hours sitting by the N&W tracks watching road, yard and branch line steam power. His was a growing fascination for these mechanical marvels. He saw the demise of steam at the age of seventeen, and not until years later did he study locomotive engineering in general and N&W steam in particular. He then plunged headlong into the two-pronged project of research and writing. The resulting interviews fueled the author's enthusiasm and put a bright crusading torch to his conviction that N&W steam is a story that should, even must, be told.

Furthermore, his convictions were strengthened as regards the outstanding performance and sound engineering of the N&W steam locomotives and their operation. Above all, the N&W personnel associated with the steam era, whom the author interviewed, were men of topmost talent and dedication—men of a worthy profession who were center stage in a drama of accomplishment.

No in-depth work of this dimension would have been possible without the help of many who cheerfully and unhesitatingly offered their own records and their knowledge in this labor of love. They are: George P. Bowman, retired general foreman, Shaffers Crossing terminal; D. J. Barton, assistant engineer locomotive design; the late Walter Budwell, retired master mechanic, Norfolk Division; Carl G. Carbaugh, engineer materials; H. Earl Cash, former locomotive fireman; H. E. Dearing, senior engineer construction; John W. Fox, Jr., assistant superintendent, Radford Division; John A. Gearhart, retired superintendent, Roanoke Shops; Voyce C. Glaze, retired mechanical engineer; the late Thomas L. Gravatt, retired yardmaster, Radford Yards; G. S. Hamilton, shop engineer; P. C. Housman, retired assistant foreman, Roanoke Shops; George H. Kelch, retired from N&W and a former U.S. government railroad inspector; Gurdon P. McGavock, retired mechanical engineer; Frank C. Miller, engineer locomotive design; Louis M. Newton, assistant general manager, transportation; Frank C. Noel, retired tool supervisor, motive power and equipment; A. L. Overstreet, manager photographic services; Charles S. Patton, retired general manager, motive power and equipment; Lewis M. Phelps, director of public relations and advertising; the late Francis D. "Bud" Ripley, retired general foreman, Radford Shops; William T. Ross, retired assistant vice-president, executive department; Hobart L. Scott, Jr., general manager, motive power and equipment; Howard G. Stultz, locomotive engineer; N. H. "Hub" Tanner, retired locomotive engineer; and Payton B. Winfree, retired director of public relations.

I am deeply indebted to the following persons for their helpfulness in this endeavor, much of which was offered while the author had moved to another region of the country and overseas. They are: Robert B. Claytor, executive vice-president, and his assistant, Sidney F. Robertson, both of whom fully supported the project; Arthur M. Bixby, Sr., historian of the Roanoke Chapter of the National Railway Historical Society and curator of the Roanoke Transportation Museum, who researched extensively and provided essential information for me before and after my departure from the Roanoke area; Clarence E. Pond, retired general manager, motive power and equipment, whose personal knowledge and records were invaluable; Robert M. Pilcher, retired engineer of tests, who spent many hours providing data and editing the text on the compound Mallet; and Mark W. Faville, retired shop engineer, for providing endless personal documents on the N&W power and, in particular, the proposed Class Y7.

Finally, a sincere thanks to my family for the sacrifices they have endured while I was researching and "putting it all together." Without the loving support of my dear wife, Mary Ann, this project would not have been undertaken, for it caused me to be away no little bit from her and my children, Jennie and John.

Robert B. Claytor, Executive Vice-President, Norfolk & Western Railway Company. *Courtesy N&W.*

Foreword

For over a century after the birth of the railroad industry, the reciprocating steam locomotive was its dominant form of motive power. Indeed, the railroads and the steam locomotive developed and prospered together, with steam being the undisputed form of power from the late 1820s until about the time of World War II. Steam power was usually custom built to perform a particular task, and in many cases a railroad's locomotives became its trademark.

As railroads expanded, a number of locomotive manufacturers sprang up during the latter half of the nineteenth century to supply power to a rapidly growing industry. In addition, some of the carriers elected to construct their own power in their system shops. Notable among the roads that took such a course, and one of the few in the South, was Norfolk and Western Railway Company (N&W), whose locomotives are the subject of this volume by Major Jeffries. Although N&W in the steam era was a comparatively small regional carrier, its contribution to the era of the steam locomotives was considerably out of proportion to its size.

The rich coalfields served by N&W are located in the rugged mountain territory of southern West Virginia, southwestern Virginia and eastern Kentucky. The combination of heavy coal tonnage and steep mountain grades meant that the railroad needed to equip itself accordingly, and its locomotives, almost from the very beginning, were designed to produce maximum drawbar pull with the highest degree of efficiency. As the railroad developed into a prosperous coal and merchandise hauler, its physical plant was upgraded to accommodate heavier rolling stock, and the size of its locomotives increased correspondingly.

As time went on, N&W experimented, developed, refined and tinkered, sometimes through trial and error processes, until it found the locomotives best suited to its needs. For a number of years, N&W purchased some of its power from outside manufacturers, while at the same time it was building other locomotives in its own shops. Those shops were an outgrowth of an organization known as the Roanoke Machine Works, established in 1884 in its namesake city in Virginia about the time that the road's headquarters were established there.

Through the years the locomotives produced in Roanoke Shops found increasing favor with the railroad, so that during the last quarter century of the steam era N&W did not buy a single new reciprocating steam locomotive from an outside builder. During those years the company concentrated its efforts on refining the basic steam locomotive to suit its own needs. It produced three principal types of company designed road locomotives and later added a fourth type of switching locomotive that ironically was not of its own design.

With an emphasis on tonnage hauling capability, N&W locomotives generally had what some would consider a rather austere outward appearance. Except for classes of power assigned primarily to passenger service, they were painted black and were usually completely lacking in ornamentation, except for the road's name and engine number. If they were short on glamour, they were not short on tractive effort since N&W locomotives hauled some of the heaviest trains in the world. As a further consideration, N&W locomotives were a special source of pride to N&W people of all ranks, who could look upon them as "their own" engines.

In this book Major Jeffries follows the development of N&W locomotives along with the railroad itself. He traces the evolution of power from the hand-fired engines of the late 1800s through the early part of the twentieth century to the peak of N&W steam power development in the early 1950s. He follows the development of the Mallet compound design into the fleet of one hundred modern Y5 and Y6 "workhorses" that formed the backbone of the N&W motive power roster.

The Mallet compound, of course, was not an original N&W idea. In fact, it was not even an

American idea, having first been introduced in Europe, but N&W took the basic design and carried it through to its highest degree of development. After most other railroads had abandoned the Mallet compound, and even after some of them had completely discarded the steam locomotive, the N&W Roanoke Shops were still building modern "workhorses" in Roanoke.

The author also describes the Class A, four-cylinder simple articulated locomotives introduced in the mid-1930s, which many locomotive enthusiasts believe, pound-for-pound, were the finest steam locomotives ever built. In addition, he gives appropriate attention to N&Ws one great gesture toward elegance, the Class J streamlined passenger locomotives introduced in 1941. The streamlining, which was subdued and in good taste, did nothing to detract from the Js tremendous weight, tractive effort and speed capabilities, and N&W fans agree that the Js were the apex of steam passenger locomotive development.

Major Jeffries does not omit the Class S 1a switchers, which included the last steam locomotive built for service by a major American railroad. Nor does he overlook N&Ws electrification project in the Pocahontas coalfields, which maintained the carrier's dependence on coal by using energy generated in a coal-fired power plant.

Through the years, Norfolk and Western's locomotives reflected the characteristics of their owner. Like the railroad, they were rugged, solid, conservative and efficient, lacking in frills, but of sound and proven design. Further reflecting the character of their owner, they were paid for in cash, rather than the present method used by most railroads of issuing equipment obligations to finance locomotive acquisitions.

Those who saw N&W steam in action will never forget the sights and sounds of, say, a Class A leaving Williamson, West Virginia, with 190 loads of coal on a nonstop run to Portsmouth, Ohio, or a Class J, with seemingly little effort, moving "The Pocahontas" along the New River in Virginia. Such sights and sounds, of course, have now passed into history, but the reader has an opportunity to learn of the power behind them in this book in which Major Jeffries very capably describes the contributions made to the age of steam by the carrier that remained loyal to that form of power longer than any other major American railroad.

Robert B. Claytor
Roanoke, Va.

Contents

Prologue

Norfolk and Western—The Giant of Steam, is a book about a great railroad and in particular its steam motive power. This railroad possessed then—as it does now—an intangible sense of great pride, for it is in reality a landmark of the American free enterprise system. This book can best be summed up in the words of Clarence E. Pond, retired N&W general manager, motive power and equipment: "It is a story of vision, of human effort toward that dream and of accomplishment. The facts speak for themselves."

Because of the heavy tonnages moved and the rugged profile of the N&W, its locomotives have long been synonymous with power. The N&W was an early user of Mallet locomotives, which were capable of moving heavy tonnage trains by brute force. The Mallet remained as one of the primary locomotive types for freight operations to the end of N&W steam. For the last two decades of steam, the railway developed just three basic designs for its main line work, both freight and passenger. To move the heavy freight over the mountains, the 2-8-8-2 Mallet was improved upon until it represented the final development of the Mallet in America and was ideal for the work assigned to it.

For the more level portions of the system, the four cylinder, single expansion articulated was the primary power for time freights, coal and empty hopper trains. These 2-6-6-4s were labelled

To move heavy freight over the mountains, the 2-8-8-2 Mallet was improved upon until it represented the final development of the Mallet in America; it was ideal for the work assigned to it. *Courtesy Harold K. Vollrath.*

1

On more level portions of the system, the four-cylinder, single expansion articulated was the primary power for the time freights, coal trains, and empty hopper trains. These 2-6-6-4s pulled an occasional passenger train, but most of their mileage was in freight service. *Courtesy Earl Palmer.*

The mechanically superb, streamlined 4-8-4s regularly handled 15 to 16 cars on grades up to 1.4% and then could run at or near 100 mph on the flatter portions of the railway. The streamlining scheme was considered by many the "most tasteful." *Courtesy C. W. Jernstrom.*

N&W employees' pride in "their" products at work cannot be overstated. This feeling, though enhanced by many factors, was anchored by the great performances these locomotives turned in. *Courtesy N&W.*

"dual service" machines since they occasionally wheeled heavy passenger trains. Most of their mileage, however, was in freight service.

As for a passenger locomotive, the N&Ws famed streamlined 4-8-4s could be termed the most versatile passenger power ever. They regularly handled fifteen to sixteen cars on grades up to 1.4 percent and then would run at or near one hundred miles per hour on the flatter portions of the railway. Mechanically, they were superb. They achieved outstanding levels of availability going frequently from one monthly inspection to the next without missing a regular assignment. The streamlining was considered by many the "most tasteful" in this country and perhaps in any country. The scheme was not carried to extremes, so these locomotives retained the essential contours of steam power.

Although these three great classes of road power were strictly N&W in design and appearance, there was something more that set them apart. First, the N&W steam power was designed and constructed in the company's own Roanoke Shops. After 1927, the N&W never bought any new reciprocating steam locomotives from private builders. The sense of pride that employees had for their products at work cannot be overstated. This feeling of pride, though enhanced by many factors, was anchored to the great performances these locomotives turned in. Second, the N&W steam power was serviced and maintained in the most modern facilities and shops. This increased their availability because the locomotives were designed to run long distances with a minimum of attention for lubrication, servicing and shopping. Third, the N&W had a superb physical plant for its steam locomotives. In certain respects, steam power is about as good as the track it runs on. N&W steam power had few restrictions from right of way conditions or supporting systems. Last, the Norfolk and Western had in operation a large fleet of modern steam locomotives that was more than half of the railway's total locomotive roster in the mid-fifties. These modern steam "iron horses" performed most of the work on the system. They handled virtually all of the main line and even some of the branch line trains.

The Norfolk and Western was committed to steam longer than any other major U.S. railroad. It vigorously championed the coal-burning locomotive to the very end. Why? Because back in many hollows, hoppers were loaded with bituminous coal and these same hoppers were made up into heavy trains that followed the valleys and rivers, crossed mountains and coursed rolling hills in their trek from mine to market. This day-to-day ritual was the N&Ws main source of revenue, so the railway wanted to do what it could to promote the coal industry, and thereby insure its own profits. N&W steam power was "modern" in every way, and the company harbored the claim that the steam locomotive could compete with the diesel—and then proved it. For many years the company's operating records and profits provided the clincher.

The N&W invested heavily in the coal-burning experimentals before the arrival of the diesel, but this effort was a little late to perfect the technology needed. Finally, the diesel arrived to stay. The N&W acquired the most modern diesel fleet in the nation at the time and operated it in a manner that was just as professional as that accorded to the steam fleet.

Keep in mind, if you will, that this book deals with the motive power of the Norfolk and Western and that motive power policies are dictated by the operating conditions of the railroad. This story tells of the history and operating conditions of the N&W and why a certain type or class of power came into existence. Furthermore, to appreciate fully the motive power of this great railroad, it is necessary to have an understanding of the philosophy that was developed when Roanoke produced its own power. Specifically, this saga spans the years from 1896, when the present railway company came into existence, until the 1964 merger, when the railroad was expanded into a major eastern carrier. After 1964, the N&W developed a new, somewhat different character—but that is another story in itself!

For the rail fan, an abundance of pictures depict the N&W and its mighty locomotives. The text is for the historian, the rail student and the mechanical engineer. Thus, there is much for all to enjoy. However, the main intention of the author is to put on record what this extraordinary railroad accomplished. The railway having destroyed most of its records of the steam era, this information was available mainly from the memory and personal records of those men who actually worked the steam power. This book, then, is a tribute to these N&W men "of vision . . . and of accomplishment."

Yes, the Norfolk and Western was indeed the Giant of Steam. It attained that splendid stature because of the efforts of all members of the N&W railway family! It was also U.S. standard railroading at its best.

Part 1

The Railway

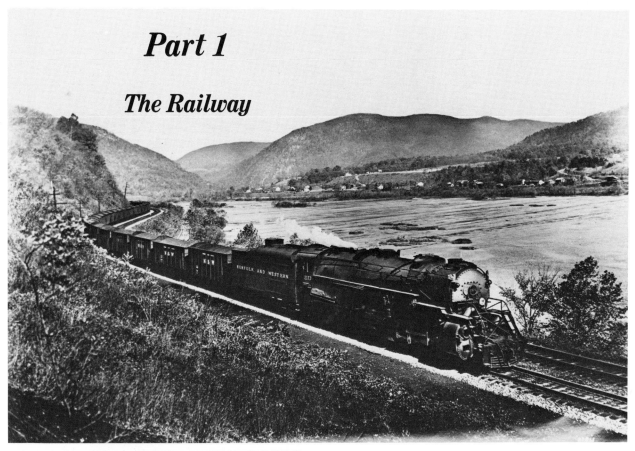

TRAINLOAD OF COAL ALONG THE NEW RIVER

This famous picture depicts the steam era N&W—its motive power, freight traffic, and operating conditions. The giant homebuilt Mallet was unsurpassed in economy, power, and reliability, and the type formed the backbone of N&W's steam motive power. Bituminous coal was the primary freight commodity and source of revenue; and, the setting indicates a well maintained railway operating in mountainous territory. Moving these heavy trains on this hilly railroad dictated motive power policy. As for the future era N&W, the railway would merge with the Virginian, whose tracks are across the New River. After that merger, more than motive power would change. *Courtesy C. W. Jernstrom.*

To study a railroad's motive power is a rewarding experience to the rail student and fan alike. But to appreciate fully that road's motive power and how well it performed can only be gained by a look into the railway itself and the operating climate the locomotives worked in. The N&W operated remarkable steam locomotives that achieved some very commendable records. However, these records were not a result of the motive power alone. The Norfolk and Western had many unique characteristics that set it apart from other railroads, and these qualities had a great effect on the design, construction and operation of its home produced steam power.

Specifically, bituminous coal became the predominant traffic on a previously noncoal carrying railroad. Furthermore, the N&W operated heavy trains over three mountain ranges and other varying terrain. Probably the most unique feature of N&W steam was its steam servicing facilities—an asset that helped bring about high locomotive availability and minimized servicing time. These same steam locomotives had been designed and constructed in the railway's own Roanoke Shops. Thus, a design philosophy developed, and an overview of the N&Ws version of locomotive engineering shows vividly that sound engineering made its steam competitive with other types of motive power for years. This progressive, well-managed, well-maintained railroad applied proven engineering principles and achieved an efficiency of operation that enabled its motive power to attain many record-breaking feats. A background look into the Norfolk and Western gives one a fine appreciation of its steam power and its accomplishments.

5

Background History

It would be logical to assume that a railroad is built by constructing a main line between two important areas or points, with branch lines being extended to other places where business beckoned. In almost all cases, this was not the way it was done. Usually many smaller railroads merged to form the present, modern systems. The Norfolk and Western was no exception. Conceiving and building the modern N&W entailed a series of struggles that spanned more than sixty years. More than a score of railroads were eventually in the network that made up the N&W in the steam era. Their building had been accomplished as a variety of independent projects, nearly all of which faced two dilemmas: the unique engineering problems of their time and strictly limited capital.

First forerunner of the N&W was the nine-mile City Point Rail Road, incorporated in 1836 and completed from the James River to Petersburg in

The *George Washington* was identical to two locomotives bought by the City Point Rail Road, the beginning of the present N&W. The two 7½-ton engines, named "Powhatan" and "Pocahontas," were considered the best then obtainable and were built by William Norris of Philadelphia, a famed pioneer engine builder. The City Point's first train for revenue service ran on September 7, 1838. *Courtesy N&W.*

FIRST LINE TO THE COALFIELDS

In 1886 a passenger train prepares to leave West Radford on the new main line down New River westward. The New River line was completed in 1883 so the predecessor N&W Railroad could tap the rich Pocahontas coalfields, thus literally changing the character of the railroad. The formative years of the N&W had many tribulations, but the outcome of those years is still felt today. Yet changes have occurred. The curved bridge at the right is long gone, since the New River line, which began at Radford, was relocated five miles north to Walton in 1900. The stone piers of this bridge still stand today. The other bridge remains in use on the Bristol line, which was part of one of the N&W's four original predecessor systems. The rich history of the Norfolk & Western dates back to 1838. *Courtesy N&W.*

1838. This provided Petersburg with a link to the Port of City Point, with boat connections to Norfolk and Baltimore. It was the beginning of the Norfolk and Western.

Logically, tracklayers would move west from Petersburg or west from Norfolk to Petersburg. Actually, the next planning for a railroad took place in Lynchburg, a town on the James River some one hundred and fifty winding miles from Richmond. Lynchburg was a seaport at the time, for mule powered boats were plying the new canal to and from Richmond, so the citizens saw little need for rail connections from the east. They envisioned a rail route across the mountains to connect the James River canal with the northward-flowing New River, thus opening a "quick" trade route via Lynchburg to the Middle West. After the New River had been declared unfit for navigation, Lynchburgers harbored the idea of making a real overland route to connect eventually with the Mississippi River region. Then they did something about it. The "Virginia and Tennessee" (V&T) was chartered in 1848 and construction began in 1850.

The building of the V&T was a truly outstanding feat of its time. This herculean task was accomplished without accurate maps, with no earth

7

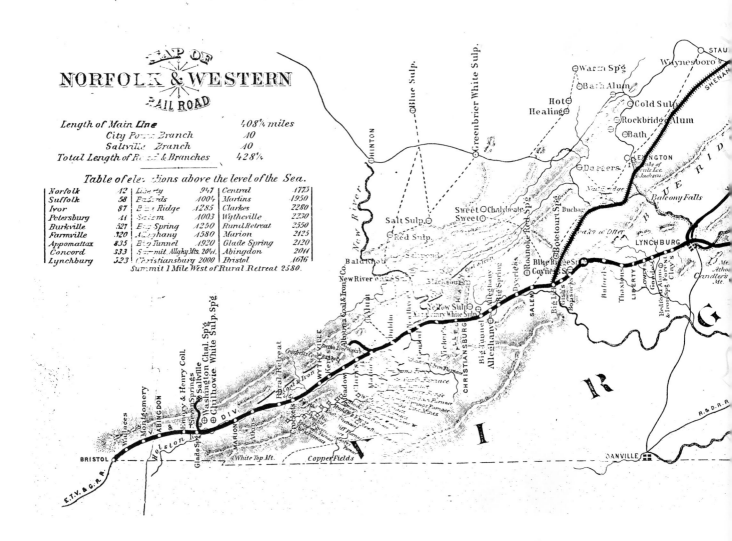

This old 1883 map depicts the predecessor N&W Railroad that linked Norfolk with Bristol. Later in the decade a line would extend along the New River to tap the rich Pocahontas coalfields. The New River line eventually reached the Ohio Valley, opening the heartland of America to Pocahontas coal. *Courtesy N&W.*

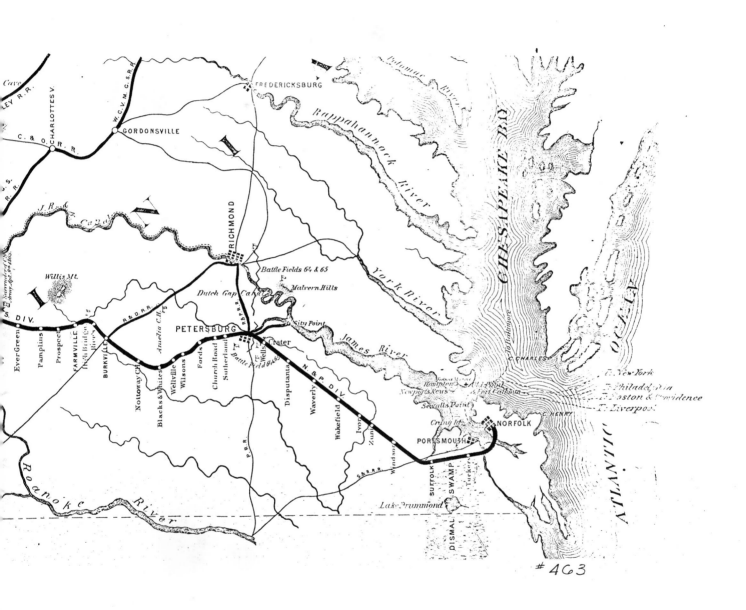

#463

9

moving machinery, no railroad connections, and no pattern of mountain railroad building to go by. And this was all done before the invention of dynamite. The line, with its sharp cuts, its fills, its tunnels and trestles, was forged with black powder, men, mules and sweat. The V&T crossed the Blue Ridge, surmounted the eastern continental divide and pushed on to the new town of Bristol in 1856. The next year a connecting line from Knoxville reached Bristol, and this link completed the first all-rail route from New York to New Orleans. Until the transcontinental lines were built, it was the quickest way to travel and ship to California via the narrow isthmus of Panama.

This route had been made possible by the coming of the Southside Railroad between Petersburg and Lynchburg. The Southside had been chartered in 1846 and the line completed in 1854. This company was formed in direct competition with the James River Canal, and the new railroad was bitterly fought by the established canal interests. The outstanding engineering feat of the Southside's construction was the bridging of the Appomattox River with a timber-truss, brick-pier bridge more than one-half mile long and towering 125 feet above the river.

Now the traffic was flowing over this new series of lines by way of Richmond, Petersburg and Lynchburg. The old seaport of Norfolk was being bypassed, its land route blocked by the Great Dismal Swamp, diverse and seemingly bottomless. The Norfolk and Petersburg Railroad, chartered in 1851, hired a young engineer named William Mahone to conquer this obstacle. This he did by clearing a wide right of way through the swamp, digging drainage ditches and laying a deep matrix of swamp trees and roots and, atop all, the fill. The engineering accomplishment still supports the railway today, carrying much heavier and longer trains over the years. After great difficulties due to acute labor shortage and a yellow fever epidemic, the right of way was pushed through Suffolk. Then Mahone turned toward Petersburg with a perfectly straight railroad of fifty-two miles—the longest tangent on the N&W and among the longest anywhere at that time. With the completion of the line in 1858, the future Norfolk and Western had become a reality with one line from Norfolk to Tennessee.

These predecessor lines of the N&W formed a necessary link in the first rail route from the industrial north to the lower Mississippi River valley. This brought only a short-lived prosperity before the Civil War began. In that war, these lines became a vital supply link for men and materials and were constant targets for Union raids and full-scale attacks. The V&T was raided con-

The *Roanoke* was typical of engines that ran on the Virginia & Tennessee in the 1850s. Built January 1854, it was the eighth engine on the road and weighed 39 tons. By comparison a century later, the future Y6b weighed 13 times as much. All V&T locomotives had names instead of numbers, with the *Roanoke* being named for the county. There was no town of Roanoke until 1882. *Courtesy N&W.*

The herculean task of building the V&T was an outstanding feat of its time. To build a mountain railroad without modern machinery, explosives, accurate maps, or mountain railway construction experience required black powder, men, mules, and sweat. Typical of the topography encountered is this 1941 photo showing a time freight descending the Alleghanies on Christiansburg Mountain, eastbound into Roanoke Valley near Shawsville, along a portion of the original V&T line built in 1853. *Courtesy N&W.*

tinually in the latter years of the war. After the siege of Petersburg, the Southside Railroad was a total wreck. Confederate forces retreating from Norfolk did much damage to delay the Northern forces along the Norfolk and Petersburg route.

The crippling damage sustained by these predecessor lines during the Civil War presented another challenge after hostilities ceased—that of rebuilding. William Mahone, now a defeated but famous Confederate general, had become president of the Norfolk and Petersburg before the war. In 1865, he also became head of the Southside and skillfully started the reconstruction of his railroads. In 1867, Mahone was elected president of the V&T.

Now as the head of three profitable railroads, each feeding traffic to the other, it was only natural for him to advocate that all three should be consolidated into one railroad. Finally in 1870,

Mahone's consolidation program was accomplished: the Atlantic, Mississippi and Ohio, Virginia's greatest railroad stretching 408 miles from Norfolk to Bristol, was born. The new company, striving to upgrade and modernize its physical plant and rolling stock, was hit hard in the Panic of 1873 and by 1876 was in receivership. In 1881 the entire company and its possessions were sold at public auction. It was reorganized as the Norfolk and Western Railroad—the immediate predecessor of the present N&W.

The new owners of the N&W also controlled a defunct property called the Shenandoah Valley Railroad (SV), which had started to build south from Hagerstown, Maryland. President of the SV was Frederick J. Kimball, a young engineer who finished the road to Waynesboro, Virginia, and drew up a plan to join the new N&W somewhere between Bedford and Salem.

11

TIME TABLE-V. & T. R. R. -On and after May First, 1856.

RUNNING WEST, OR UP.

STATIONS.	Miles.	Mail Train ARRIVE.	Mail Train LEAVE.	Accom. Train ARRIVE.	Accom. Train LEAVE.	Freight Train ARRIVE.	Freight Train LEAVE.
Lynchburg,			12.55 P.m				5. a m
Clay's,	8	1.16				6.	
Forest,	10½	1.23	1.26			6.20	6.30
Goode's,	16	1.40				7.10	
Lowry's,	19	1.49				7.30	
*Liberty,	24½	2.5	2.9			8.5	8.20
Thaxton's,	30	2.23				8.55	
*Buford's,	37	2.43	2.46			9.45	10 5
*Bonsack's,	47	3.15	3.19			11.5	11.20
Gish's Mill	50	3.27				11.38	
Big Lick	53	3.36	3.39			12.	12.10
Salem,	60	3.57	4.			12 45	12.53
*Thomas',	70	4.26				1 50	
Big Spring,	73	4.35	4.38			2 10	2.20
Shawsville	76½	4 47				2.38	
Christiansburg	86	5.20	5 24			3 50	4
Central Depot,	96½	5 54	6.14	SUP-	PER.	5.	5. a m
*Newbern,	104½	6.38	6.41			5.45	6. 5
Martin's,	112	7. 2				6.45	6.50
Max Meadow,	124½	7.42	7.45			8. 5	8 15
Wytheville,	132½	8.10	8.13			9.	9.10
Mount Airy,	145½	8.52	8 55			10.20	10.30
Marion,	160	9.40	9.43			11.45	
Seven Mile Ford,	167	10. 5					

*Passing places.

RUNNING EAST, OR DOWN.

STATIONS.	Miles.	Mail Train ARRIVE.	Mail Train LEAVE.	Accom. Train ARRIVE.	Accom. Train LEAVE.	Freight Train ARRIVE.	Freight Train LEAVE.
Lynchburg		12.				5.25	
Clay's		11.33				4.25	
Forest,		11.28	11.26			4.	4.10
Goode's		11. 7				3.15	
Lowry's,		10.58				2.50	
*Liberty,		10.40	10.44			1.50	3.20
Thaxton's,		10.24				1.10	
*Buford's		10. 2	10. 5			12 20	12 30
*Bonsack's,		9.28	9 32			11. 2	11.20
Gish's Mill,		9.18				10.42	
Big Lick		9. 7	9.10			10.12	10.27
Salem,		8.46	8.49			9.20	9.30
Thomas'		8.17				8.	8.20
Big Spring,		8. 6	8. 9			7.35	7.45
Shawsville		7.53				7.10	
Christiansburg		7.15	7.19			5.55	6.10
Central Depot,		6.25	6 45	Break-	fast.	7.30	5. a m
Newbern,		6.	6. 3			6.20	6.42
Martin's,		5.37				5.35	5.40
Max Meadow,		5.	5. 3			4.13	4.23
Wytheville		4.35	4.38			3.18	3.30
Mount Airy,		3.54	3.57			2. 3	2.13
Marion,			2.10 am				12.45 a m
Seven Mile Ford.			2.46				

READ UP.

*Passing places.

Up Mail train passes Up Freight train at Central Depot.

Up Mail train meets Down Freight train at Liberty.

Up Mail train meets upper Down Freight train at Newbern.

Down Mail train meets Up Freight train at Buford's

Down Mail train passes Down Freight train at Thomas'.

Down Mail train meets Upper Up Freight train at Newbern.

Freight trains meet at Bonsack's.

RULES AND REGULATIONS.

1. Wood, Material, Extra and Special Trains will avoid all Regular Trains.

2. In case of an accident or detention to a Passenger Train, where it will be detained over three hours, a messenger must be immediately dispatched to Lynchburg.

3. In case of the engine attached to the Mail Train being disabled, any engine that may be on the road shall be used to supply her place.

4. Freight Trains will wait for Passenger Trains one hour after their time of arrival, (unless they pass sooner,) and then proceed, keeping one hour behind time, until the train looked for is passed or heard from.

5. If either Freight Train shall arrive promptly at the meeting place, and the other Freight Train does not arrive, it shall wait one hour, after its departing time and then proceed, having prior right to the track, keeping one hour behind time.

6. When Freight Trains, by losing time in case of accident, find they cannot arrive at the next passing place in time, they shall proceed cautiously, with a man one-third of a mile ahead with a red flag or lantern.

7. Passenger Trains, after being one hour behind time, must wait one hour longer for Freight Trains, [which will run according to Rule 4,] unless it arrives sooner, and then proceed, sending a man one-third of a mile ahead, with a red flag or lantern.

8 Should two trains meet on the way, advantage shall be given to the one which has the greatest distance to run back.

9. All trains will leave Lynchburg, Central Depot, and the West end of the Road promptly, by Card time, though trains of the same class then due have not arrived, and the delayed trains must avoid them.

10. In case of an accident to any train, a man must be sent both ways, with a red flag or lantern, to give notice to any approaching train.

11. A blue flag or lantern on the engine will signify, that an Extra Train will follow the train to which it is attached.

12. When a messenger is sent to give intelligence of an accident, he must, in all cases, be a responsible white man.

13. All Bridges to be passed at a speed *not exceeding four miles per hour, under any circumstances.*

14. Be sure you are right, and *run no risk.*

15. No one allowed to ride on the engine or tender but the Engineer, Fireman, Master Machinest, and Road Master, *and the Engineers are required to keep all other persons off.*

16. Freight and Material Trains are not allowed to carry passengers.

H. H. GILL, Gen. Supt.

Timetable, rules and regulations of old V&T. The line was completed to Bristol on October 1, 1856. *Courtesy Earl Palmer.*

The outstanding engineering feat of the Southside Railroad was construction of a bridge across the Appomattox River in 1853. The timber-truss "High Bridge" was considered the biggest bridge built up to that time—3,400 feet long with 20 piers made of 3,766,000 bricks. Early travelers were fearful for their safety when crossing, but no accident, not even Civil War battles, destroyed it. The sturdy piers still stand beside the modern steel bridge now used. *Courtesy N&W.*

The seemingly bottomless Dismal Swamp was quite an obstacle to overcome for the Norfolk & Petersburg Railroad. But a young engineer, William Mahone, used a unique method to build a wide right-of-way through the swamp. This engineering accomplishment still supports the railway today, carrying much heavier and longer trains over the years. Here 1206 rolls with Time Freight 86 in 1949 across the Dismal Swamp. *Courtesy N&W.*

The original SV owners hired a geologist to report on the resources of southwestern Virginia. The report also included resources along the Virginia-Kentucky-West Virginia borders. After Kimball verified the accuracy of this report, he immediately set out to tap the rich coal deposits. After the SV rails junctioned with the N&W in 1882 at Roanoke, Kimball, now an N&W vice-president, projected a branch down the New River and over the mountains to the area now known as the Pocahontas coalfields. The first carload of coal was dispatched to Norfolk on March 13, 1883, and a new era began.

In the meantime, coalfield branches and spurs were being extended. One notable extension was the Clinch Valley line connecting Bluefield with the Louisville & Nashville (L&N) interchange at Norton, Virginia. This line originated much of the coal that was produced subsequently in Virginia. Another development was the North Carolina Branch. It was constructed south from Pulaski on the Bristol line in the belief that rich iron ore deposits existed at the North Carolina line. Such deposits did not materialize, and the branch ultimately reached Galax and no farther.

Once the coalfields were tapped, Kimball urged

that a line be constructed to the Ohio River to open new markets. His greatest project was the Flat Top Tunnel, west of Bluefield. This was necessary to reach additional coalfields and to provide a main route west to the Ohio. The tunnel was completed in 1888, and the line pushed westward. Although money was tight in 1890, construction was started east from Kenova, West Virginia, on the Ohio River to meet the line pushing west from Bluefield. Real engineering troubles were encountered on this extension with numerous tunnels, unmapped country, the Ohio River Bridge (the present-day successor was the largest on the steam-era system) and another financial depression.

In 1875, the building of a railroad began down the Scioto River Valley from Columbus, Ohio, through Chillicothe and Portsmouth east, reaching Coal Grove by 1881. This line, known as the Scioto Valley and New England, was purchased by the N&W. The physical connection between the parent road and the line was made in 1892.

This created a 706-mile road from a leading port on the Atlantic to the heartland of the nation.

The N&W leased both the Roanoke and Southern Railway and the Lynchburg and Durham in 1892. These two lines were purchased in 1896 to become the Winston-Salem and Durham lines, respectively.

The territory of the Norfolk and Western had great traffic potential but was mostly undeveloped. In 1893 a serious business depression occurred at a time when the railroad had not stabilized after continuous and costly expansion. The Norfolk and Western *Railroad* went into receivership in 1895, and on September 24, 1896, the Norfolk and Western *Railway* was created. This is the same prosperous and progressive carrier that is in existence today.

The Cincinnati, Portsmouth and Virginia Railroad was purchased by the N&W in 1901. This is now the Cincinnati line. Since that time, numerous terminal and track relocations and scores of coal and industrial branch changes have

Atlantic, Mississippi & Ohio 4-4-0 37 was placed in service in 1871 as a woodburner. This engine was rebuilt about 1877 at Lynchburg, where it was converted into a coalburner. The railroad saw the advantage of coal as locomotive fuel and began the changeover from wood to coal in 1876. This photo shows the coalburner. *Courtesy N&W.*

This drawing depicts the first carload of N&W coal. Actually, the first load was used by the railroad company as fuel and the second load was dispatched to Norfolk. During the first year 81,890 tons of coal were shipped. A new era had begun. *Courtesy N&W.*

been made. But the basic framework of the Norfolk and Western remained intact throughout the steam era. One additional note of interest for this period is that Frederick J. Kimball, often considered the father of the first N&W, returned as president in 1902, but died in office the following year.

Starting with the N&W merger with the Virginian Railway on December 1, 1959, a new age dawned for the Norfolk and Western. And the day was never brighter than on October 16, 1964, when the N&W merged with the Nickel Plate, leased the Wabash, and bought other property to become a large railroad stretching from the Mis-

sissippi to the Atlantic. This last merger is another story and will not be dealt with here.

The growth of the N&W can be told, too, by the never-ending expansion and modernization of its physical plant. What better way is there to tell this than to study N&W steam locomotive development. The N&W steam motive power may well be the most important feature of its growth. Nonetheless, it was only one of many aspects. This study of the N&Ws steam development is indicative of how this progressive railway went about modernizing all facets of its operations and all parts of its physical plant.

NORFOLK & WESTERN RAILROAD COMPANY.

F. J. KIMBALL and HENRY FINK, Receivers.   Form C. T. 48

[31]   Telegraphic Train Order No: 69   [31]

Superintendent's Office, *April 3* 1897

For *Dry Branch* _____ Station.   To Conductor and Engineman

of 1st 90 *Eng* 189 271 286 2d No 88 *eng* 248

Eng 193 & *Eng*

After assisting Eng No 88 *eng*
286 *will* run extra Hickmans *Crk*
to Belspring 2d No 88. *eng*
248 and Extra 286. *will* Meet
at Belspring After assisting No 88
eng 189 271 & 286 *will*
run Extra Hickmans to Dry Branch
1st No 90 *eng* 193 &
Extras 189 271 & 286. *will*
Meet at Dry Branch

J. C. C.   Superintendent.

Time Received 406 P.M.   CR   Given at 409 P.M.

CONDUCTOR	ENGINEMAN	TRAIN	MADE	AT	RECEIVED BY
	Sweeten X189	Carpenter	409		
	Virginia 271	Carpenter	409		
		286	Carpenter	409	
			Carpenter	409	

CONDUCTOR AND ENGINEMAN MUST EACH HAVE A COPY OF THIS ORDER.

Before the modern era of automatic signals and Centralized Traffic Control, train orders governed the movement of all trains. This order controlled several trains between Dry Branch and Belspring, Virginia, in 1897. *Courtesy Earl Palmer.*

Above: In the early eighties, the 2-8-0 became the N&W's standard heavy-duty locomotive. This old Class F reflects railroading in the late 1800s—the engineer's individual touch to "his" assigned engine. This engineer placed an Indian figure and deer antlers on the engine front. The stovepipe stack was characteristic of that era. *Courtesy Earl Palmer. Below:* Many engines of the predecessor N&W Railroad enjoyed years of service on the N&W Railway. Later renumbered 43, Class D 207 performed until the coming of much larger, more efficient steam power. Number 207 at Bluefield about 1895. *Courtesy C. W. Jernstrom.*

Route Profile & Operations

HEAVY TRAIN ON A STEEP GRADE

Heavy tonnage coal trains and mountainous grades dictated N&W motive power requirements. Steam locomotive development on the railway produced remarkable engines—some for mountain work, others for flatter portions of the system. The railway also made line changes that eased severe grades and curvature. Along with the opening of the new Elkhorn Tunnel, there were extensive route improvements on 5.3 miles of track. The track realignment consisted of reducing maximum curvature from 12 to 6 degrees, the building of two bridges, and the reduction of maximum grade from 2% to 1.4%. Powerful locomotives, heavy trains, severe mountain grades, and sound engineering were characteristics of this well-managed railway during the steam era. In June 1951, a Y6b works a coal train on the newly relocated Elkhorn line. *Courtesy N&W.*

Prior to the era of modern mergers, the Norfolk and Western Railway was a relatively small railroad. Its track mileage connected the Midwest and the Norfolk port to the coal bin of America. Its main line ran 663 miles from Norfolk to Columbus with important lines between Portsmouth and Cincinnati, Walton and Bristol, Roanoke and Hagerstown, Roanoke and Winston-Salem, Lynchburg and Durham and Bluefield and Norton. With a total of 2,134 road miles in six states, the Norfolk and Western Railway was synonymous with the origination and transportation of bituminous coal.

Moving this coal and merchandise required long heavy trains that could cross mountains some railroads chose to bypass. Once the mountains were crossed, these same heavy trains would proceed through relatively flat country either to market or to port. As a result, some of the most remarkable American steam locomotives ever produced were designed and built by the Norfolk and Western. These met admirably the awesome demands made of them. As for passenger service, the N&W served an area of relatively sparse population density, yet produced fine passenger trains powered by the most powerful 4-8-4 ever produced. These 4-8-4s were so well designed that they were equally at home on the more level stretches and the most mountainous portions of the system.

The N&W traversed some of the most varied terrain in this country. The segment from Norfolk to Roanoke, known as the Norfolk Division, crosses the Dismal Swamp and proceeds through flat sandy country into the Piedmont region to Crewe. In the days of steam, all heavy tonnage trains were stopped at Crewe for a change of motive power. Through passenger trains and manifest freights—called time freights on the N&W—usually proceeded west on to Roanoke, or to Norfolk if eastbound. Westward from Crewe, the main line continued through the rolling Piedmont hills, and then crossed the first mountain barrier, the Blue Ridge. Eastbound coal trains had to be assisted by a pusher from Bonsack, just east of Roanoke, to the Blue Ridge summit. On the Norfolk Division, the 2-6-6-4s were the predominant heavy freight power east of Crewe,

In the distance, a mighty N&W steam engine is speeding a trainload of bituminous coal to market. In 1950, coal represented 75% of the N&W's total freight tonnage, accounting for 62% of total freight revenue. This coal originated about midway in the system on the Pocahontas Division, with 37% moving east and 63% to the midwest gateway. *Courtesy N&W.*

Streamlined 4-8-4 Class Js were primary passenger power. Good in the mountains and on the flatlands, these sleek beauties pulled top-rated passenger trains. In pool service, the tireless 600s routinely worked from Roanoke to the ends of the system and returned without engine change. *S. Mailer Photo, Courtesy C. T. Felstead Collection.*

The 2-8-8-2 classes Y5 and Y6s were heavy-duty freight locomotives ideally suited for Pocahontas, Radford, and Shenandoah division work. The most powerful engines on N&W, these compound Mallets developed tremendous force at lower speeds using steam and coal more efficiently. Here is Y6b 2178 with auxiliary water tender at Hagerstown, Maryland, in February '54. *Courtesy Charles E. Winters.*

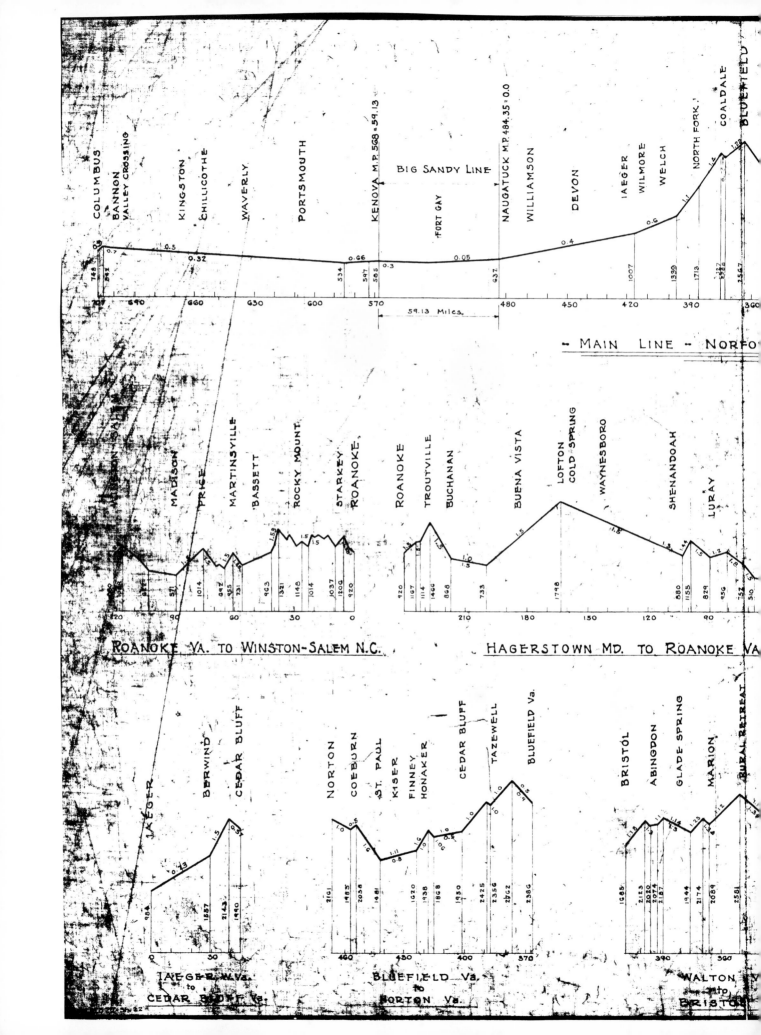

MAIN LINE - NORFO

BIG SANDY LINE

COLUMBUS · BANNON VALLEY CROSSING · KINGSTON · CHILLICOTHE · WAVERLY · PORTSMOUTH · KENOVA M.P. 568=59.13 · FORT GAY · NAUGATUCK M.P. 484.35=0.0 · WILLIAMSON · DEVON · IAEGER · WILMORE · WELCH · NORTH FORK · COALDALE · BLUEFIELD

59.13 Miles

ROANOKE VA. TO WINSTON-SALEM N.C.

MADISON · PRICE · MARTINSVILLE · BASSETT · ROCKY MOUNT · STARKEY · ROANOKE

HAGERSTOWN MD. TO ROANOKE VA

ROANOKE · TROUTVILLE · BUCHANAN · BUENA VISTA · LOFTON COLD SPRING · WAYNESBORO · SHENANDOAH · LURAY

IAEGER W.Va.
to
CEDAR BLUFF Va.

IAEGER · BERWIND · CEDAR BLUFF

BLUEFIELD Va.
to
NORTON Va.

NORTON · COEBURN · ST. PAUL · KISER · FINNEY · HONAKER · CEDAR BLUFF · TAZEWELL · BLUEFIELD Va.

WALTON V
to
BRISTOL

BRISTOL · ABINGDON · GLADE SPRING · MARION · RURAL RETREAT

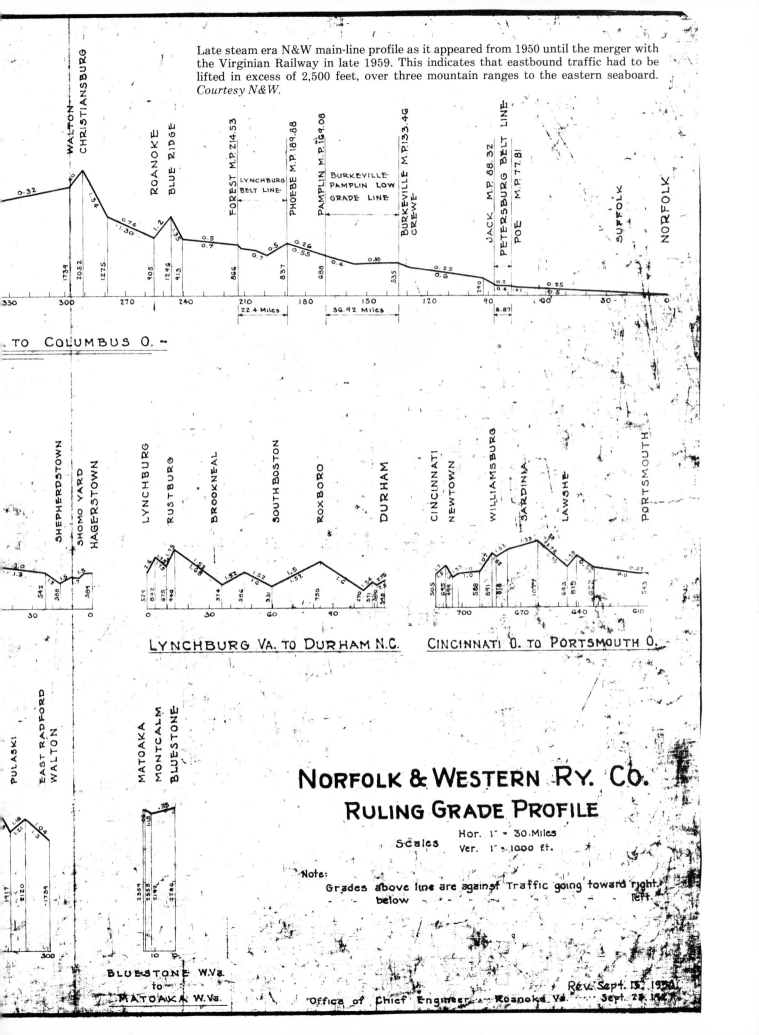

Late steam era N&W main-line profile as it appeared from 1950 until the merger with the Virginian Railway in late 1959. This indicates that eastbound traffic had to be lifted in excess of 2,500 feet, over three mountain ranges to the eastern seaboard. *Courtesy N&W.*

TO COLUMBUS O.

LYNCHBURG VA. TO DURHAM N.C.   CINCINNATI O. TO PORTSMOUTH O.

NORFOLK & WESTERN RY. CO.
RULING GRADE PROFILE

Scales
Hor. 1" = 30 Miles
Ver. 1" = 1000 ft.

Note:
Grades above line are against Traffic going toward right.
below   left.

BLUESTONE W.Va.
to
MATOAKA W.Va.

Rev. Sept. 15, 1950.
Office of Chief Engineer, Roanoke, Va.   Sept. 28, 1...

On flatter portions of the system, the Norfolk and Scioto divisions, Class A 2-6-6-4s were primary freight power. These single expansion locomotives were used not only in manifest freight service, but also on loaded coal trains. In the late steam era, 190 loaded hoppers was the rating for a single 1200 from Crewe to Norfolk and Williamson to Portsmouth. The 1210 at Crewe in December '56. *Courtesy C. W. Jernstrom.*

Class K2 4-8-2s, modernized and streamlined in the mid-forties, performed almost all the late steam secondary passenger work. The 120 at Petersburg, Virginia, in September 1945. *Courtesy Charles E. Winters.*

while the modern 2-8-8-2s were used in pusher and freight service on the Blue Ridge and performed all heavy freight duties on the rolling Lynchburg to Durham line of this division.

Roanoke was the focal point for three divisions: the Norfolk Division to the east; the Shenandoah Division north to Hagerstown, Maryland, and south to Winston-Salem, North Carolina; and the Radford Division westward. The Shenandoah Division follows its valley namesake northward for 238 miles to the interchange with the former Pennsylvania and Western Maryland railroads at Hagerstown. The grades are steep and the route tortuous on both the Shenandoah Valley line and the Winston-Salem line. As a result, only the modern 2-8-8-2s were called upon to handle the through freight traffic on this division.

Westward from Roanoke to Bluefield the Radford Division spans the most mountainous segment of the N&W. Proceeding west from Roanoke Valley, the main line climbs for thirty-three miles to the summit of the eastern continental divide at Christiansburg. This climb has a maximum gradient of 1.34 percent and constitutes a rise in elevation of 1,060 feet from Roanoke to the top of Christiansburg Mountain. From the summit, the line drops down the west slope for seven miles to Walton, on the New River, where the main line splits—one line to Bristol and the other on to Bluefield.

Bristol was an important connection with the Southern Railway for both passenger and freight operations. The line to Bluefield followed the easy gradient of the New River to Glen Lyn and then upgrade for the final twenty-three miles to that city perched on a mountain top. The westbound trains of freight and empty hopper cars out of Roanoke went unassisted on this tough portion. But the heavy tonnage eastbound trains—of loaded hoppers totalling 10,300 tons—were assisted from Walton to Christiansburg by one of the modern 2-8-8-2 compound articulateds acting as a pusher. These 2-8-8-2s, the most powerful locomotives on the railway, became the impres-

Eastbound J 610 at Alleghany summit, while the Y6 has almost conquered the mountain with a time freight. This depicts N&W mountain railroading at its best. *Courtesy C. W. Jernstrom.*

Powerful Mallet 2168 working hard as it blasts through the peaceful mountains. One can feel the ground tremble as it passes by. *Courtesy Earl Palmer.*

sive trademark of motive power on the Radford Division. They were very powerful at relatively low speeds and thus were perfectly suited to the heavy work required on the mountainous Allegheny grades.

The Pocahontas Division encompasses not only the main line from Bluefield to Williamson, West Virginia, but also most of the numerous branches to coal tipples in Virginia, Kentucky and West Virginia. The main line ascends west from Bluefield to Bluestone up a short grade and then descends a steep grade to Iaeger. This Bluefield to Iaeger portion of the line was electrified beginning in 1914 to reduce the usage of steam in its single-track, 3,015-foot Flat Top Tunnel.

In 1950, a new 7,110-foot tunnel was bored at Elkhorn, and a portion of the line was relocated to ease the grade from 2 percent to 1.4 percent and eliminate numerous curves. After the construction of this new line, electrification was scrapped and steam reinstated as the mainstay freight power from Iaeger to Bluefield. This represented one of the very few cases where steam replaced another type of motive power in operations, and

this was a milestone in steam railroading. All westbound trains then moved unassisted on the mostly downhill slope on this division, but all eastbound tonnage trains required pusher assistance from Farm to Bluestone. West from Iaeger, the line follows the Tug Fork River to Williamson. The 2-8-8-2s were the main line freight power on this division.

Williamson, a large coal collection yard, was the eastern terminus of the Scioto Division. At Portsmouth this division extended northward to Columbus, Ohio, and westward to Cincinnati. The large and efficient classification yard at Portsmouth was one of the most modern yards anywhere. N&W coal bound for the Great Lakes proceeded to Columbus for the Pennsylvania Railroad to haul it to the Port of Sandusky on Lake Erie. Until the late 1950s, more coal was transported from the coalfields westward than to the eastern seaboard. To haul this heaviest of coal traffic on the N&W, the 2-6-6-4s were the primary source of power on the flat Scioto Division.

All main line through passenger trains were pulled by the streamlined 4-8-4s. In the last

Class A 1206 nearing Blue Ridge summit with westbound time freight. Engine at right is a Y6 pusher that has just finished assisting a heavy eastbound train from Bonsack to the top. *Courtesy Earl Palmer.*

27

Doubleheading with an A led by a Y6 on heavy eastbound trains across the Blue Ridge was normal procedure in the 1950s. The double-tracked main added flexibility as seen by this train approaching on the "left hand" track. *Courtesy Earl Palmer.*

decade of steam passenger service, streamlined 4-8-2s were used on locals and other secondary passenger trains, on the lighter passenger-density lines of the system, such as the Shenandoah Division, and on the Norfolk to Richmond "Cannonball." In addition to the Powhatan Arrow, the Pocahontas and the Cavalier—the N&Ws top-rated passenger trains that graced its own rails—the Southern Railway and N&W jointly routed three "name" passenger trains each way over the N&W tracks between Lynchburg and Bristol. These "name" carriers were the Tennessean, the Pelican and the Birmingham Special. These prestigious passenger trains of the N&W and of the Southern were always assigned one of the beautifully proportioned black and Tuscan red 4-8-4s of the N&W.

A good measure of a railroad's operating performance is how well and to what extent it makes use of its road and equipment. In 1955 the Norfolk and Western handled more net ton-miles of freight per day for each mile of road it operated than did any other American railroad of more than 340 miles in length. This traffic density and good performance of the N&W is further attested to by the fact that the system moved more tons per train-mile in 1955 than any other U.S. railroad of equal or greater length.

To handle this vast tide of through freight traffic as well as local and passenger trains, the entire N&W main line from Norfolk to Columbus had been double tracked in the early 1900s and in more recent years laid with rail weighing 131 pounds per yard or heavier. This allowed each set

Although much is said of N&W's main-line operations, branch lines added a picturesque and romantic railroading touch to backwoods communities. Perhaps most scenic was the Abingdon Branch and its daily mixed train named "Virginia Creeper," powered by a Class M 4-8-0. Today the line and steamers are gone, "but the silent canyons and cloud-bound mountains traversed by the mixed-consist 'Creeper' will always be peopled with memories of the steam powered trains that shared in their romance." (Quote from Earl Palmer). *Courtesy Earl Palmer.*

of tracks to handle traffic moving predominantly in one direction. Furthermore, the installation of centralized traffic control coupled with adequate sidings and crossovers facilitated movement of the faster passenger trains past the slower freights en route. Remember, the heavy coal traffic was the primary reason for double tracking the Norfolk-to-Columbus main line. Loaded coal trains moving to port or market and empty hoppers returning to the coalfields around the clock were the N&Ws answer to the conveyor belt. After the merger with the Virginian, a portion of the original double tracked N&W main line was not needed, however, for loaded coal trains could use some of the easier Virginian

route to Norfolk and the empties return on the old N&W line. But the concept remained in practice.

Starting in 1928, the Norfolk and Western began using Centralized Traffic Control (CTC). This complete modern system was developed to provide a safer, more economical means of directing the movement of trains by signal indications without the use of train orders. The position light signals and switches are operated remotely from a central location where the movement of rolling stock on possibly hundreds of miles of track is controlled. The N&W was one of the extensive users of CTC in the United States from the 1930s to the present.

To illustrate the effectiveness of CTC, in 1943

Modern 2-8-8-2 compound Mallets were used as pushers on main-line grade districts as well as on coal branches. On Raitt "hill" in the coalfields, often three Y6s worked a single train. These modern "workhorses" were distinctive in appearance and operation—to hear one at work left no doubt as to its capabilities. *Courtesy Earl Palmer.*

Class A 1209 awaits a call for road service on "ready track" while an 0-8-0 switcher rests between yard assignments. The shifter was the mainstay of yard operations in last decade of N&W steam. Portsmouth 1958. *Courtesy C. W. Jernstrom.*

Older power accomplishing unglamorous tasks was often obscure to the casual observer, but these "horses" of another era performed their work without apology. M2 1117, like her sisters, was used in one-trick switching, on branch lines, and on work trains. Roanoke 1953. *Courtesy Charles E. Winters.*

much of the line from Roanoke up the Shenandoah Valley to Hagerstown was upgraded to better handle the heavy World War II traffic to the Northeast. Freight traffic on this line had increased to more than six times the 1939 volume, the last prewar year. By March of 1943 the total gross ton-miles was exceeding 600,000,000 per month. By installing CTC and double tracking one helper grade, the operating capacity was increased thirty percent to over 840,000,000 gross ton-miles per month. It is evident that these improvements were a major contribution to the war effort, for much coal went to the fuel-hungry industrialized Northeast via the Shenandoah Valley route instead of the hazardous wartime rail-water route through the Port of Norfolk. Such modernization and improvements took place on other portions of the system also, such as

the Bristol line. Through sound technological upgrading of the physical plant, the N&W was able to make a significant increase in its hauling capacity with essentially the same physical plant.

In 1958, there were twenty-seven railways in the United States longer in road miles than the N&W. But due to its location and coal traffic, the Norfolk and Western was a "big" railroad of vital importance. It connected with twenty-one other railroads for freight interchange at eighty-four junctions and with oceangoing vessels at the port of Norfolk.

But nothing can bring the significance of the N&W into sharper focus than studying the steam motive power of this progressive, well-managed railway that was built on the effective application of both good engineering and sound economics.

Locomotive Servicing
& Utilization

MOST MODERN STEAM SERVICING FACILITIES

The most unique aspect of N&W steam was the thoroughly modern servicing facilities, which enhanced higher locomotive availability. The railway designed its motive power incorporating the latest technology to reduce maintenance and to extend time between servicing. Y6 2181 is being lubricated and light running repairs are being made in Blue-field's engine servicing facility. High pressure grease and oil dispensing lines were accessible throughout the building to lubricate locomotives. On the other track is a streamlined 4-8-2 being serviced. *Courtesy N&W.*

As the previous chapter stated, the steam era N&W was a highly efficient railroad as judged by the criteria used by the U.S. railroad industry. The criteria of tons handled per train-mile and net ton-miles of freight per day for each route-mile showed the Norfolk and Western achieving results that were at or near the top for any American railroad in 1955. Probably one of the best gauges of a railroad's performance and efficiency is gross ton-miles per train-hour, since it is based on both train speed and tonnage. In 1955, the N&W produced more gross ton-miles of freight per train-hour than any other U.S. railway of comparable or even greater length.

All of the aforementioned indicators of outstanding efficiency using steam can be attributed to a number of reasons. First, the predominant traffic or commodity hauled was a bulk cargo—bituminous coal. Secondly, such cargo facilitated fully loaded tonnage train operations. Third, N&W was a progressive rail carrier making calculated improvements to increase productivity.

Finally, the steam motive power used was designed for service best suited to its capabilities. Particularly noteworthy, this good performance was achieved on a railroad that was forced to operate on heavy grades over three mountain ranges—the Blue Ridge, Allegheny and Elkhorn.

Having steam locomotives of very sound design coupled with the most modern servicing facilities resulted in high locomotive availability. This enabled the N&W to attain these record highs of performance despite the rugged grades. Convincing evidence of its locomotives' performances is that the N&W in 1955 had the lowest fuel consumption per ton-mile of freight ever achieved in the railway's history. The steam locomotives had been improved to the extent that less than half as many locomotives moved twice as much traffic as three decades earlier.

Why is 1955 pinpointed so often to illustrate the N&W steam locomotive performance? This was the year that diesels were first added to the N&W roster; it marked the zenith of N&W steam.

The N&W recognized early that modern servicing facilities were required to gain the full potential utilization of the railway's steam giants. With "long houses" for lubricating and making light running repairs, N&W steam power was routinely serviced and made ready for the next assignment in a matter of minutes instead of hours. *Courtesy N&W.*

Portsmouth's extensive and modern engine terminal viewed from coaling station toward the roundhouse. Date: 1953. *Courtesy N&W.*

Class A 1213 being lubricated in Williamson's "long house." The 1200s had mechanical lubrication to 238 points from oil reservoirs. Additionally, 98 points were greased through pressure fittings. *Courtesy N&W.*

The road's heavy freight locomotives were averaging 6,000 miles a month in mountain drag service, and its fast passenger engines were doing 15,000 miles a month without long distance engine runs.

How did the Norfolk and Western achieve such results? By "dieselizing" *in theory* before the first diesels were acquired. Specifically, this included better locomotive servicing facilities, faster turn-around times for these engines at the terminals, and the elimination of intermediate stops between terminals. The N&W was the first railroad to install modern centralized servicing facilities for completely lubricating its steam power. The idea was to provide a modern assembly line for servicing the locomotives, and these locomotives would rarely enter a roundhouse except for periodic inspections and heavier repairs.

At larger terminals where there was a concentration of steam motive power, a modern engine service building, called a lubratorium, was constructed over one or more of the servicing tracks. Called "long houses" by the railway personnel because of their configuration, these locomotive servicing buildings were as modern as any in the country. Constructed of brick with all windows of glass blocks, they were well ventilated, well lighted, had heat controls and electrically operated rolling doors at each end and a full-length inspection pit. The latest pressure lubrication equipment dispensed oil and various greases used in lubricating locomotives through hoses suspended from the ceiling, thus allowing easy access to the many lubricating points of the locomotive.

Servicing a locomotive at a terminal began with

cleaning the fire, washing the engine and taking on water, coal and sand. Next the locomotive would be moved to the "long house" and inspected over the inspection pit. While being inspected, it would be lubricated and light repairs made. Then the engine would be moved to the ready track to await dispatch. Thus a freight locomotive could arrive at a terminal, be cut off its train and be serviced, returned to a train and be proceeding out on the road within two hours. With the extensive servicing required on a steam locomotive, this short time was phenomenal. On the Norfolk and Western, it was routine because of advanced servicing facilities coupled with modern locomotives carrying all the refinements needed to achieve high availability, or more miles between services.

To attain higher utilization records, the N&W set out to extend engine runs between terminals. Initially, this was done by moving through freights between major terminals with fewer stops. With the advent of CTC, such longer runs with fewer stops were achieved. Likewise, the use

of larger tenders to reduce intermediate coal and water stops was another significant step. By the early 1950s most on-line coaling stations were no longer needed, though it was still necessary to stop heavy tonnage trains for additional water. Water stops were situated to take advantage, whenever possible, of a normal stop such as those to couple on a pusher, make train inspection and for cooling hot wheels on the train cars after descending a heavy grade.

By 1953, after an intense and successful effort to eliminate cast iron wheels on train cars and the resulting stop to allow cooling, the N&W began connecting an auxillary water tender behind the regular locomotive tender. This extra 20,800 gallons of water enabled the large capacity freight locomotives pulling heavy tonnage to proceed between major terminals without a stop except for pusher grades. After the addition of the extra tank, water stops were required only in case of unusually high water consumption en route. The extra water cars not only made possible non-stop runs between major terminals, but they also

1207 with new auxiliary water tender in May 1952. With an extra water tender, N&W steam road giants pulled heavier freight trains between major terminals without an intermediate water stop. Before the auxiliary tenders, Class As worked 175 loaded hoppers from Williamson to Portsmouth; afterward, 190 loads. This had to be steam's finest hour! *Courtesy N&W.*

permitted power formerly used in starting after an intermediate water stop to be used to keep a heavier train rolling. Thus, gross ton-miles per train-hour (locomotive utilization) rose significantly since this takes into account both train tonnage and time-distance (average speed).

Its heavy freight locomotives equipped with thirty ton coal capacity tenders, the railway's need for many of its on-line coaling stations dwindled. However, large and modern coaling stations were used to the end of steam at three strategic locations: Vicker, Virginia, at the foot of the eastbound Allegheny climb to Christiansburg; Farm, West Virginia, at the foot of the eastbound climb to Bluefield from Williamson; and Prichard, West Virginia, between Portsmouth and Williamson.

The stations at Vicker and Farm were at the foot of steep mountain grades where heavy eastbound trains normally stopped for helper assistance. These stations served the helper locomotives and the train locomotives, too, if additional coal was needed. Many of the freight trains running between Roanoke and Bristol stopped at Vicker for coal and water because of this long and hilly 151-mile run that included the Allegheny climb as well as two other heavy grades on the Bristol line.

The coaling facility at Prichard, the largest of the three, had 2,000 tons coal capacity with four approach tracks. This station met the occasional need for intermediate coaling stops by very heavy trains moving between Portsmouth and Williamson. There also the passenger locomotives out of Roanoke on runs to and from Cincinnati took on coal and water each way, thus eliminating the

Two modern steamers being "turned" at Portsmouth's thoroughly modern engine terminal. If anything set N&W steam apart, it was servicing facilities and techniques that substantially boosted engine availability. *Courtesy C. W. Jernstrom.*

Smoke pollution was a major concern at large steam terminals. At Bluefield, the railway constructed large vents that routed engine smoke through water sprayers removing most fly ash before emission to the atmosphere. Here 1239 is being positioned under a vent. *Courtesy C. W. Jernstrom.*

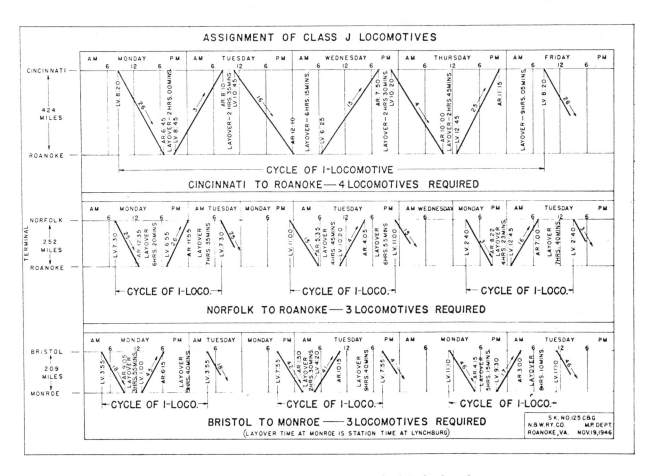

Quick turn arounds demanded of Class J 600s resulted in high mileage passenger engines on a rather short and hilly railroad. The design excellence of the Js also contributed to this achievement. *Courtesy N&W.*

need to buy more expensive coal at Cincinnati Union Terminal. For the occasional coal going to the Ohio River to be loaded into river barges at Kenova, the Prichard coaling station met locomotive recoaling needs.

With improved servicing facilities and the elimination of on-line halts, the Norfolk and Western achieved utilization records that were unequalled by steam freight locomotives in similar service on any other U.S. railroad. As for the steam passenger locomotives, those superb streamlined 4-8-4s ran without engine change between Roanoke and either Cincinnati or Norfolk, or between Bristol and Lynchburg. This accounted for higher mileage and utilization. In the mid-1950s, the all-steam N&W operating efficiency substantially exceeded the national average when all other major U.S. roads were either partially or totally dieselized. This speaks for itself!

The following article was published in the September 1951 issue of the *N&W Magazine*. The article traces the workings of locomotive 2184 for two days and vividly describes the high utilization of the N&W steam locomotives. The techniques of servicing set forth took place routinely to the end of N&W steam. However, this was before the era of adding extra water cars to eliminate the water stops indicated in the article. Particularly noteworthy was the reliability of the home-designed and home-built "work horses of the N&W."

Our Modern Workhorses and How They Work

In 1950 our railroad made an all-time N. & W. record with respect to one of the best measures of transportation performance—gross ton-miles of freight traffic handled per train hour. That figure—64,766 gross ton miles per train hour—not only was the best we have ever achieved, but it was the best performance of any railroad in the United States more than 900 miles in length. It ranked sixth among all Class I railroads.

An important factor that made the record possible was the N. & W.'s expert and intensive use of modern equipment and facilities, notable among which is a fleet of modern coal-burning freight locomotives. As of August 15, 1951, the Norfolk and Western owned 286 freight locomotives. Of these engines 137 have been built since 1936. They are modern* locomotives, and represent less than 48% of the railway's freight

locomotive ownership. However, during the first six months of this year they accounted for approximately 91% of the total freight gross ton miles.

*A modern locomotive is defined by the N. & W. as one which is designed with a high capacity boiler, equipped with roller bearings on all tender and engine wheels, one piece cast steel bed frame, improved counter-balancing and complete mechanical and pressure lubrication.

Number 2184 is the subject of the accompanying article that vividly describes the reliable performance of this great locomotive. This mighty Y6b is being prepared at Williamson for another road trip. Modern engine design coupled with latest servicing techniques meant higher locomotive availability and utilization. *Courtesy N&W.*

"Workhorse" under the coaling station at Shaffers Crossing, Roanoke. Shaffers Crossing was the center of locomotive dispatches during steam. From August '44 to steam's end, March '45 was the busiest month with 3836 engine dispatches from Roanoke—an average of 124 per day. *Courtesy N&W.*

To learn how these modern freight locomotives are used and to observe their performance on the job, a member of the MAGAZINE staff recently accompanied a typical freight locomotive, No. 2184, during two full days of operation and was greatly impressed by what he saw.

Locomotive 2184 is one of the railway's newest Y-6-b engines, of which we now have 24, and referred to as the "work horses" of the railroad because they pull heavy tonnage trains.

The 2184 is strictly a home product, designed by N. & W. Motive Power Department mechanical engineers and built by N. & W. employees at Roanoke Shops. Construction of No. 2184 started in March, 1949, and it came out of the shops on April 28 of that year, going into service on the same date. From that date until April 25, 1951, the locomotive was in almost continuous service and rolled up a total of 89,627 miles. This was an average of 172 miles per serviceable day. The system average for these locomotives during recent months has been about 215 miles per day, with one division having averaged as high as 300 miles

per day, excluding unserviceable and stored days.

On April 25 the engine went to Roanoke Shops for light repairs. It emerged from the shops on May 18 ready for another two years of steady operation. From that date to August 8, inclusive, it traveled an average of 167 miles per day and accumulated a total of 13,862 miles for the 83-day period.

The MAGAZINE writer's acquaintance with Locomotive 2184 began at the Shaffers Crossing engine terminal on the morning of August 9 when the engine was being put in readiness for pulling Time Freight Train No. 85 to Williamson. The locomotive, which had arrived at Shaffers Crossing that morning after a run from Bluefield, was then going through the procedure known as "turning" the locomotive which, at Shaffers Crossing, requires about two hours, on an average.

When we first saw it, 2184 was standing under the coal wharf where Coaler C. H. Price was replenishing its tender (capacity 30 tons of coal) and its sand boxes, each of which holds a ton of sand. Two other operations had preceded the coaling and sanding. When the locomotive arrived on the incoming track it was taken over by Hostler R. M. Overstreet, who spotted it over the ash pit. There the fire box and ash pan were cleaned by James Price and J. L. Woody. Then Hostler A. C. Fitzgerald moved the engine to the inspection pit, where Engine Inspectors S. R. Warren and B. G. Thomasson made a thorough examination of the general condition of the locomotive. After the coaling and sanding was completed, the locomotive was moved to the washing plant where the locomotive and tender were washed thoroughly by W. S. Saunders, and the tank, which holds 22,000 gallons of water, was filled.

Next stop in the "turning" procedure was the lubrication plant where all parts of 2184 were efficiently lubricated and light repairs were made as called for by the engineman who last was in charge of the engine or by the engine inspectors at Shaffers Crossing. Men on the job in the lubricating plant included: Machinist H. J. Wilson, Pipefitter R. L. Pace, Air Brake Machinist H. C. Nunn, Engine Supplymen James Patterson, Dan Reed, Jack Brown and J. R. Hampton and Box Packer J. C. Brickey.

No. 2184 then was ready for service and was moved by the hostler to the outgoing track where the road engine crew took over.

While awaiting completion of the final stages of "turning" the 2184, we were told that the locomotive was "called" for 11:45 a.m. ("Calling" time for a locomotive means the time it must be in readiness for a trip.)

The engine crew—Engineer E. J. Pifer and Fireman R. A. Leffel—were on duty promptly at

Engineer Pifer prepares to start 2184 rolling on its way to Bluefield—the classic pose of a veteran throttle artist at work. *Courtesy N&W.*

11:45 a.m., when we arrived at the outgoing track. Both men were busy with preliminaries for the run. Engineer Pifer gave his locomotive a careful inspection and saw to it that the locomotive was furnished with the necessary equipment, fuel, water and supplies, and Fireman Leffel saw to it that the fire was going good and the stoker operating properly. Both men welcomed us and seemed glad to have us aboard.

Engineer Pifer, a veteran who has served the N. & W. for more than 50 years, was almost ready to get going. By opening the gauge cocks, and glancing at the water glass, he ascertained the height of the water in the boiler and double-checked by opening and closing the low water alarm test valve. Then he observed the air and steam gauges, saw to it that the injector and feedwater pump were working properly. At 12:02 p.m., he inched back the throttle. With hardly an audible exhaust, the big and powerful engine started to move slowly out into the yard. Soon we were switched over to one of the main yard pull-out tracks and Mr. Pifer moved the reverse lever so that we could back down into the westbound forwarding yard and couple onto No. 85. As we slowed to a stop we looked out of the locomotive gangway and observed Yardmaster E. G. Snyder supervising the making up of No. 85. After receiving his train orders and the conductor's check of the train register, Engineer Pifer released the brakes, moved the reverse bar forward and pulled back the throttle a notch. The train began to move and we were on our way to Bluefield.

"We've got 65 cars—2,523 tons," Mr. Pifer remarked when the train was out on the westbound main line and he settled down with a chew of tobacco. He explained that the normal tonnage rating for a Y-6 locomotive, Roanoke to Bluefield,

"Our engine was working perfectly as we gathered speed through the level stretch beyond Salem" with time freight 85. 2184 needed only tightening of a wrist pin and a single lubrication adjustment for running repairs in its two-day, 647-mile trek. That is dependable and reliable performance! *Courtesy N&W.*

Fireman Blankenship readies 2184 before starting on the Roanoke to Crewe run. On the tough Blue Ridge climb, he and the engineer knew their jobs well in coaxing all possible power from the tireless "workhorse." *Courtesy N&W.*

is 2,800 tons but that the tonnage for No. 85 usually is less than this so as to enable the train to maintain a faster schedule.

We noticed that the locomotive was carrying white flags, indicating that No. 85 was being operated as an extra. "That's to help us get over the road," the engineer explained. "When we don't have to operate on a fixed schedule we can proceed as fast as conditions will permit and perhaps arrive at the next terminal ahead of the timetable schedule. Often this prevents terminal delays and expedites the movement over the entire run."

Our engine was working perfectly as we gathered speed through the level stretch beyond Salem. *The Powhatan Arrow* had passed us before we left the yard and the only train which could keep up with us was No. 9 which Mr. Pifer knew would have to stop at Salem. He had slight worries then about delaying the passenger train and when we reached Elliston his worries vanished completely since we were then in the C.T.C. district which extends from Elliston to Christiansburg. Sure enough, we had hardly passed Shawsville when No. 9 pulled by, going west on the eastbound track.

By now, the 2184 was settling down for the long pull up Allegheny Mountain to Christians-burg—a pull that would raise our 3,000 gross tons (including weight of locomotive and tender) a vertical distance of about 1,100 feet before we reach the summit. Every now and then Engineer Pifer would give the feedwater valve another turn and Fireman Leffel would adjust the stoker valve control. Mr. Leffel, who is on the extra list, hadn't been at his job long but he performed like a veteran. He kept as close a watch over his fire as a Boy Scout nursing a campfire. As a result, the steam pressure gauge needle never deviated from the 300-pound mark.

We gathered the full meaning of Mr. Pifer's explanation of the tonnage as No. 2184 maintained a good speed while climbing the Alleghenies. A locomotive working at full capacity is an awesome "creature", almost life-like as its whole body throbs with power. You feel as well as hear its tremendous effort as it generates and then uses the power of steam. You observe with amazement and some envy how the harder it works the more power it generates as long as it is fed with sufficient coal, and wish that humans were built that way.

Soon we were over the mountain top at Christiansburg and drifting toward Vicker and Walton. The large capacity tender makes unnecessary a stop for coal at Vicker and we passed the coal wharf at 40 miles an hour. Both the engineer and fireman were keeping close watch on the signals since these governed our operation. Each indication was called out by both members of the crew. Other than a brief stop to wait for a signal to clear just west of Walton, our only stop on the run to Bluefield was to take water at Lurich in preparation for the hard climb up the valley north of East River Mountain to the coal field capital. Here our locomotive encountered its heaviest grade of the afternoon—a 1.6 percenter, which made the sweat roll off both the engine and those in the cab. But again, No. 2184 gave a fine performance. We left Lurich at 3:15 p.m. and by 4:40 we were in Bluefield Yard. From Roanoke it had required just four hours and 20 minutes to chalk up 300,000 gross ton-miles, or nearly 70,000 gross ton-miles per hour.

Engineer Pifer stopped our great Iron Horse on the relieving track at 4:48 p.m. The moment we stopped, the Y-6-b was inspected by Engine Inspector D. H. Mauldin. The rod cups and other parts of the engine not reached by mechanical lubrication were filled with a lubricant by Engine Supplymen J. T. Haynes, J. P. Hairston, L. R. White and B. G. Williams. Moments later the engine was moved to the ash pit, where the fire was cleaned by Hillary Richardson and D. H. Adams. Hostler Joe Barlow next moved 2184 to the coal wharf for coal and water and then ran the engine across the turntable to the outgoing track.

The entire job of inspecting, servicing and refueling the locomotive at Bluefield had consumed a total of 29 minutes or no longer than would be required to have your car serviced at a filling station.

On the outgoing track we shook hands with Engineer W. D. Akers and Fireman J. P. Akers, who were to operate the engine to Williamson, and greeted 50-year Veteran Dan J. Cooper, the head brakeman. To get a different view of the operation we decided to ride the caboose to Williamson and were welcomed aboard by Conductor C. M. Anderson and Flagman J. C. Reynolds, another 50-year Veteran.

After Train 85 had been reassembled in Bluefield Yard, our locomotive started rolling again at 6:09 p.m. She had a heavier train this time—121 cars, 5,431 tons—due to the fact that the ruling grade against westbound traffic over Elkhorn Mountain is now only .5% (This grade was reduced by the construction of the new Elkhorn Tunnel and the line revision project between Cooper and Lick Branch, completed in 1950.)

Locomotive 2184 was pulling an important cargo of merchandise in the train stretched out

behind her. A look at the waybills in the hands of Conductor Anderson revealed that the cars were en route to many different destinations. There were carloads of cigarettes, plaster, chemicals, television sets, pig iron, furniture, machinery, groceries, sand, ballast, leather goods, cotton goods, and many other products. Some were going as far as the Pacific Coast, others were on their way to points in Colorado, Wisconsin, Kansas and Texas. And Engineer Akers was doing as fine a job of handling that train as we had ever observed. The caboose is the place to feel the full effects of jerks and slack action in a train's movement, but we felt not a single jerk of any consequence all the way from Bluefield to Williamson. This accomplishment included careful control of the train downgrade from Elkhorn Tunnel and stopping for train inspection at Farm.

We made a good run from a time standpoint, too, stopping in Williamson Yard at 9:45 p.m., or 3 hours and 36 minutes after leaving Bluefield. This was just 16 minutes less than the time made between the two terminals by passenger train No. 15, although the latter usually makes five more stops en route than did No. 85.

The engine terminal force quickly took over No. 2184 after its arrival. Hostler George Maynard spotted the locomotive at the coaling station at 10 p.m. and Coaler Melvin Williams promptly refilled the tender. Then the locomotive was moved to the spark track where Ashby Warren and Charles Sopher cleaned the fire. At this point Hostler Luther Farley took over the engine and moved it into position for putting water into the tank (June Dalton officiated at this job) and then moved 2184 into the engine servicing building where our engine was inspected by Machinist Inspector W. H. Hinkle and lubricated by Box Packer Baldwin Payne and Shopmen Robert J. Strother and Clyde Sherrill.

The turning operation at Williamson required just 55 minutes. So far not a single part of the locomotive had required repairs.

The next assignment for 2184 was to move a coal train from Devon (22 miles east of Williamson) to Bluefield. It was called for this job at 3:30 a.m. and doubled to Devon with locomotive No. 2116, which was to help us move the train. Again we rode in the locomotive cab—this time with Engineer R. E. Toler and Fireman W. M. Basham. Engineer Evan Moody and Fireman E. H. Blankenship were on the pusher and Conductor Rock Phillips was in charge of the train. Leaving Williamson at 4:03 a.m., we moved to Vulcan where we took water. At 5:30 a.m., we stopped at Devon where we saw on the storage

Serviced at the Shaffers Crossing long house, 2184 had mechanical lubrication to 213 points. *Courtesy N&W.*

track a string of 124 loads of coal, left there on the previous evening by a crew off the Buchanan Branch. Our pusher moved to the rear of the train while our locomotive was coupled to the head end. Shortly afterward, following passenger train No. 4, we moved out of Devon for Bluefield with an 11,000-ton train.

The most interesting part of our trip was up the new Elkhorn grade from Lick Branch and on through the new Elkhorn Tunnel. At Farm we had set off part of the train, reducing tonnage from 11,000 to 5,500 tons. With this load our locomotive and its helper had no trouble in crossing the mountain. The hardest part of the climb was not over the new line between Lick Branch and

Cooper, but over the five-mile stretch immediately preceding it, between North Fork and Lick Branch, where the grade against eastbound traffic now is being reduced from a maximum of 1.7% to 1.4%, together with elimination of heavy curvature. These improvements will make it possible to increase eastbound train tonnage.

Engineer Toler halted locomotive 2184 in Bluefield Yard at 11:20 a.m. By 12:05 p.m. the engine was ready for service again and was called to pull another coal train to Roanoke. We left Bluefield at 2:30 p.m. with Engineer A. S. Molter, Fireman R. F. Baker and Brakeman D. C. Sowder on the head end and Conductor J. A. Stump and Flagman Anderson Jones on the rear. We had 107

Washing the locomotive was part of the turning procedures. Up to date engine terminals, modern locomotive designs, and railway family pride promoted high utilization of N&W's steam giants. *Courtesy N&W.*

loads of coal, with a tonnage of 9,330. With engine No. 2174 (Engineer W. H. Williams) helping us over Christiansburg Mountain, we had no difficulty on the trip and locomotive 2184 arrived at Shaffers Crossing at 7:45 p.m.

Fit as a fiddle after its grueling, 31-hour operation over 400 miles of rail, our great engine of power and stamina was given little rest after the return to Shaffers Crossing. Another coal train was in Roanoke Yard awaiting its turn for movement to Crewe and 2184 was called upon to do the job. We pulled out of Park Street Yard at 11:10 p.m. in the locomotive cab with Engineer Harry J. Waldrond and Fireman E. M. Blankenship. Behind us were 96 carloads of coal with an official gross weight of 8,199 tons. We picked up a helper locomotive east of Vinton and then began the tough climb over the Blue Ridge.

The Y-6-b's are rugged and used to hard work, but they will give maximum performance only when they are handled properly by crews who know their jobs. That kind of a crew operated 2184 on the night we climbed the Blue Ridge. It was fascinating to watch the engineer carefully prod the locomotive to exert its maximum power as we passed Blue Ridge Station and slowly but surely advanced to the top of the mountain. His hands darted from the sanding lever over to the feed water valve, then he touched the engine brake valve to see if fully released. His left hand hauled the throttle lever back another notch while his right adjusted the reverse lever to just the correct position. Meanwhile, Fireman Blankenship was busy on his side, alternately adjusting the blower valve and the other valves which operate the stoker and distribute the coal as it enters the firebox. The steam pressure gauge registered a constant 300 pounds. The huge 2184 was doing its best, but its exhaust came slow and labored. Finally, with a great puff we crossed the top and the climb was over. Our locomotive had passed the test.

The run down the other side of the Blue Ridge was the fastest this writer has ever traveled on a freight locomotive. The engine seemed to express relief over finishing its heavy task, by letting itself roll down the grade to Montvale and beyond. However, the speedometer needle never went beyond 50 miles an hour. We made the 30-mile run to Forest in 52 minutes and at 1:25 a.m. we had stopped at Kinney for water and train inspection.

Kinney was the end of the run for this writer (who straightway hunted a bed!) but not so for No. 2184. After arrival at Crewe it was turned immediately and prepared for another trip to Roa-noke. The locomotive left Crewe at 10:35 a.m. (August 10) pulling a train of empty coal cars and arrived in Roanoke at 2:45 p.m. Fifteen minutes later it was back at the Shaffers Crossing engine terminal, having traversed within two days a total of 647 miles, or an average of 323.5 miles per day. And during all of that traveling the sum total of repairs needed was the tightening of a wrist pin and a simple adjustment of the lubrication so that more oil would be furnished to one of the cylinders. Performance like that is what our Motive Power folks mean when they say that our modern locomotives have "high availability." Performance like that helps to make ours a successfully-operated railroad, and every member of the railway Family can be justly proud of these great symphonies of steel and power, designed and built by our own people in our own shops.

ROANOKE SHOPS, THE CITY'S FIRST MAJOR INDUSTRY

Roanoke Shops, located at the east end of the railway's terminal complex, is adjacent to downtown Roanoke. These shops were not just for repair, as on most railroads, but they produced the fruits of genuis that N&W designers showed at the drawing boards. Locomotives and cars designed and built by N&W employees in the Roanoke Shops were considered unsurpassed in quality and as good in performance as any produced in this country. The shops' appearance remained essentially unchanged, from this 1939 photo, to the end of steam. In the foreground is the shops' locomotive roundhouse, behind are the smith, machine, erecting, and boiler shops with various other shops beyond. The steam era Roanoke Shops were an institution in themselves, and this reputation dates to the beginnings of Roanoke in 1882. *Courtesy N&W.*

The Roanoke Shops

The Norfolk and Western's main railway shops did the maintenance work on all of its steam locomotives needing heavy repairs. In this the road was no different from other large railroads. But the Roanoke Shops were unlike most other railway shops in that with great fidelity they produced the fruits of the genius its designers showed at the drawing boards. Their product included not only locomotives but rolling stock, too. The N&Ws Roanoke Shops were not always owned by the railway, yet their long history always included the construction and maintenance of locomotives and rolling stock.

The shops, known originally as the Roanoke Machine Works (RMW), organized on November 19, 1881, and built its plant during the next two years. The purpose of the company was to build and repair locomotives and cars for the Norfolk and Western and the Shenandoah Valley railroads, as well as to do similar contract work for other American railroads.

The RMW was Roanoke's first major industry. It employed about one thousand men and as originally constructed, comprised a smith shop, a machine shop, an erecting shop, a foundry, a planing mill, a lumber dryer, a storehouse and a

First of a long line of steam locomotives from N&W's Roanoke Shops was 117 built September 1884. The shops, then Roanoke Machine Works, were controlled by N&W Railroad until January 1897 when the reorganized N&W Railroad acquired ownership of RMW. After 1897, the works became N&W's Roanoke Shops. *Courtesy N&W.*

Boiler shop constructing Class A boilers in July 1937. *Courtesy N&W.*

twenty-one-stall car roundhouse. Nearby was the locomotive roundhouse, which was used jointly by the N&W and the Shenandoah Valley railroads. Both junctioned adjacent to the RMW. The two operated on different gauge track, so there was a freight and passenger car hoist for lifting car bodies and changing trucks to place them on the proper rails.

In 1882, the N&W Railroad purchased control of the works by acquiring its stock. Roanoke Machine Works remained under other owners until January 9, 1897, when the new N&W Railway acquired ownership. In the meantime, the new N&W owners steadily expanded and modernized shop facilities until they occupied an area of approximately ninety acres and were employing about 2,850 persons during World War II. During 1925 and 1926, the machine shop was rebuilt. As a result, in the last three decades of steam, it was considered as modern and efficient as any railway machine shop in the world.

From September 1884 to December 1953, the Roanoke Shops constructed 447 new locomotives, which is indeed an eye-catching statistic! Much has been written about the imposing parade of conventional steam locomotives built by the N&W from 1930 onward. Except for thirty purchased in 1950, all were created in the company's own shops. When the first diesels were bought, there were still 224 Roanoke-produced engines in service. But what is not generally known is that the N&W from 1930 on also built most of its own fleet of coal hopper cars plus some other types. Since coal cars (hoppers) comprise virtually two-thirds of the road's freight cars, the N&Ws Roanoke Shops not only made practically all of its modern steam locomotives but also most of its rolling stock too!

The railway had good reasons, of course, for doing its own construction. R. H. Smith, then N&W president, set them forth in 1956:

. . . in addition to giving heavy repairs to our vast fleet of freight cars in a better way and with maximum economy, we may also build most of our new cars with our own men and according to our own notions. Incidentally, doing both of those jobs with the same force should help in our ever-continuing aim to give uninterrupted employment to our men.

This philosophy extended right on to the building and maintenance of its steam locomotives. Here was an example of sound economics and good leadership—the company could build its own hoppers cheaper than commercial builders could to the N&Ws specifications. Also, the N&W was looking after its own employees and seeing to their welfare.

Upon completion of the new freight car shop in 1956, the open shop method of constructing hopper cars gave way to an enclosed assembly line method. In 1957, the freight car shop was turning out twenty hoppers per eight-hour shift (one every twenty-four minutes). Since then, sixteen hoppers per shift has been considered the optimum. In the early fifties, the seventy-ton hoppers became the standard, and in the early sixties the eighty-five-ton capacity car was introduced.

The Roanoke Shops was credited with some significant firsts. To extend boiler flue life, beginning in March 1912 the shops electrically welded a replacement segment to a used flue. This is called "safe-ending" a flue. Prior to then, when a portion of the flue was unserviceable, the entire

Boiler shop forces applying staybolts to the firebox of the first streamlined Class J600, during its construction. Boiler barrel and firebox is inverted for convenience of workmen. *Courtesy N&W.*

New Y6 boiler construction nearing completion in April 1940. The boiler will soon be tested, then moved to the erecting shop for the attachment to bed casting and the application of lagging and boiler jacket. *Courtesy N&W.*

flue was discarded. The first completely electrically welded locomotive firebox turned out in the United States was built in the Roanoke Shops and was put in service July 1, 1914, in locomotive Number 778. In 1922, the first large firebox with crown, sides and combustion chamber formed from one piece of steel was constructed. One master boilermaker for the N&W held the patents for the auxiliary firebox flue sheet, reinforcing ribs for back firebox flue sheets, boiler wash-out plugs and the banded electrically-welded front flue sheet.

Building a modern steam locomotive was quite an undertaking, for it required the coordinated effort of numerous workers in various shops. Before actual construction began, materials for items

produced locally had to be procured and component parts that the N&W did not make in its own shops obtained. Examples of the latter are air pumps, feedwater heater systems, superheaters, safety valves, lights, lubricators, roller bearings, tires and similar items. With the advent of bed castings, a great deal of work was eliminated that had previously gone into the construction of the built-up frame. These cast steel frames were produced and machined by a nationally known supplier. The locomotive-to-be was assembled in the erecting shop, with other shops supplying basic component parts.

The first component to reach the erecting shop floor was the bed casting(s). Various riggings, lubricators and certain parts of the valve gear

With boiler jacket, piping, and fittings installed, the engine is "wheeled." After the rear drivers are secured by binders, this giant Mallet will be moved again by these overhead cranes to connect 2185 to its front engine. Date: May 1949. *Courtesy N&W.*

Another steam giant almost ready for service. The building of one new locomotive per month, together with classified repairs to maintain existing power, stabilized the shops' manpower. Over the years, this new construction almost completely replaced older steam. 2131 was completed May 16, 1938. *Courtesy N&W.*

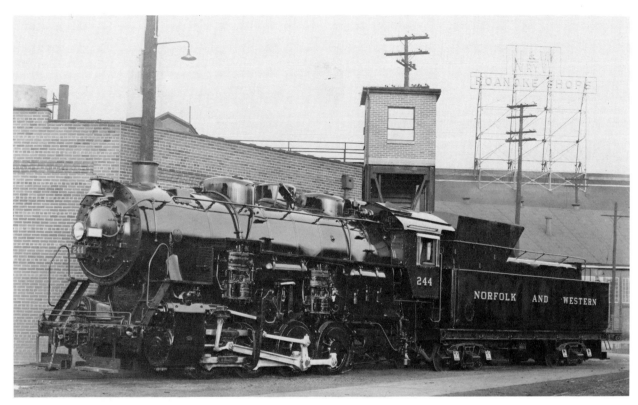

The last steamer constructed in Roanoke Shops was Class S1a 244 in December 1953. All total, Roanoke built 447 new engines, reboilered 2 others, with 203 of the new locomotives being constructed from 1930-53. The railway harbored the claim that its homebuilt steam power was unsurpassed in quality and was a major factor in the company's well-being. *Courtesy N&W.*

were attached to the frame(s) except for wheels. Meanwhile, the foundry was casting wheel centers, piston centers, cylinder heads and many other locomotive castings. The smith shop forged the driving, piston and valve gear rods. In the boiler shop, flat plate steel was being rolled to form the boiler shell. After the boiler shell was welded and riveted together, the mud ring, firebox and flues were installed, and the cylinder saddle attached to the boiler shell. Next, the new boiler was sand blasted to clean out all mill scale and other extraneous matter. A hydrostatic test was then conducted at 125 percent of working pressure, followed by a steam test at working pressure to check for leaks. Now the boiler was transferred to the erecting shop on two freight-car-like trucks. In the erecting shop the boiler was attached to the bed casting, the lagging and boiler jackets applied, and all other boiler fittings installed.

About one or two days prior to completion, the new locomotive was "wheeled" or more precisely the complete boiler with frames was picked up, then lowered onto the wheels. When the driving wheels were secured by binders, the brake rigging

was hung, the driving rods attached and then the final attachments were added. The tender was constructed by the tank and boiler shops. Finally, the new locomotive was pulled to the nearby shops' roundhouse and fired up. After setting the valve gear and safety valves, a few minor adjustments were made and the new locomotive was ready for service. In addition, other shops or departments such as the machine shop and electrical department were on the production "team," too.

The Roanoke Shops had the capacity to complete one large modern steam locomotive each month, although on occasion they could average more than one per month for a short duration and during wartime. The smaller 0-8-0 switchers were completed at the rate of about three every two months. The new locomotive construction was worked into the normal schedule of overhauling the older locomotives. Over the years, the N&W almost completely replaced its steam locomotive fleet with modern power by the efficient use of shop forces for both overhauling and new construction.

While steam locomotives were being con-

54

structed, others were being sent to the Roanoke Shops for periodic heavy repairs. Government regulations and N&W maintenance procedures required annual and biannual inspections and that the subsequent repairing be performed. Every four years the flues were renewed, although a two-year extension could be granted. And every five years, the boiler had new lagging applied. Once in a great while, the firebox had to be replaced and other very extensive repairs made.

N&W steam locomotives were not shopped on the basis of mileage, but on condition—were heavy repairs needed? If heavy repairs were required, the locomotive was moved to the erecting shop where the rods, brake rigging, piston and cylinder heads were all removed from the engine for reworking. When the locomotive required new wheel centers, the journal boxes renewed or turned, the entire locomotive was lifted from the wheels and the repair work accomplished; then the locomotive was "wheeled" again. When general repairs to the machinery were made, the running gear, wheels and cylinders were com-

pletely taken apart, worked on and reassembled. All of the heaviest repairs were made at the Roanoke Shops, though the Portsmouth Shops helped out by doing some of the heavier repair work until the 1940s.

During World War II, the Roanoke Shops performed service not to the N&W alone but also to the country's far-flung war effort. No less than 284 locomotives of eight other railroads were repaired and kept rolling. Likewise, the N&Ws own shops produced thousands of other items the nation needed in its march to victory.

Interestingly, the N&W Railway sponsored the 755th Railway Shop Battalion for the Military Railway Service in Europe during the hostilities. This shop battalion was composed primarily of men from the railway's own Roanoke Shops. This distinguished unit was cited for meritorious service. And why not? Here was a military unit composed of skilled personnel from the most efficient railway repair shops anywhere, performing a duty they knew so very well.

In July 1958 the last of the N&Ws steam locomotives received heavy repairs. With the steam

Hoppers being constructed by open shop method along freight car line. This system of car construction gave way to the enclosed assembly line method in 1956. *Courtesy N&W.*

Twenty hoppers, like this 70-ton type, were being built each eight-hour shift in 1957. Later 16 hoppers per shift were considered optimum. The 70-ton hopper was the standard type built during the fifties. *Courtesy N&W.*

Y2a 1712 undergoing classified repairs in June 1928. Not only was existing power repaired at Roanoke, but many older classes were rebuilt and upgraded, such as the original Y2s into Y2as in the twenties. In late steam, high mileage Class Js were shopped annually, while the freight engines were given heavy repairs "on condition"— when needed. *Courtesy N&W.*

A portion of the old steam construction shops are today the diesel shop. Although new diesels are not built at Roanoke, complete disassembly, reassembly, and rebuilding of them is routinely done. GP9 649, one of N&W's early diesels, is being extensively rebuilt in 1974 due to a mishap. *Courtesy N&W.*

engines running out their serviceable miles or being retired as each order of diesels rolled in, the Roanoke Shops took on a new look. At first, during early dieselization, few overhauls were needed, for this was definitely the most modern diesel fleet in the land. With age, the diesels began receiving engine overhauls; generators required maintenance, and wheels were renewed. The Roanoke Shops set up an assembly line for fast, efficient repair work. The long-established freight car assembly line continued to turn out a never ending stream of hoppers and some covered hoppers and gondolas as well. In 1963 the 100-ton capacity hopper was introduced. This continues to be the standard coal-carrying car today.

The N&Ws Roanoke Shops is not just a shop for the building and maintenance of locomotives and cars: it is an institution in itself. The pride of the shop's employees in their railway and in their work clearly shows in the products they have rolled forth from its floors. These great "iron horses" stemmed the flood of dieselization longer than any other steam power. The service rendered by the shops to the Railway, and in time of war to the nation, is a tribute to the workers who performed it. They earned and gained a reputation that ranks them with the finest anywhere. A reputation such as this is not easily made, nor is it easily forgotten.

Locomotive Engineering

HOMEBUILT STEAM POWER

Roanoke terminal's Shaffers Crossing roundhouse and long houses seem to be over-flowing with steam locomotives on an October night in 1943. Almost all engines observed were designed and built by N&W employees in the railway's shops. Thus a design philosophy and concept of locomotive engineering evolved over the years that was N&W through and through. *Courtesy N&W.*

Design Philosophy

The Norfolk and Western Railway, like some other railroads, had faith in and admiration for the coal-burning locomotive. Almost all other railroads, in order to meet their requirements for new motive power, contracted with commercial builders to construct their new locomotives. Each railroad would make minor changes to the basic design offered by the builder and then assign the new motive power to the tasks at hand. The N&W, unlike most railroads, designed and built its own new steam locomotives in its own shops. Thus, a design philosophy emerged that resulted in the N&W being regarded as the epitome of standard steam railroading. This philosophy was evident in the N&Ws definition of the term

"modern steam locomotives" and in the railway's ability to design the most powerful locomotives in both tractive effort and horsepower rating with a given engine weight. The N&W, by recognizing the advantages and disadvantages of steam, designed modern locomotives to capitalize on merits and minimize shortcomings.

Defining the modern steam locomotive, the N&W declared that the term meant a locomotive built with a large, high capacity boiler, roller bearings on all the engine and tender axles, one-piece cast steel engine frame with the cylinders cast integral, complete mechanical and pressure lubrication and improved cross-counterbalancing of the reciprocating and rotating parts. The

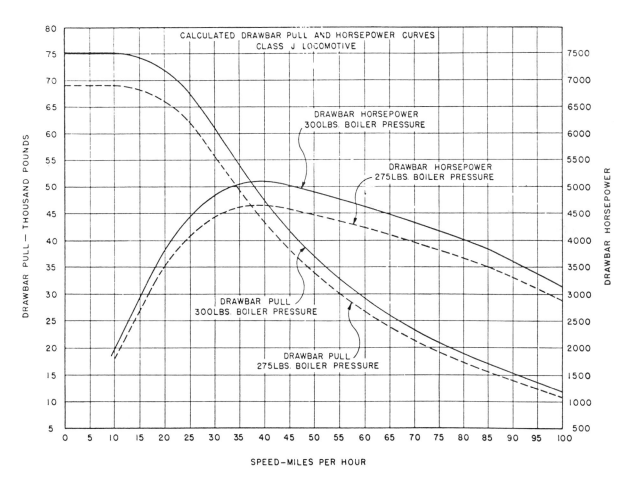

Late era N&W steam road power was set for 300 psi boiler pressure, which was considered about maximum for conventional steam. The first 10 As and 11 Js were built with 275 psi but subsequently were raised to 300. This diagram indicates the resultant increase in the Js drawbar pull and horsepower at the higher working pressure. *Courtesy N&W.*

The versatile Class A 2-6-6-4, a totally N&W-designed locomotive, could handle the heaviest coal trains on the level stretches of the system, step out with a time freight, and wheel a heavy passenger train at 70 mph where operating conditions permitted. *Courtesy Charles E. Winters.*

N&W super-power boilers of its most modern road locomotives all had three hundred pounds per square inch steam pressure, very large grate areas with combustion chambers to increase firebox volume and the maximum heating and superheater surfaces possible for a given boiler size.

The three hundred pounds boiler pressure was regarded as a maximum for the conventional steam locomotive. To attain higher pressure and higher temperature steam to gain more horsepower from a given quantity of water, a new type boiler and a different type of converter of steam energy into motion energy was needed. Subsequently, the steam turbine electric evolved. Finally, the diesel electric eliminated the problem altogether. As for roller bearings, the N&W was the first railroad to use roller bearings extensively on all modern road engine and tender axles and on the reciprocating and rotating parts of its fast road locomotives—the 4-8-4s and the 2-6-6-4s.

Why did the N&W continue to operate steam locomotives, and to build new ones, when other roads turned to different forms of motive power? The answer emerges in a statement in 1951 by H. C. Wyatt, then the assistant general superintendent motive power, to the railway's employees:

> Our situation differs from that of most other roads in two respects—first, we had available along our railroad, in almost unlimited quantities, the cheapest of any known fuel—coal. It is coal of the finest quality for power generation. Second, when other railroads began to turn to other types of power, we already had in service a substantial number of modern coal-burning steam locomotives. The railroads on which the greatest number of steam locomotives are replaced by other types did not have fleets of steam power as reliable, efficient or as modern as our own J's, A's, or Y6's.

This was a typical statement made by the N&W in that era promoting the coal-burning locomotive. In the final analysis, the N&Ws modern steam locomotives represented steam's finest hour both in design and in road service.

60

One reason for the success of the Y5/Y6s was that almost all of the locomotive weight was used for adhesion—90% to be exact. For brute power, there were no finer engines for heavy-duty mountain freight service. *Courtesy Charles E. Winters.*

For years the N&W championed the steam locomotive because for fuel it burned coal, which was the major source of traffic and revenue for the railway. With its superbly designed, home-built steam giants, N&W thought it could effect no economy or improvement in service by switching to other modes of power. *Courtesy C.W. Jernstrom.*

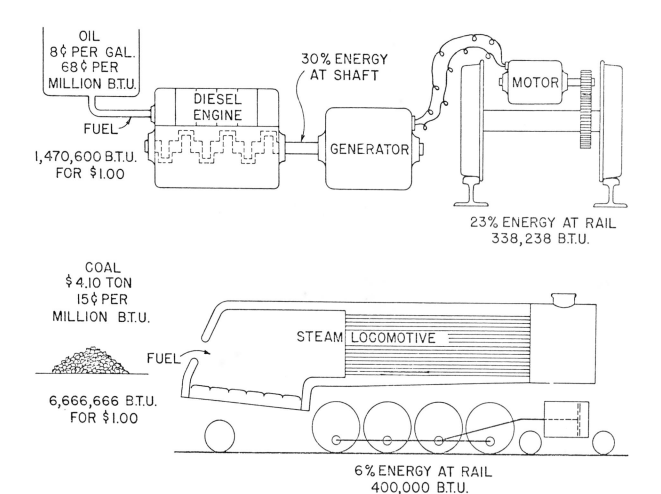

OIL
8¢ PER GAL.
68¢ PER
MILLION B.T.U.

30% ENERGY
AT SHAFT

MOTOR

DIESEL ENGINE

FUEL

GENERATOR

1,470,600 B.T.U.
FOR $1.00

23% ENERGY AT RAIL
338,238 B.T.U.

COAL
$4.10 TON
15¢ PER
MILLION B.T.U.

FUEL

STEAM LOCOMOTIVE

6,666,666 B.T.U.
FOR $1.00

6% ENERGY AT RAIL
400,000 B.T.U.

The economics of continuing with modern, coal-fired locomotives justified the construction of N&W home-built steam power in the late '40s. This schematic shows that for equal dollar amounts of fuel compared, steamers could get 18% more work at the rail. Furthermore, diesels initially cost more for a given capacity, and their availability for service was not better than N&W's modern steam. *Courtesy N&W.*

The heavy grades over three mountain ranges and the heavy coal traffic dictated motive power requirements on the N&W. For freight service, the locomotives had to pull with an enormous force on the frequent, adverse grades, while on the flatter portions of the system they moved these same trains at near passenger train speeds. This requirement necessitated locomotives of both high tractive effort and high horsepower ratings. For mountain work, the World War I era 2-8-8-2 compound Mallet was improved upon, updated and refined to the point that it could develop 152,206 pounds starting tractive effort and produce more than 5,600 drawbar horsepower in the twenty-five miles per hour range.

The idea of using steam twice in the Mallet compound was not discarded by the N&W as it was by other railroads. The N&W knew that the Mallet was slow, but nonetheless very powerful. For mountainous work where heavy train speeds were low, the Mallet compound's advantages of brute power with steam economy was capitalized upon. Thus the economy of using steam twice paid off. As for the versatile 2-6-6-4, a totally N&W designed locomotive, it could handle the heaviest coal trains on the level stretches of the system, step out with a time freight in mountain regions, and wheel a heavy passenger train at seventy miles per hour. The 4-8-4 passenger locomotive could cruise routinely at ninety miles per

Roanoke built 157 roller-bearing-equipped steam locomotives. Primary advantages of modern roller-bearing steam power over that with conventional bearings were relatively low fuel consumption, high availability, and low maintenance costs. *Courtesy N&W.*

hour on the straight portions of the main line, and yet accelerate a heavy passenger train up steep mountain grades as well as any steam locomotive ever produced.

If there was one word to describe these giants of the N&W steam era, that word would be *versatility*. Each of these three types of locomotives was suited to various duties and was designed for system-wide use. How did the N&W design the 2-6-6-4 and 4-8-4 locomotives for such versatility? It was done by using the seventy-inch driving wheel for high horsepower at higher speeds and by using larger cylinders to attain the high tractive effort needed in the lower speeds.

With these high horsepower and high tractive effort locomotives, the N&W achieved more power to total weight ratio than was characteristic of most U.S. locomotives. Likewise, the drawbar pull and drawbar horsepower ratings were the maximum possible with a given locomotive total weight and weight on drivers. This was achieved with high boiler pressures, the seventy-inch driving wheel and the large cylinders. The cylinder starting tractive effort was so high that the driving wheels would slip before the maximum cylinder power was developed. In this way, the railway produced locomotives that used all possible power for starting a train with a given locomotive weight. The same train was then propelled with the maximum power possible from the high capacity boilers in combination with the seventy-inch drivers (or fifty-eight-inch drivers for the 2-8-8-2).

Furthermore, to get the maximum power possible from a given locomotive size, the maximum practical number of driving axles were employed for the intended service, thereby bringing more of the locomotive's weight to bear on the driving wheels. To keep as much of the locomotive's weight as possible for traction, the least number of lead and trailing truck axles were used. This could be illustrated by the latter-day 2-8-8-2 whose total weight was 611,520 pounds. Of this total weight, 548,500 pounds were on the drivers, leaving only 63,020 pounds on the lead and trailing trucks.

As for proposed power on the N&W, the Y7 2-8-8-2 would have been a four cylinder, single expansion locomotive with a boiler potential very similar to the 2-6-6-6s and 4-8-8-4s in use on other railroads. The Y7 would have weighed considerably less than the 2-6-6-6 and 4-8-8-4, yet roughly with equal horsepower and probably higher tractive effort than either. The diesel, on the other hand, had all of its weight on the driving wheels

and as many units could be coupled together in tandem for the horsepower needed for a particular job. This leaves little doubt why the diesel was very attractive to motive power personnel and was in fact one reason for N&W dieselization.

Although the N&W was passionately dedicated to the coal-burning steam locomotive, it was fully cognizant of conventional steam motive power's advantages and disadvantages. The steam locomotive was an extremely rugged and simple machine with the capability to withstand more abuse than other types of power. For a given power rating, it was relatively inexpensive to build. Another outstanding characteristic was its ability to develop quickly its maximum power when needed. This is best illustrated by the fact that the steam locomotive could evaporate, in a given time, ten times as much water as the most efficient stationary steam plant boiler of the same weight as the locomotive.

In spite of the steam locomotive's virtues, the railway was realistic about conventional steam. It recognized the relatively low overall efficiency attained in conventional steam power and realized that any substantial improvement of the reciprocating steam locomotive was extremely difficult. This was a result of using water as a medium of converting heat units in fuel to work units in moving the pistons. A tremendous amount of heat is required to convert water at the boiling point to steam at the same temperature. Since the final exhaust from the locomotive's cylinders is in the form of steam, a further loss of potential work units occurs.

To help overcome this problem, the N&W experimented with the steam turbine electric for higher efficiency with a significant increase in steam pressure. The railway also researched the possibility of developing a coal-fired gas turbine electric to eliminate the medium of water altogether as a converter between the coal heat units and the work units. The steam-turbine electric was unsuccessful, and the coal-fired gas turbine electric never got off the drawing board after preliminary tests of certain components.

The diesel provided the best solution for all types of operations—main line, light service lines, and yards—simply by coupling units together and working in tandem for a particular job. The diesel, although more expensive to acquire than steam, is significantly more efficient and does not require the frequent servicing and extensive servicing facilities of the steam era.

Finally, the question arises, "If steam locomotive component parts peculiar to the steam locomotive had been available in the mid-1950s, would the N&W have dieselized when it did?" The opinions of the N&W officials during the late steam and early dieselization era differ widely on this. One opinion is common, though, and that is the diesel would have come sooner or later. Its advantages could not be overlooked. But the N&W officials' opinions differ from here on. One extreme is that the diesel would have come when it did anyhow. The other is that it would not have been adopted if the N&W could have gotten the many parts in quantity not manufactured in the Roanoke Shops, such as stokers, valve gears, air compressors, injectors, feedwater heaters, safety valves and other components peculiar to the steam locomotive.

In the mid-1950s, the N&W was the only all-steam Class I railroad. Commercial manufacturing firms were curtailing the production of many of the needed steam component parts. The railway found itself still capable of getting parts, but, as some of the officials stated, it became increasingly more difficult and costly to obtain them. Yet, considering the dual servicing facilities required for both steam and diesels at terminals during the transition from steam to diesel and the growing opposition to steam locomotives due to smoke, fly ash and air pollution along the right-of-way, the demise of steam was hastened.

Maybe, just maybe, the N&W modern steam locomotives, produced and operated in the last three decades of steam, did delay the diesel longer than is generally known. The N&W modern steam locomotive did lose out to the diesel in the end, but it held out longer than any other. This is to the credit of the locomotives themselves, and, above all, to those who designed, built, operated, serviced and maintained them. All who did certainly have a right to be proud—proud of themselves, proud of their steam locomotives, and proud of the Norfolk and Western!

Improvements on the Compound Mallet

The N&W used the compound Mallet locomotive to the end of the steam era. In this it was different from other railroads. The very last road engines the Norfolk and Western built were of this type. Yes, other roads did use the compound Mallets for secondary work, but few roads ever bought a new Mallet after 1930. The Norfolk and Western, on the other hand, did not just continue building the same old Mallet, it improved the basic, old United States Railway Administration (USRA) 2-8-8-2 compound to the point that it could give any single-expansion X-8-8-X articulated a "run for its money" when engaged in heavy mountain operations. This evolution extended from the 1920s to 1955.

The compound Mallet referred to here is the term applied to the articulated locomotive that has a rear set of cylinders and drivers using high-pressure steam and a front set of cylinders and drivers using the low-pressure steam exhausted from the rear cylinders. This system of the compound expansion of steam was the only successful such system adopted in U.S. railroading and was named after its Swiss designer, Anatole Mallet. Thus the term "Mallet" refers only to the compound expansion articulated type of locomotive.

The first Mallet produced in the U.S. was built in 1904. The Norfolk and Western received its first Mallets in 1910 on primarily an experimental basis. But the N&Ws first successful compound Mallet was the Class Z1, wheel arrangement 2-6-6-2. These highly successful articulateds were only eclipsed by the larger 2-8-8-2 in an effort to gain more power. The 2-8-8-2s initially were of two classes: the Class Y2, designed and built both by the N&Ws shops and by a commercial builder; and the Class Y3, a product of the United States Railway Administration of World War I. The Class Y3s were superior in actual performance, and these became the basis for the N&Ws improvements on the compound Mallet.

The advantage of compounding was its economy and high tractive effort at low speeds on heavy grades requiring high drawbar pull. Under operating conditions requiring relatively long cutoff, the use of steam twice before exhausting it into the atmosphere meant more work from a given quantity of steam. Since it operated in simple for starting and at low speeds on heavy grades, the Mallet had a significantly higher starting tractive effort than single expansion power of comparable weight.

Unfortunately, this type of locomotive had some striking disadvantages. One, the Mallet, because of the low pressure cylinders, was a slow speed engine with its maximum horsepower developed at about fifteen miles per hour. Above this speed, drawbar pull and drawbar horsepower fell off sharply. Therefore, the compound locomotive was well suited only for mountain service with heavy trains. Secondly, a Mallet locomotive operating simple was very uneconomical and not

This Baldwin switcher was less than two years old when C&O dieselized its yard operations. N&W saw the chance to overhaul its yard fleet, purchased C&O switchers, then built 45 copies in Roanoke Shops. Although not a N&W design, these shifters had high tractive effort and high availability ideally suited for yard work. *Courtesy A. A. Thieme, C. T. Felstead Collection.*

satisfactory except on relatively short ruling grades under unusual conditions. To improve the operation of the Mallet, the N&W set out to increase the drawbar pull, horsepower and economy of this power at higher speeds; and, when on tough grades at lower speeds to operate in compound with increased drawbar pull and horsepower. The N&W wanted to use the simple operation only for starting and as a last resort to keep the train moving under adverse circumstances.

To gain this additional power and speed of the compound Mallet, it was necessary to determine the reasons the drawbar horsepower decreased rapidly as the speed increased over fifteen miles per hour. It was discovered that excessive back pressure was being exerted on the low pressure pistons during exhaust stroke and that incoming steam was restricted during admission stroke. These undesirable conditions were caused by restricted valve port openings as cutoff was reduced to get expansive work from the steam and to excessively high back pressure at the exhaust nozzle. Originally, the Mallets had a maximum cutoff of ninety percent in the high pressure and eighty-eight percent in the low pressure cylinders. (Note: cutoff means the length of the piston

stroke during which steam is admitted before expansion starts.) During road tests it was found that there was practically no improvement in drawbar pull by using a longer cutoff above seventy-five percent. However, when the maximum design cutoff was ninety percent, a cutoff of seventy-five percent meant reduced valve travel and consequently reduced valve port openings.

With the causes that retarded speed and power of the Mallet identified, the N&W mechanical engineers set out to correct these shortcomings. As the Class Y5 and Y6 engines were built, the front low-pressure cylinders received eighteen-inch piston valves, instead of the original fourteen-inch valves, to provide greater valve port area so the partially expanded steam could enter and leave these cylinders with less restriction. After much experimentation from 1937 to the late forties, the valve design was changed to increase valve port opening for a given cutoff and valve travel. This was accomplished by increasing steam lap to limit cutoff at eighty percent in the high pressure and seventy-five percent in the low pressure cylinders with 6½ inches full valve travel. (Note: steam lap is the amount the admission portion of the valve overlaps the steam port when the valve is at the midpoint of its travel.)

Due to relatively low overall efficiency and difficulty in improving the reciprocating steam locomotive, the railway tried to develop for years a new form of coal-fired motive power. The result was the steam turbine electric in the mid-fifties. This was N&W's last bid for a coal-fired successor to conventional steam. Diesels provided the final solution. *Courtesy C. W. Jernstrom.*

This 4-8-2 Class K1 was just one of many classes developed over the years that ultimately led to N&W's giants of the steam era. Number 105 was one of 16 K1s designed and built by Roanoke Shops in 1916-17. *Courtesy Harold K. Vollrath.*

Class Y3s, as 2027, were superior in performance, and these became the basis for N&W's improvements in its Mallet compounds. The advantages of compound engines were their economy and high tractive effort at low speeds, which made them ideal for heavy grades that required high drawbar pull. *Courtesy N&W.*

Compound Mallets were superior to single expansion locomotives in service that required relatively long valve cutoff. Since N&W profile was very hilly, Mallet's steam economy reduced operating costs in the mountains. The Class Y5 design, as that of 2097, was refined later into the Class Y6. *Courtesy N&W.*

Y5 and Y6 front low-pressure cylinders had 18-inch piston valves instead of the 14-inch valves on earlier classes. The bridgepipe allowed a larger exhaust pipe to the stack. These improvements provided less restriction to steam entering and leaving the front cylinders as well as freer exhaust passages. Number 2120 was the first Y6, built in 1936. *Courtesy N&W.*

To reduce exhaust back pressure further, bigger stacks with larger area exhaust nozzles were installed that cut back pressure at the nozzle to about twelve pounds per square inch maximum. The new stacks and exhaust nozzles provided better drafting and freer steaming boilers.

The redesigned valve events, stacks and exhaust stands were originally applied to the Class Y6b as built. These improvements boosted maximum drawbar horsepower to 5,600 at twenty-five miles per hour. All of these improvements, coupled with the Y5 and Y6's larger grate area, extended combustion chamber and higher boiler pressure, substantially increased performance of the modern Mallets over that of classes Y3 and Y4. But none of these aforementioned modifications gave any extra power, in compound, at low speeds normal on steep grades with heavy tonnage.

One way of obtaining the desired added power was by getting more work from the large, low pressure cylinders. This could be done by raising the receiver pressure with a small amount of superheated boiler steam, thus increasing the pressure and temperature of the steam entering the low pressure cylinders. On the conventional Y5/Y6 engines, this exhaust steam from the high pressure cylinders was eighty-five to ninety pounds per square inch in the receiver pipe. As originally built, these locomotives had internally located reducing and intercepting valves. These valves gave considerable trouble from carbon deposits and were difficult to get to for cleaning and maintenance; thus, a study of these components was made for improving their design.

After experimentation in the early 1950s, the N&W developed an externally located reducing valve and positively controlled intercepting and high pressure cylinder exhaust valves. The external reducing valve was designed to automatically operate when the Mallet was working in simple for starts or while running. Furthermore, it could be put in operation even if the locomotive was operating in compound. When used in compound, the reducing valve allowed a *relatively small* amount of superheated boiler steam to be added to the receiver, thereby raising the pressure and temperature of the exhaust steam from the high pressure cylinders. The cab valve used by the engineer to place the reducing valve in service while operating the Mallet in compound was known to engine crews as the booster operating valve, or "booster valve" in short. With the "booster" on, the superheated boiler steam raised the receiver pressure to about 100 to 110 pounds

Y5/Y6s had 126,838 pounds tractive effort compound, or 152,206 pounds simple. This additional 20% starting tractive effort enabled them to make successful starts on heavy grades or under adverse conditions that otherwise could not be done with an engine of this capacity. *Courtesy Charles E. Winters.*

The external reducing valve, located above the right rear cylinder, was installed to all 100 Y5 and Y6s in the mid-fifties. The 2100s also received redesigned valve events and larger stacks. Note 2122's larger stack compared to 2149. *A. A. Thieme Photo, Courtesy C. T. Felstead Collection.*

per square inch and added considerable temperature to the steam supplying the low pressure cylinders. The result was a gain in tractive effort and work from the low pressure engine on heavy grades at low speed when the going was tough. With the booster on, the Mallet was not quite as economical as if in straight compound operation but was much more efficient than working in simple on the ruling grades.

The application of the externally located reducing valve and its manually operated booster operating valve to all of the modern Mallets took place in 1953-1955. When the Y5, Y6 and Y6as received the booster valves, they also got the redesigned valve events, stacks and exhaust stands so successful on the Y6bs. These "booster valve" equipped Mallets were officially classed as the "Improved Y5/Y6." The two most significant improvements were the installations of the external reducing valve with the manual control and the valve change to limit the cutoff to eighty percent in the high pressure and seventy-five percent in the low pressure cylinders at full valve travel, which gave larger valve port openings for a given cutoff. These modifications boosted maximum drawbar horsepower by more than 1,000 with the maximum reached at a higher speed of 25 miles

per hour; and, while still in compound with the booster on, train speed increased on the grades from about eight miles per hour to twelve to fifteen miles per hour depending on the severity of the ascent. Likewise, train tonnage on the heavy grade districts was increased by as much as 500 tons with the "Improved Y5/Y6s." The higher receiver pressure made the low pressure engine slippery. To best use the added power with the booster on, lead was added to the front bed casting of the Y5/Y6s to get better traction.

These improvements were coupled with a high capacity boiler, roller bearings on all engine axles, cast steel frames with cylinders cast integrally, improved counter-balancing and pressure and mechanical lubrication. These features applied to the modern Mallet made this locomotive competitive with any X-8-8-X locomotive up to, say, thirty miles per hour. A look at the Y6b horsepower and drawbar pull curves in the next section on "Steam versus Diesel Tests of 1952" clearly indicates the power of these locomotives. As can be seen from these curves, the Y6b had more drawbar pull and a higher maximum drawbar horsepower than the Class As, although the Y6b had sixteen less square footage of grate area. Only by introducing the proposed single expansion Class Y7 2-8-8-2, could the N&W have gained the high drawbar pull of the Y6 with a flatter drawbar horsepower curve at the higher speeds. But it was felt by the officials that dual service Class As were more suitable for the heavy flat land trains, and to use the Y7s in the mountains would not be an advantage on the Y6s in economy.

The Class A had a maximum thermal efficiency of about seven percent when being operated at capacity. This was about the average in the age of steam but was especially good with the extremely heavy trains pulled by this type of locomotive. The Y6bs, on the other hand, had an overall efficiency in actual operation equal to or slightly better than the A. This does not seem very sig- nificant until one considers that the single expansion Class As operated at the higher speeds best suited to that type of power. If the single expansion locomotive is operated in slow, heavy work, its efficiency drops rapidly. The N&Ws compound Mallets equalled the As in efficiency while working in slow, heavy mountain service. This performance of the Mallet meant a substantial savings to the company.

I wonder if other railroad companies engaged in mountain operations with high speed single expansion locomotives may have secretly wished, in view of the N&Ws Mallets, that they had reconsidered their motive power policy. Economically, there were no finer locomotives for the service they performed.

The following four illustrations depict the operation of the modern Mallet locomotive. The heart of the modern Mallet locomotive is the intercepting valve, which determines if the engine is simple or compound, and the reducing valve, which regulates boiler steam to the low-pressure cylinders at a reduced pressure, when simple. The engineer starts the Mallet in simple. When underway he puts the simpling valve in compound position. To use or not to use booster steam depends if laboring on a heavy grade or working a very heavy train. *N&W Drawings. Courtesy Robert M. Pilcher Collection.*

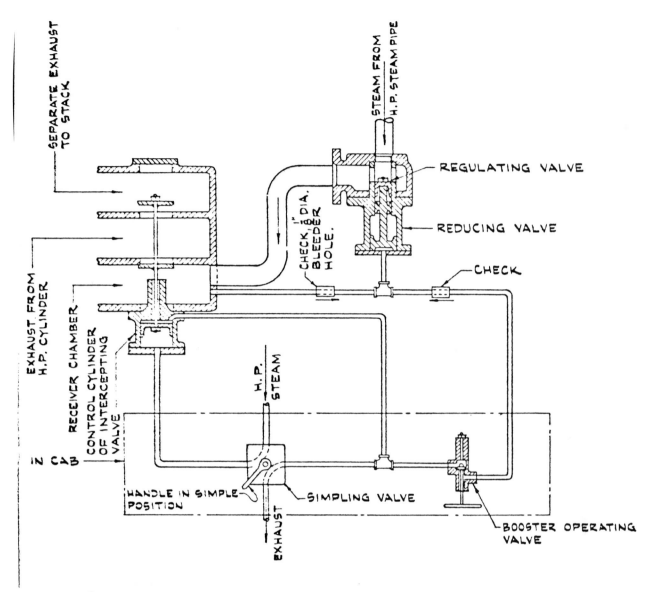

SEPARATE EXHAUST TO STACK

STEAM FROM H.P. STEAM PIPE

REGULATING VALVE

REDUCING VALVE

CHECK, ⅛ DIA. BLEEDER HOLE.

CHECK

EXHAUST FROM H.P. CYLINDER

RECEIVER CHAMBER

CONTROL CYLINDER OF INTERCEPTING VALVE

IN CAB

H.P. STEAM

HANDLE IN SIMPLE POSITION

SIMPLING VALVE

EXHAUST

BOOSTER OPERATING VALVE

Simple Position

Note:—

When handle on Simpling Valve is pointing to the left, the Intercepting valve is in simple position. Exhaust from H.P. Cylinders passes through a separate exhaust pipe to stack instead of into receiver chamber. No steam is being delivered to the Booster Operating Valve and the position of the Booster Valve Handle has no effect on the operation. H.P. steam moves through the Regulating Valve in the Reducing Valve to the L.P. cylinders through the receiver chamber and receiver pipe. When the pressure in the receiver chamber is too high, the Regulating Valve in the Reducing Valve will close. When this pressure is too low, the Regulating Valve will open.

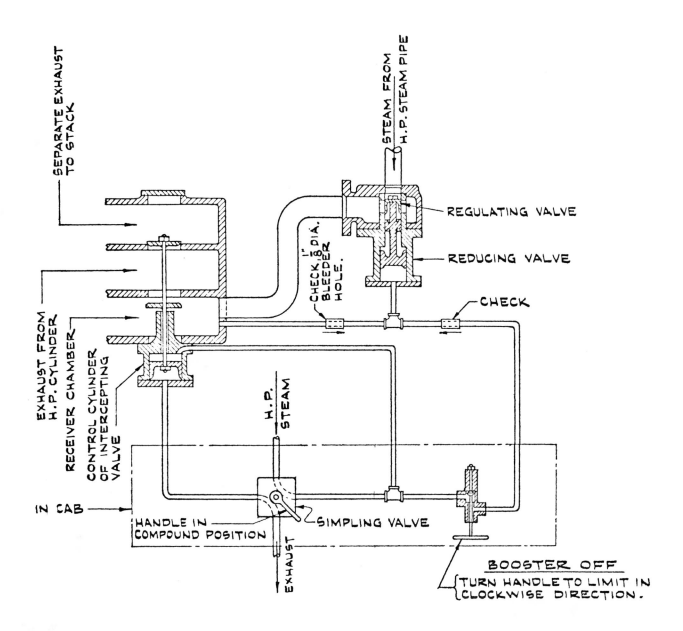

Compound Position Without Booster Steam

Note:—

When handle on Simpling Valve is pointing toward the engineer, the Intercepting Valve is in compound position. The exhaust from H.P. cylinders passes to the L.P. cylinders through the receiver chamber and receiver pipe. Booster Operating Valve is in "Off" position (Handle turned to limit in clockwise direction), steam flows through Booster Operating Valve to control cylinder in Reducing Valve, forcing the Regulating Valve to its closed position.

Operation of Intercepting Valve, Reducing
Valve and Controls—
Mallet Locomotives

Office of General Supt. Motive Power,
Norfolk and Western Railway Company,
Roanoke, Virginia, July 13, 1953.

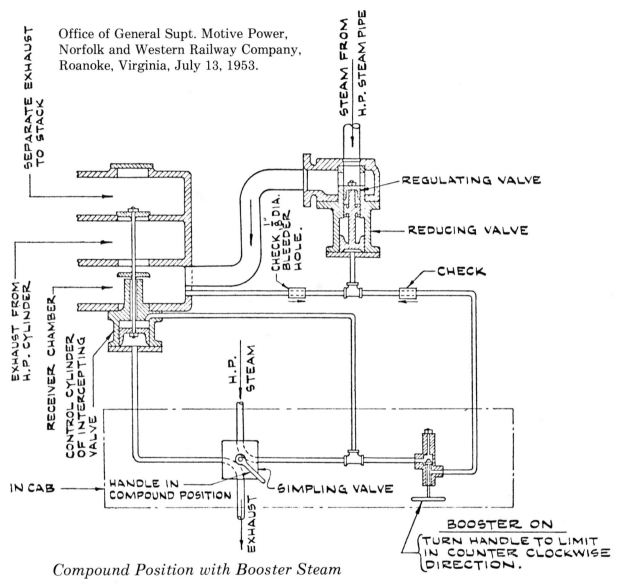

Compound Position with Booster Steam

Note:—

When handle on the Simpling Valve is pointing toward the engineer, the Intercepting Valve is in compound position. The exhaust from H.P. cylinders passes to the L.P. cylinders through the receiver chamber and receiver pipe. Booster operating valve is in "On" position (Handle turned to limit in counter clockwise direction). Steam cannot flow through the Booster Operating Valve so the Regulating Valve will remain open and permit steam from H.P. steam pipe to pass into the receiver chamber. The correct pressure is automatically maintained in the receiver chamber by the balance between the high steam pressure on the regulating valve and the receiver steam pressure on the reducing valve control cylinder.

Operating Instructions For Simpling Valve and Booster Valve in Cab, Mallet Locomotives

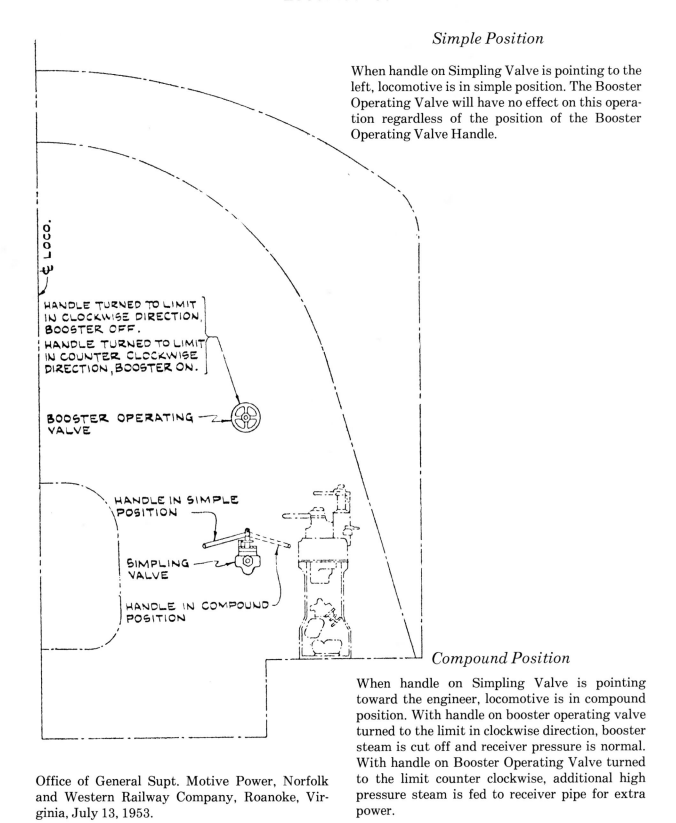

Simple Position

When handle on Simpling Valve is pointing to the left, locomotive is in simple position. The Booster Operating Valve will have no effect on this operation regardless of the position of the Booster Operating Valve Handle.

LOCO. ℄

HANDLE TURNED TO LIMIT IN CLOCKWISE DIRECTION, BOOSTER OFF.

HANDLE TURNED TO LIMIT IN COUNTER CLOCKWISE DIRECTION, BOOSTER ON.

BOOSTER OPERATING VALVE

HANDLE IN SIMPLE POSITION

SIMPLING VALVE

HANDLE IN COMPOUND POSITION

Compound Position

When handle on Simpling Valve is pointing toward the engineer, locomotive is in compound position. With handle on booster operating valve turned to the limit in clockwise direction, booster steam is cut off and receiver pressure is normal. With handle on Booster Operating Valve turned to the limit counter clockwise, additional high pressure steam is fed to receiver pipe for extra power.

Office of General Supt. Motive Power, Norfolk and Western Railway Company, Roanoke, Virginia, July 13, 1953.

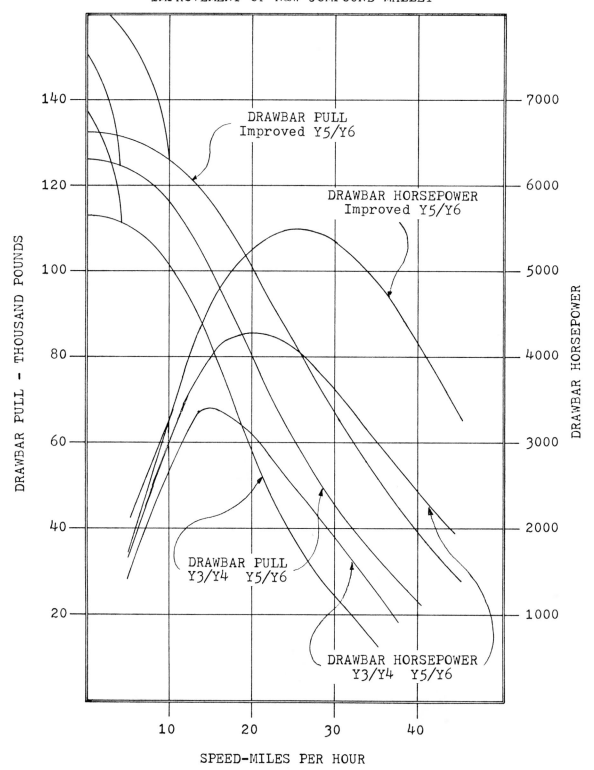

DRAWBAR PULL AND HORSEPOWER CURVES
IMPROVEMENT OF N&W COMPOUND MALLET

Drawbar pull and horsepower curves comparing Y3/Y4 and early Y5/Y6 with the improved Y5/Y6 of the late steam era. This graph vividly shows development of N&W's compound Mallets. *Drawing by H. St. Amont.*

Steam versus Diesel Tests of 1952

The motive power policy of the N&W in the early 1950s was one of total dedication to the coal-burning steam locomotives. This policy was not a result of the romance of railroading with steam but was based on sound economics, good engineering and a desire to promote the coal industry—the N&Ws greatest source of income. The Norfolk and Western was so confident of steam motive power that it continued building new steam units while all other major railroads were dieselizing. To illustrate this calculated approach, R. H. Smith, then president of the N&W, made this statement in 1951 to the N&W employees:

> As for locomotives, your own Roanoke Shop continues to add steadily to our fleet of modern steam locomotives. Last year this contribution was 18 new engines which I believe are as good performers as any type produced anywhere in this country.

> It has been said that the fact that the Norfolk and Western is the only fairly large railroad which does not today own a single locomotive of any type except coal-burning engines is suggestive that our railroad is not progressive. But when one examines the figures of 23 principal railroads in this nation and finds that again in 1951 your railroad—against the handicaps of unusually hard grades over three mountain ranges between the Ohio Valley and the Atlantic Coast, and against, with one exception, the lowest average freight charge per net ton mile of freight traffic handled—produced the lowest C. T. ratio and the highest number of ton-miles per freight train hour of any of those 23 railroads, the soundness of our confidence in our present type of motive power is confirmed. I do not suggest that we will never use other types of locomotives, but I do say that before we adopt them they will have to prove by performance that under our conditions they will do a better all-around job for us than those we build ourselves.

Is this fantasy? No. It is very convincing evidence that the steam locomotive could be, and was, competitive with other forms of power. Did it mean that all other forms of power were out altogether? A very emphatic No! Smith was once reported as saying that as long as he was president, the N&W would never own a diesel. In this 1951 statement, such a reported prediction is not substantiated. It should be remembered that the first diesels were ordered in 1955 and that almost one-half of the N&W steamers were retired during the presidency of Smith.

The Norfolk and Western was not oblivious to other types of power. As outlined in the design philosophy portion of this chapter, the railway was aware of steam's disadvantages and was continually comparing on paper the N&W steam power with the newer types of locomotives. But actual tests to compare the N&W modern steam locomotives with the diesel were sorely lacking. So the decision was made to conduct a test in 1952 on two completely different operating districts—one a mountain area and the other a near-level stretch.

The Electro-Motive Division of General Motors accepted the challenge to stack up an "off the shelf" four-unit diesel capable of 6,000 horsepower against some of the N&Ws own "homegrown" articulateds. The railway started looking around for its own competitors for the test and came up with two new locomotives "just itching" for a race. One, a Class A, Number 1239, was to be used between Williamson and Portsmouth. The other, a Class Y6b, Number 2197, prepared for the tough run between Williamson and Bluefield.

Before the test these two locomotives were overhauled at the Roanoke Shops to make them "fit as a fiddle" for the upcoming competition. Even though these two engines could not realize that their continued existence was possibly riding on the outcome, such was not true of the N&W shop force working on 1239 and 2197. These workers had watched these new locomotives roll from the famous shops ready for service within the previous three years. Number 2197 had been completed in January of 1952 and was so new that the "mill scale" was still present. This Y6b was equipped with an innovative device that had been experimented with on other engines for about a year to perfect it—the externally controlled reducing valve, called the "booster valve." This valve had not yet been adopted as standard equipment. Now was a good time to see what a "booster valve" Mallet could do against the much-talked-about diesel. The recently built 2197 only needed a good tune up before the test.

The 1239, on the other hand, received a major shopping since it was some two and one-half years old. The 1239 was one of the new Class As that had been equipped with the lightweight rods with roller bearings on the crank and wrist pins. This super articulated was the last word in heavy freight operations. To prepare the locomotive for the test, a handpicked shop force was selected. It

Class A 1239's performance was exemplary in that it could equal or better just about anything the brace of 6,000 horsepower diesels could do on a level district. Here 1239 is seen at Crewe in February 1953 soon after the tests. *Courtesy C. W. Jernstrom.*

In the 1952 tests, the booster valve equipped Y6b was very competitive with the diesel, especially at speeds the Mallet developed most of its drawbar horsepower. Modern N&W steam were most competitive for heavy tonnage mainline work at higher speeds. Y6b 2195 in mountain service February 1956. *Courtesy C. W. Jernstrom.*

was one eminently qualified for this job. As C. S. Patton, Jr., then general foreman of the Roanoke Shops, noted, "The pride of the workers for this job was something else." And why not! Here was one of their products going out to compete with a type of locomotive that many acclaimed as the best. These workmen had faith that their railway had the finest power possible, and that it was superior to other roads' power, which already had succumbed to the diesel invader. And this faith was evident in the worker's approach to the tasks performed on 1239. New rings, needed for the pistons, were procured from the manufacturer and were handcarried in a suitcase back to the Roanoke Shops for installation.

The test in each district was divided into two parts. On the Pocahontas Division, the 2197 versus EMD 459 test took place between Williamson and Farm, West Virginia, eastbound with loaded coal trains on near-level, heavy curvature, limited-speed track. The other part was on the steep climb from Farm to Bluefield eastbound, again, with a loaded coal drag. On the Scioto Division, the 1239 versus EMD 459 test went westbound with loaded hoppers from Williamson to Portsmouth and then returned with empties on this same near-level, relatively straight track. The N&W steamers were being tested in their normal habitat for the type of service each was so ably suited to.

Results were roughly a standoff: the diesel better at the lower speeds and the big articulateds better at the higher running speeds. The fuel cost was a little higher for the coal-burning locomotives when figuring for gross ton-miles. The 1239's performance was exemplary in that it

Although the 1952 steam versus diesel test was roughly a standoff, it did indicate to N&W there was no need to look further for a steam replacement if that should occur. The diesel was already developed, in mass production, reasonably priced, powerful, reliable, and had high availability. Furthermore, the electric drive principle was attractive on heavy grade districts. When steam became too expensive to continue with, the diesel was ready and waiting. EMD GP9 725 in 1958. *Courtesy Harold K. Vollrath.*

could equal or better just about anything the diesel could do. (*See* Figures 1 and 2 for a summary of the 1239 versus EMD 459 tests.)

As for the Y6b, given an equal tonnage train as the diesel, 2197 could perform as well as 459 at higher speeds. However, the diesel was clearly faster on the steep Elkhorn Grade with like tonnage. (*See* Figures 3 and 4 for a summary of the 2197 versus EMD 459 test.)

The drawbar horsepower and drawbar pull curves in Figure 5 tell much of the steam versus diesel capabilities as experienced in these 1952 tests. The fact is that steam was very competitive with the diesel if the coal-burning reciprocating steam locomotive was worked at near capacity and at speed. If the speed dropped too low, then steam could not develop its maximum horsepower. And if steam was not worked at capacity, the reduction in fuel consumption was not directly proportioned to the reduction in work required. Thus, modern N&W steam power was only competitive and economical for the big, heavy tonnage, main line jobs. In contrast, the varying power demands on the lighter service lines or yard operations did not give steam a chance.

What effects did the "Steam versus Diesel Tests of 1952" have on the N&Ws motive power policy? Initially, very little. Since the tests indicated essentially a standoff, there was no need, as the N&W saw it, to change to diesels with no significant decrease in cost and with a modern steam fleet already in existence. It did show, however, that the diesel was the only practical and economical replacement to conventional steam power when that should occur. But there was one factor that was not considered: from the end of World War II on the cost of labor had become more and more significant in motive power operation. With the wages for labor spiralling, and with steam motive power's extensive requirements for labor, this one factor weighted the scales toward dieselization.

When the decision for the initial phase of dieselization was made, the first districts dieselized were those that were light service lines requiring

SUMMARY SHEET "A"
ROAD TESTS – KENOVA DIST. – 1952
WESTBOUND AVERAGES
COMPARATIVE PERFORMANCE – CLASS "A" NO. 1239 AND GM DIESEL NO. 459

SHEET A.

AVERAGES – WILLIAMSON TO PORTSMOUTH			
	CLASS "A" LOCO. 1239 JULY 1952 AVG. 6 TEST RUNS	GM DIESEL – 459 SEPT. 1952 AVG. 4 TEST RUNS	CLASS "A" LOCO. 1239 OCT. 1952 AVG. 3 TEST RUNS
1. Number Revenue Cars	175	176	175
2. Tons (Incl. Dynamometer and Caboose)	14985	15763	16028
3. Total Time – Yd Board to Yd Board	3:13	3:16	3:12
4. Total Time – Start to Stop	3:32	3:33	3:31
5. Running Time – Start to Stop	3:31	3:33	3:31
6. Speed MPH (Running Time)	31.6	31.4	31.6
7. MGTM Per Hr. (Running Time)	472.5	493.9	506.0
8. MGTM Per Train Hr. (Total Time)	470.5	492.5	504.6
9. Fuel – Coal as Fired (Tons) Fuel Oil (Gallons)	19.48	1028	18.4
10. Fuel Per MGTM – Coal as Fired Fuel Oil (Gallons)	23.47	.589	20.7
11. Fuel Cost per MGTM	$0.0723	$0.0617	$0.0638

October 15, 1952..

Figure 1. "A" versus diesel test summary westbound on Scioto Division. *N&W Summaries, Courtesy Robert M. Pilcher Collection.*

SUMMARY SHEET "B"
ROAD TESTS- KENOVA DIST. 1952
EASTBOUND AVERAGES
COMPARATIVE PERFORMANCE - CLASS "A" NO. 1239 AND GM DIESEL NO. 459

SHEET B.

AVERAGES - PORTSMOUTH TO WILLIAMSON			
	CLASS "A" LOCO. 1239 JULY 1952 AVG. 6 TEST RUNS	GM DIESEL - 459 SEPT. 1952 AVG. 4 TEST RUNS	CLASS "A" LOCO 1239 October 1952 AVG 3 TEST RUNS
1. Number Revenue Cars	175	175	175
2. Tons (Incl. Dynamometer and Caboose)	4117	4126	4130
3. Total Time - Yd. Board to Yd. Board	2:45	2:48	2:42
4. Total Time - Start to Stop	3:15	3:11	3:08
5. Running Time - Start to Stop	3:12	3:11	3:08
6. Speed - MPH (Running Time)	35.3	35.8	36.3
7. MGTM Per Hr. (Running Time)	145.2	147.5	149.9
8. MGTM Per Train Hr. (Total Time)	143.2	146.9	149.9
9. Fuel - Coal as Fired (Tons)	15.3		15.1
- Fuel Oil (Gallons)		831	
10. Fuel Per. MGTM - COAL AS FIRED (Pounds)	65.9		64.5
- FUEL OIL (Gallons)		1.776	
11. Fuel Cost per MGTM	$0.2030	$0.1861	$0.1987

October 15, 1952..

Figure 2. Road test A versus diesel summary eastbound with empty hopper train.

SUMMARY SHEET
ROAD TESTS - POCAHONTAS DIV. - 1952
EASTBOUND AVERAGES - WILLIAMSON TO FARM
COMPARATIVE PERFORMANCE - CLASS Y6b No. 2197 AND GM DIESEL NO. 459

Sheet - D

AVERAGES - WILLIAMSON TO FARM			
	GM DIESEL - 459 SEPTEMBER 1952 Avg. 2 Runs	GM DIESEL - 459 SEPTEMBER 1952 Avg. 3 Runs	CLASS Y6b LOCO. 2197 NOVEMBER 1952 AVG. 5 Runs
1. Number of Revenue Cars	116	88	85.6
2. Tons (Incl. Dynamometer) Est.	10218	7481	7422
3. Total Time - Yd Board to Yd Board	2:45	2:20	2:18
4. Total Time - Start to Stop	2:56	2:31	2:29
5. Running Time - Start to Stop	2:55	2:31	2:29
6. Speed - MPH (Running Time)	21.58	24.91	25.36
7. MGTM Per Hr. (Running Time)	220.09	186.40	188.22
8. MGTM Per Train Hr. (Total Time)	219.09	186.40	187.51
9. Fuel - Coal as Fired (Tons)			13.63
Fuel Oil (Gallons)	964	796	
10. Fuel Per MGTM - Coal as fired (lbs)			58.44
Fuel Oil (Gallons)	1.509	1.697	
11. Fuel Cost Per MGTM	.1581	.1778	.1800
12. Minimum Speed, Alnwick Grade	13.95	19.5	20.8

Nov. 19, 1952..

Figure 3. Summary of Y6b versus diesel on flat portion of Pocahontas Division.

SUMMARY SHEET
ROAD TESTS - POCAHONTAS DIV. - 1952
EASTBOUND AVERAGES - FARM TO BLUEFIELD
COMPARATIVE PERFORMANCE - CLASS Y6b NO. 2197 AND GM DIESEL NO. 459

	AVERAGES - FARM TO BLUEFIELD		
	GM DIESEL - 459 SEPTEMBER 1952 AVG. 2 TEST RUNS	GM DIESEL - 459 SEPTEMBER 1952 AVG. 3 TEST RUNS	CLASS Y6b LOCO. 2197 NOVEMBER 1952 AVG. 3 TEST RUNS
1. Number of Revenue Cars	39.5	58.7	41.7
2. Tons (Incl. Dynamometer & Auxiliary Tender)	3512*	5136*	3818
3. Total Time - Yard Board to Yard Board	1:26	1:50	1:40
4. Total Time - Start to Stop	1:35	2:03	1:50
5. Running Time - Start to Stop	1:35	2:03	1:50
6. Speed - MPH (Running Time)	22.65	17.55	19.33
7. MGTM PER HR. (RUNNING TIME)	79.55	90.07	73.78
8. MGTM PER TRAIN HR (Total Time)	79.55	89.60	73.78
9. Fuel - Coal as Fired (Tons)			9.6
Fuel Oil (Gallons)	445	670	
10. Fuel Per MGTM - Coal as Fired (Pounds)			141.61
Fuel Oil (Gallons)	3.539	3.640	
11. Fuel Cost Per MGTM	$ .3709	$ .3815	$ .4362
12. Minimum Speed, Elkhorn Grade	16.6	10.9	12.1

Nov. 18, 1952..   * No auxiliary tender

Figure 4. Y6b versus diesel summary on heavy grade portion of Pocahontas Division.

twenty-four-hour steam servicing facilities for a relatively small number of steam locomotives. So the first eighty-three diesel-electric units, which had the characteristic of being readily combined and worked in tandem to make any size locomotive for the particular job demands, were used on the Durham, Cincinnati and Shenandoah districts with the elimination of almost all locomotive servicing needs. The 1952 test showed the advantages of each type of motive power, and when the diesel did arrive to stay, steam remained in use where and how it was best suited to the task—heavy main line work at full capacity in the higher speeds. The older power for both yard and road work went to the scrap lines first.

The "Steam versus Diesel Test of 1952" was the N&Ws last bid for conventional steam. This was the glory period of the Norfolk and Western's most modern steam, and this steam power fought the diesel "down to the wire." On the "day" of this test, the diesel was not better than steam. How could the N&W steamers lose out with a proud shop force showing pride in their locomotives as they had when preparing their 1239 for its "hour of decision?"

One might say the encounter was a no-decision bout. Yet labor costs soon provided the diesels with a knockout punch in the N&W arena.

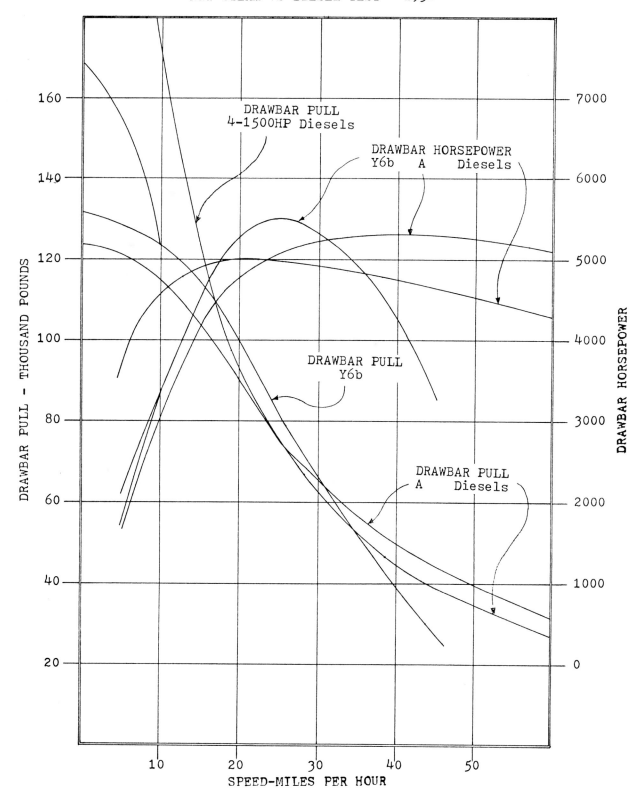

Figure 5. A, Y6b, and nominal 6,000 horsepower diesel drawbar and horsepower curves. Diesel curves developed by R. M. Pilcher, engineer of tests, from diesel test data obtained later during dieselization. *Drawing by H. St. Amont.*

Part 2

Older Steam

FORERUNNER TO THE STEAM GIANTS

Older N&W steam power was not as well known as the A, J, and Y6s, yet this older power was used to develop N&W's motive power policy of the late steam era. Number 1399 was unique in appearance and had a career different from all other older steamers. This engine vividly represented the effect of older steam on N&W's steam policy. This locomotive originally was one of the 190 Class Z 2-6-6-2s, the railway's first successful Mallet, and the compound Mallet remained a N&W power principal to steam's end. 1399 was rebuilt with four simple cylinders in an effort to develop a higher speed engine than the compound. Although not successful in subsequent road tests, this experiment ultimately led to the Class A 2-6-6-4. Each class of older power made a contribution to the evolution of N&W steam, ending with those magnificent homebuilt giants. *Courtesy N&W.*

N&W giants of the steam age were well known, but they did not just come about incidentally. The Norfolk and Western Railway, like other roads, acquired standard steam motive power at the turn-of-the-century, but they were always experimenting here and testing there with certain specialty features of locomotives. There emerged a philosophy wherein the N&W chose to apply fundamental and proven technology to a few basic locomotive designs. Much of the N&Ws success was due to the fact that when it found something good, that feature was developed further and was then applied on a comparatively large scale.

It is a fascinating story to follow the develop-

ment of older N&W steam power and to see the evolution that resulted finally in three types of steam road power. The three classes of power—the N&W giants of the steam era—were all outstanding. Each in its own right was a remarkable design. Most significantly, they "held the dike" against other forms of motive power longer and better than any other steam power in U.S. railroading. The design, construction and operation of the locomotive fleet were refined through the years, and so the older steam era provided the foundation for the last three decades of N&W steam. The compound Mallet and Mountain types constituted this foundation, and they became the very basis for the N&W steam giants.

2-8-0

The newly organized Norfolk and Western Railway Company in late 1896 found itself in a position of owning a conglomeration of power. Much of this power was relatively new, having been acquired in the preceding decade by the predecessor Norfolk and Western Railroad. The other motive power on hand either had been around much longer or had been procured through a number of mergers effected in the eighties and nineties.

The new N&W immediately set out to standardize motive power to the maximum extent possible. The predecessor N&W had some large classes of power, yet the locomotive art was advancing at such a pace that power just five years of age was at times considered obsolete. What was needed was a locomotive that could be used all over the system—an engine of sound design incorporating the latest technology and with increased power for the mountains. It must be remembered the 2-8-0 was the standard freight engine at the turn of the century, and that the N&W tracks were literally crawling with 2-8-0s in three major classifications (F, G & T). What was needed was bigger, more modern power, not just a new wheel arrangement.

Evidently as an interim measure, a group of seven 2-8-0s, later known as the G1s, were bought soon after the new N&W took over. In what must have been a test, the railway next bought two groups of Consolidations, each group with major differences. One group comprised cross-compounds, the other conventional single expansion

"A VERY PROFITABLE ENGINE"

Class Ws were light, easy to maintain, and capable of performing a wide range of duties for more than fifty years. These sturdy and dependable locomotives were used for years in road and yard service, while four lasted to the end of steam as "shop shifters." Being "a very profitable engine" meant the N&W had a type readily adaptable to varying demands with a minimum of upkeep. *D. W. Johnson Photo, Courtesy C. T. Felstead Collection.*

engines. The compound engines were not wholly successful, but the 2-8-0 Class W single expansion units performed so well the N&W bought or built 277 of them. These 2-8-0s "were very profitable locomotives" stated Walter Budwell, master mechanic of the Norfolk Division. This was Walter Budwell's way of saying they were useful for many years and were likewise the ancestors of a long line of N&W power that would ultimately be regarded by most as U.S. steam railroading at its best.

G1 7 (Baldwin 1897), with 13.8 ton, 6,000 gallon tender in 1934. *Courtesy N&W.*

B 62, new at Baldwin 1898. *Courtesy Harold K. Vollrath.*

W 819, new at Baldwin 1899. *Courtesy Harold K. Vollrath.*

W2 904, new at Baldwin 1902. *Courtesy N&W.*

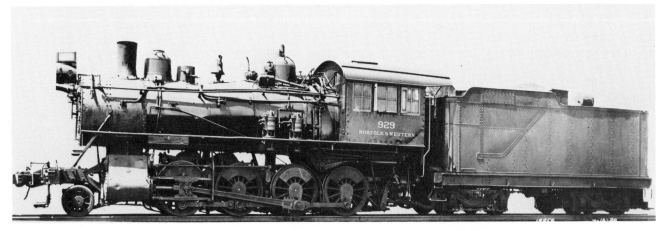

W2 929 (Patterson 1903), with 9,000 gallon tender in 1934. *Courtesy Harold K. Vollrath.*

W5 839 (originally W1, Roanoke 1900) in 1925. *Courtesy Charles E. Winters.*

Class G1

The original Consolidations purchased by the railway were simply the early Class Gs with an increased boiler pressure. This new power, classed as G-h, was built by Baldwin Locomotive Works in January 1897 and numbered 352 through 358. These engines had 20-by-24 inch cylinders, a grate area of thirty-one square feet, and fifty-inch drivers. The total engine weight was 120,785 pounds with 107,000 pounds on drivers. The boiler pressure was 180 pounds per square inch, and this developed a tractive effort of 29,376 pounds. An 8.5 ton, 4,000 gallon capacity tender was attached.

In appearance the Class G-h engines were typical of that period. They had the narrow inside firebox, the extra oversize cab, the oil lamp on top of the smokebox and the flat top steam chest characteristic of the slide valve cylinders. With newer power being built in the early 1900s, the G-hs were steadily downgraded until by 1920 they were strictly very light branch line power. They played that role to the end.

This class went through a haphazard renumbering on several occasions. Between 1903 and 1909,

they became numbers 200 through 206 and were reclassed as G1. Number 202 was dropped from the roster by 1912. As for the rest of the class, numbers 200, 201, 203 and 205 were sold in May 1917 to the Virginia Carolina Railway and were renumbered 6, 7, 4 and 5, respectively. In January 1920 the N&W took over the operation of the Virginia Carolina (the line became the Abingdon Branch) and the G1s were retained as the 4 through 7. To make numbers available to the new 4-8-2s being built at the Roanoke Shops, number 204 became the 301 in December 1925 and the 206 became 302 in January 1926. The G1's appearance remained essentially unchanged in later years except for a new pilot, electric headlights and a slightly larger tender.

Numbers 301 and 302 were both sold to the U.S. government in January 1944, and numbers 4 and 5 were scrapped in April 1947. Numbers 6 and 7 met a happier fate. In 1955 the former was donated to the city of Roanoke, the latter to the city of Bluefield, where the two stand proudly on display today.

Class B

Between February and September 1898, Baldwin delivered seven larger 2-8-0s classed as B, numbered 62 through 68. These new engines were cross-compounds that were being experimented with. The slide valve cylinders were twenty-three inches in diameter on the high pressure side and thirty-five inches on the low pressure side by a thirty-two-inch stroke. The thirty-five square foot grate produced 200 pounds pressure of steam, and with fifty-six-inch drivers, the locomotive could develop 40,304 pounds tractive effort. Each weighed 185,685 pounds with 165,585 pounds on the drivers. They were equipped with the Stephenson link valve gear. The tender was of 8.5 tons and 4,000 gallons capacity.

Even while the single expansion 2-8-0s were being bought or built in quantity by the railway, two more Bs were purchased from Baldwin in March 1900, and they were numbered 69 and 70. Strangely, one last B, number 61, was bought in March 1904. These last three were all built almost identical to the first seven.

The Bs, like other cross-compounds, did not prove satisfactory, so they were converted to single expansion locomotives in 1915. When converted, they also received Baker valve gear and piston valves; both cylinders became 21-by-32 inches, and a new tractive effort rating of 42,840 pounds resulted. As rebuilt, they were mostly used on the Pocahontas Division. Number 62 was retired in October 1933, and all others of this class were dismantled in July 1934.

Class W and Class W1

The railway had tried the Class B compounds, but now was the time in management's view to again try a "conventional" engine. Baldwin was called on to build the new class. Numbers 800 through 809, completed in December 1898, were classed as W. These engines weighed 167,830 pounds total and had 149,530 pounds on the drivers. Boiler pressure was 200 pounds per square inch, and with the 21-by-30 inch cylinders, they could develop 40,163 pounds tractive effort

W2s were primarily switchers and light branch-line engines during their last two decades of existence. 788 doing yard chores near Petersburg, September 1946. Footboards on this engine show that is was used mostly in switching assignments. *Courtesy Charles E. Winters.*

884 being stored April 1936, which may have been fairly common in Depression years. "Ole 884" was put back into service and was not dismantled until April 1950. *Courtesy Harold K. Vollrath.*

Number 825 was unique from all other W6s. Used at Roanoke's passenger car shop, this shop shifter was too long with a passenger car on that shop's turntable. 825's length was reduced considerably by shortening the frame in front of the cylinders, which required removing a portion of the smokebox too. *Courtesy Harold K. Vollrath.*

Roanoke, Shaffers Crossing's own terminal goat, 821. Date: July 1948. *Courtesy C. W. Jernstrom.*

with the fifty-six-inch drivers. The grate area of 32.6 square feet was a narrow type between the drivers. Cylinders were of slide valve construction, and the valve gear was the Stephenson. The tender was of 9.7 tons and 5,000 gallons capacity.

These new locomotives were so successful that the railway had Baldwin deliver another identical twenty, numbers 810 through 829, from April to July 1899. The Roanoke Shops produced numbers 830 through 842, 844 and 865 (construction numbers [c/n], 153 through 165, 167, 168) between January 1900 and April 1902, but they differed some, being equipped with the piston valve and classed as W1. The piston-valved W1s were the superior performers, so Baldwin rolled out another ten 2-8-0s, this time W1s numbered 845 through 854, during February and March 1901. Richmond Locomotive Works next built two groups of ten each. Numbers 855 through 864 were erected in June and July 1901, while 870 through 879 were not built until December of the same year.

All of the Ws (numbers 800 through 829) underwent rebuilding to receive piston valve cylinders and were reclassified as W1 by 1922. The W1s weighed slightly less than the Ws, having a total engine weight of 165,500 pounds with 147,300 pounds on drivers. The W and W1s with their narrow fireboxes gave way soon after construction to the wide firebox W2s. Except for the rebuilding of the Ws and the addition of electric headlights to all, these seventy W and W1s remained unchanged throughout their existence. Upon successive downgrading, all but a handful were in yard work by 1920. Between 1920 and 1926, twelve were converted into 0-8-0T "shop goats," but the rest were retired starting in 1925. Other than the "shop goats," all were gone by 1933 with most (thirty-eight) going in 1926.

Class W2

The Roanoke Shops had built the first Ws having piston valves, classed it W1 and now would improve the W1 by enlarging the firebox. This wide firebox class, designated as W2, became the N&Ws standard 2-8-0 and maintained its leadership for years. The N&W then set out in a whirlwind building campaign to acquire or build in its own shops 202 Class W2s. The numbering scheme was puzzling. At first, the W2s were numbered above the W1s to 949, then were assigned blocks of numbers backward from 800. These W2s had the same running gear dimensions as the earlier Ws, but had the wide firebox located above the drivers. The new grate area was 47.3 square feet; also this class was a little heavier, having an engine weight of 175,100 pounds and 157,850 pounds on the driving wheels. Tractive effort and tender data remained unchanged from the previous 2-8-0 Ws. The following table outlines the construction of the class by number and by builder:

Numbers	Builder	Built	Total
843	Roanoke (c/n 166)	1901	1
866-869	Roanoke (c/n 169, 173-175)	1902-04	4
880-899	Richmond	1902-03	20
900-918	Baldwin	1902-03	19
919-922	Richmond	1902	4
923-925	Roanoke (c/n 170-172)	1902-03	3
926-927	Richmond	1903	2
928-947	Patterson	1903	20
948-949	Baldwin	1903	2
791-799	Baldwin	1903	9
778-790	Richmond	1903	13
776-777	Roanoke (c/n 176, 177)	1904	2
766-775	Patterson	1903	10
754-765	Baldwin	1903	12
734-753	Baldwin	1903-04	20
730-733	Roanoke (c/n 178-181)	1904	4
722-729	Baldwin	1904	8
715-721	Richmond	1904	7
708-714	Baldwin	1905	7
699-707	Richmond	1905	9
682-698	Richmond	1905	17
673-681	Baldwin	1905	9

W2s were the line's main freight power, along with the newer Ms, until advent of the Mallets in 1912. The Ws then were mostly assigned to the lighter branch lines and some eighty-five went to

One of four W6s lasting to 1958, number 809 was originally a W, subsequently a W1, W5, and then W6. 809 worked Bluefield Terminal until the decision to totally dieselize. *Courtesy Charles E. Winters.*

W6 800 had a most distinctive and distinguished career. It worked Roanoke Shops from 1920 to 1958, greeting each new homebuilt giant during those intervening years, and it had the longest career of any N&W steamer—almost 60 years. 800 is shown in view of the motive power office building. From that building poured forward the genius of N&W's design boards. *Courtesy Harold K. Vollrath.*

yard work by 1919. By the mid-twenties, the class was surplus and started appearing in the scrap lines. During the late twenties and the first half of the thirties, a tremendous number were retired from N&W service. Eighteen were sold to other railroads where they saw service for many years. By 1937, only forty-seven were left on the N&W roster. When the 0-8-0s were purchased in 1950, thirty W2s were in use as light switchers. The 0-8-0 was a thoroughly modern type and took over all light switching duties, most of the 2-8-0s being retired before the end of 1950. The last three W2s (numbers 746, 758 and 778) ended their service in 1953.

The W2s changed little in appearance during their service. One notable alteration was the installation of the electric headlights (it was relocated several times) and substituting footboards for the pilot. Tenders were changed to the 13.8 ton, 6,000 gallons, or the 14 tons, 9,000 gallons variety. The larger version was most prevalent in the W2s in latter days. At least seventeen were equipped with the Baker valve gear, and nine (numbers 769, 771, 778, 779, 885, 887, 891, 910

and 925) got Schmidt superheaters during 1914-17. And to increase the drafting efficiency, many received an enlarged exhaust nozzle and a "fatter" stack that gave a heavier appearance to the class. Some weights and specifications changed in later years.

The W2 served the railway well. Being a "very profitable locomotive" it enjoyed a distinguished career. It was light, easy to maintain, yet large enough that it was useable for a long time—fifty years to be exact. This class was not affected by dieselization.

Class W3

A Class W, number 823, was shopped before 1909 and had an Allfree-Hubbell device installed on the slide valve cylinders. The device increased exhaust-port opening, but with the demise of slide valve engines, further experimentation with it was unnecessary. Number 823 was reclassed as W3 with this device installed, and it was retired and scrapped in 1926. All dimensions and specifications were identical to the Class W.

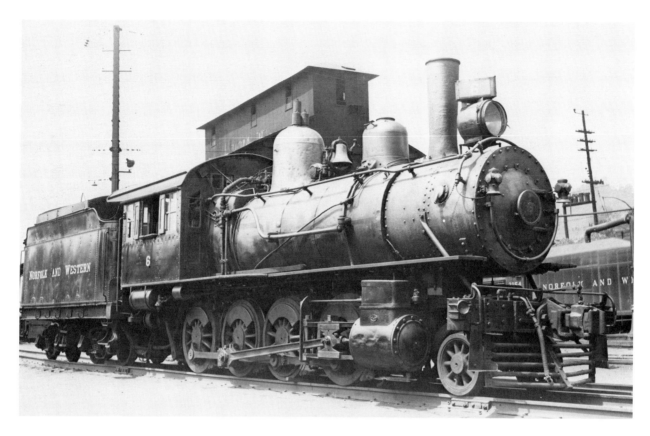

Above: Two 2-8-0s, numbers 6 and 7, were kept around for special use. These G1s were the heaviest engines allowed on a short line between Honaker and Blackford, Virginia, known as Honaker Branch. The consolidations lasted until 1955 when Honaker Branch was abandoned. Number 6 at Bluefield, August 1948. *Courtesy Harold K. Vollrath. Below:* The slide valve Class Ws later received piston valve cylinders and were reclassed as W1s. Former W 813 is in yard service in July 1924. Note the enlarged stack. *Courtesy N&W.*

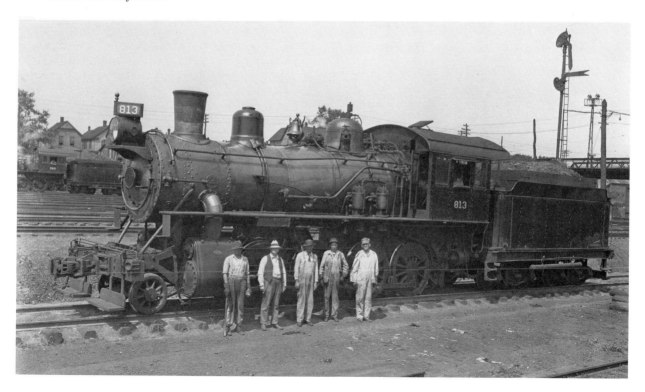

The "very profitable" W2s served N&W for years in a wide range of work. This particular old-timer, built in 1902, worked main lines, branches, and yards until 1949 when dismantled at Roanoke Shops. *Courtesy N&W.*

Class W4

Probably about the time the later Class M1s were being built with Walschaert valve gear applied, Class W2, number 776, also received this Walschaert gear as an experiment. This engine was reclassed as W4. All weights and specifications were identical to the W2 class. The Walschaert valve gear was not popular with the N&W, and subsequently the 776 was scrapped in 1930 along with many other Ws that were passing from the scene at this time. No other Walschaert gear was applied to a 2-8-0.

Classes W5 and W6

"Shop goats" were needed at a few selected terminals and shops for varied shifting duties in restricted areas. In the early twenties, the N&W had an aging fleet of these shifters that needed replacing. With the class W1s about to be retired, here was a chance to transform some existing

power into the needed shop switchers. So numbers 800 and 834 were sent to the railway's shops in mid-1920 for the complete rebuilding required. The tenders were stripped from the engines and water saddle-tanks were placed over the boilers at the steam dome. On each, the generator was placed ahead of the stack while the single-piston air pump was moved forward along the boiler to be even with the sandbox. The engine frames were extended back for the installation of small two-ton capacity coal bunkers. The saddle tanks held 2,000 gallons of water. As rebuilt, the engines were reclassed as W5, and all data remained unchanged except that the engine weight was now 186,900 pounds. With the lead truck deleted from the engines, all weight was applied to the drivers.

Between 1922 and 1924, six more W1s were converted to Class W5. In 1924, number 806 was converted to an 0-8-0T but was classed as W6. The W6 was shorter in length than the W5, and some other minor modifications or improvements

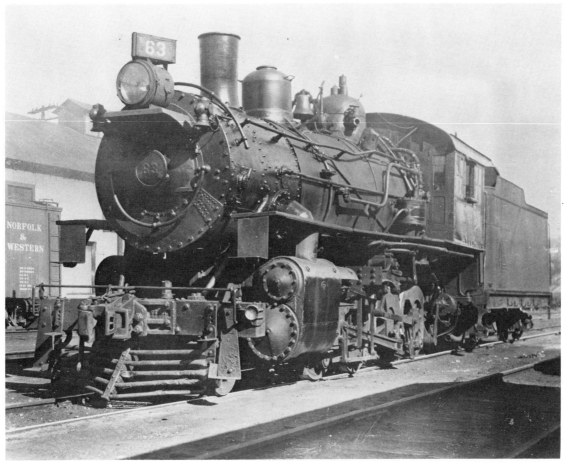

When built, the cross-compound Class Bs were thought to be a decided step forward in steam economy. It was soon discovered that the compound cylinder limited speed and starting qualities of the engine. The class received simple cylinders and Baker valve gear in 1915. Here is 63 viewed after being simpled. *Courtesy N&W.*

were made because of the experience gained from the first eight conversions. After the out-shopping of number 806, the W5s were all reclassed as W6s by late 1925. Finally, numbers 804, 825 and 842 were converted to W6s from W1s in 1926. A listing of each locomotive, when converted, where assigned and when retired follows:

No.	Converted	Assigned	Retired
800	8-23	Roanoke Shops	7-58
802	1-24	Portsmouth Terminal	3-54
804	1-26	Williamson Terminal	11-35
806	7-24	Portsmouth Shops	7-34
809	2-23	Bluefield Terminal	3-58
821	12-22	Roanoke Terminal	4-58
825	3-26	Roanoke Terminal	6-53
830	3-23	Williamson Terminal	4-58
834	7-20	Portsmouth Terminal	7-34
839	2-24	Unknown	6-41
842	7-26	Unknown	11-34
860	1-24	Roanoke Shops	5-36

The last four W6s in existence, numbers 800,

809, 821 and 830, were renumbered 10 through 13 in April 1957 to make room for new diesel invaders being bought in quantity. These shop shifters were retired and scrapped in March and April 1958, except for number 10 (alias 800), which hung on until July.

Number 800 had the distinction of being the locomotive with the longest continuous service ever in N&W history—almost sixty years from December 1898 to July 1958. And, very fitting indeed that she worked from 1923 to her end in the Roanoke Shops. This means she "greeted" each new locomotive built there for her last thirty-five years. Certainly, this venerable locomotive had as much to do with the "making" of the N&W as any engine this proud railroad ever had. Gallant old 800 deserves a place alongside those other N&W giants of the steam era—the As, Js and Y6s!

4-8-0

"THE HUCKLEBERRY"

One of the best known Class M. powered, mixed trains was "the Huckleberry" along the Blacksburg Branch. 449 had the honors shortly before the demise of steam on this branch. Soon both steam and the mixed consist would be gone, closing a romantic chapter of N&W branch-line railroading. In late steam, the 4-8-0 Ms were used on branch lines, work trains, one-shift switching, and in territory with weight restrictions. The M was the standard light class and, being an excellent engine, was forced into retirement only by the diesel. *Courtesy Earl Palmer.*

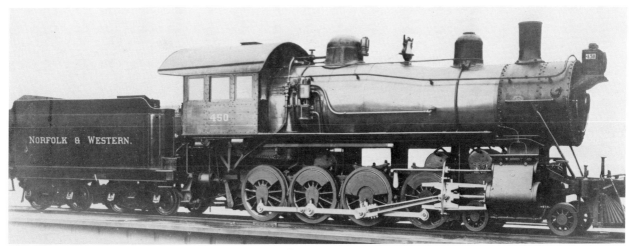

M 450, new at Baldwin 1906. *Courtesy N&W.*

M1 1000, new at Baldwin 1907. *Courtesy Harold K. Vollrath.*

M1 1091 (Richmond 1907) with 9,000 gallon tender in 1942. Class Ms looked similar to M1s in same era. *Courtesy N&W.*

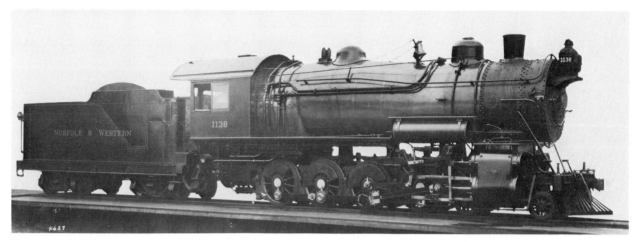

M2 1138, new at Baldwin 1910. *Courtesy N&W.*

M2 1147 (Baldwin 1911) with N&W 12,000 gallon tender in 1945. *Courtesy N&W.*

M2 Experimental Switcher 1112 (Baldwin 1910) rebuilt by Roanoke Shops 1948. *Courtesy N&W.*

Class M

As the century turned, the N&W produced and acquired a stable of 277 2-8-0s, Class Ws, to be its standard freight locomotive. These locomotives were successful and were immensely popular with the crews and the railway alike. At this same time, coal trains became heavier, so doubleheading could not be avoided. Immediately, the railway was looking for more potent power. The Mikado was being produced now, but the N&W evidently wanted a type of power that brought more total weight to bear on the drivers, would be easier on the track curvature and would have a larger boiler to increase the running speed if possible. Mindful of these specifications, the motive power people ushered in a class that gained little favor on other roads but would please the N&W by its performance until the end of steam. That was the 4-8-0!

The N&W called on two commercial builders to build a fleet of one hundred and twenty-five locomotives, classed as M. Richmond Locomotive Works built seventy-five, numbered 375 through 449, from July 1906 to February 1907. Baldwin Locomotive Works delivered fifty, numbered 450 through 499, between May and September 1906. These new engines proved to be an improvement over the then ubiquitous 2-8-0.

Running gear of the M was similar to the W's, having fifty-six-inch drivers and twenty-one-inch bore by thirty-inch stroke cylinders. The tractive effort was the same at 40,163 pounds and boiler pressure at 200 pounds per square inch. The only difference was the main rod was connected to the second driver on the M, and its twelve-inch piston valve was two inches larger than the W's. The grate area was forty-five square feet (two square feet less than the W), but the bigger boiler with almost five hundred more square feet of heating surface, along with a good firebox volume above the grate, was a free steaming one. The Stephenson valve gear, as well as the large-style cab found on the Ws, was used. Tenders were 13.8 tons and 6,000 gallons capacity.

The Ms were a better locomotive than the Ws because they incorporated improvements the smaller power did not have. A bigger boiler, with the main crank being on the second driver, meant more speed and heavier hauls. The extra lead axle carried part of the added weight of the larger boiler, yet the drivers carried more weight than did those of the Ws. The engine total wheel base was less than three feet longer, while the driving wheel base was the same as the W's. One can see the N&W design philosophy forming here: Place the least weight possible on other than driving axles. This philosophy would reach its zenith three decades later in the form of much larger power—the articulateds. The 4-8-0 had the same number of axles as the Mikado, but more of the total weight was on the drivers of the twelve-wheeler. These 200,000-pound locomotives had 168,000 pounds on the drivers. Later the 2-8-2

After the arrival of modern 0-8-0 yard shifters, most 4-8-0 Class Ms were retired, except those needed for one-trick yard assignments, branch lines, and work trains. M 422 is mostly in yard work since it has footboards. *W. Krawiez Photo, Courtesy C. T. Felstead Collection.*

Crew posing with its well-maintained 1027, Class M1, at Portsmouth in 1921. M and M1s were used extensively in manifest freight service in the twenties. *Courtesy Harold K. Vollrath.*

would grow larger, but in 1906, the N&Ws philosophy was just sound engineering in adopting the M.

All Class Ms were main line freight power until the 1920s. They handled much of the local work, doubleheaded time freights, worked the coal tipples and branch lines. With the railway acquiring many Mallets in the mid-twenties, the sturdy little Ms were sent off to the scrap lines in larger numbers, starting in 1927. By the end of WWII, only thirty-nine of this proud breed remained.

This class received some modifications while in service. Electric headlights replaced the original oil-burning type. At least thirty-one of these locomotives that lasted into the thirties had the Baker valve gear installed. Engine weight was increased slightly. All of the Ms that remained by 1938 had their original tenders replaced by the fourteen ton, 9,000 gallon tenders that were discarded from other power. Those that remained into the fifties received the 10,000 gallon USRA tenders, or the 12,000 gallon tenders that were originally assigned to the Y2s. Eight (numbers 382, 386, 439, 447, 457, 482, 493 and 495) were equipped with superheaters in 1915. Numbers 429 and 459 were to receive superheaters, probably those from the 386 and 493, scrapped in 1927 and 1928, respectively.

Those that stayed on after the war were primarily switching and branch line power. With the N&W buying thirty new 0-8-0 switchers in 1950, and then building forty-five more in the next three years, most of the Ms used in switching chores were retired. At the start of dieselization, only fifteen remained, but these fifteen were used mostly in faster branch line work not suited for the new 0-8-0 switchers. All were retired from service by the end of 1958, and number 475 was kept around and outfitted for the centennial celebration of the old predecessor line, the Virginia and Tennessee. Number 475 was retired shortly after 1959. Fortunately, one M has been kept for posterity. Number 433 was donated to the town of Abingdon, Virginia, on November 25, 1958, and is on public display there.

Class M1

Baldwin delivered fifty more 4-8-0s between September and December 1907, numbers 1000 through 1049. Richmond got an order for the N&W twelve-wheeler, and it delivered another fifty in November and December numbered 1050 through 1099. These were identical to the earlier one hundred and twenty-five except for the use of the Walschaert valve gear; and behind the sandbox there was a small dome that received the

On a wintry March day in 1956, M2c 1155 moves about Shenandoah, Virginia, yards between switching assignments. *Courtesy Charles E. Winters.*

feedwater from the injectors. These new locomotives were classed as M1. All other specifications of the M1s were the same as for the Ms.

The M1s were used interchangeably with the Class Ms, although the Walschaert valve gear was unpopular on the N&W. Those that lasted long enough received improvements right along with the Ms. In 1925, some M1s went to the scrap lines, and many more shortly thereafter. Only nineteen were in service in 1937, and the last nine were retired at the end of World War II. Number 1070 was the last to go in 1948. Only the 1092 was ever equipped with the superheater.

Class M2

The 225 Class M and M1s were proving good performers, but it was felt that more power was needed for the mountains. So an enlarged version of the 4-8-0 was produced in an attempt to gain more power. Baldwin built fifty monsters of a 4-8-0 wheel arrangement. These were numbered 1100 through 1149, built between September 1910 and January 1911, and were classed as M2. This new power weighed 262,000 pounds and had 221,780 pounds on the drivers, which was more than the older Ms total weight. The grate area was the same but the boiler was ninety-one inches in maximum diameter with 3,569 square feet of heating surface with no superheater. Boiler pressure was 200 pounds per square inch, the cylinders were twenty-four inches in diameter by a thirty-inch stroke, thus producing 52,457 pounds tractive effort. The drivers were fifty-six inches. All of the M2s had the Walschaert valve gear.

The Roanoke Shops built numbers 1150 through 1160 (c/n 182-192) from April 1911 to April 1912. This new Roanoke power was grouped in three subclassifications because of minor variations, as follows:

Numbers	Class	Description
1150-1152	M2a	Baker valve gear, stoker
1153-1154	M2b	Baker valve gear, stoker, Hobart-Allfree cylinders
1155-1160	M2c	Baker valve gear, stoker, superheater

This was the first application of superheaters, stokers and the straight Baker valve gear to any N&W power. By 1920, the M2as and M2bs were reclassed as M2c with the addition of superheaters. The fourteen ton, 9,000 gallon capacity tenders were standard for all sixty-one M2s.

It is suspected that the arrival of large numbers of Class Z, 2-6-6-2 Mallets, put a stop to the M2 production. The new Mallets dominated the heavy freight service motive power roster from 1912 on. That the M2 reign was shortlived is an understatement. By 1920, all but a handful were on the Norfolk Division. As the 2-6-6-2s were downgraded from main line duties, the M2s were relegated more and more to yard and secondary

Backwoods railroading added another touch to the folklore along the Abingdon Branch. The train crew is helping friends beside the line "putting up hay." Maybe the unusual was the usual for life and railroading along the route of the mixed consist, the "Virginia Creeper." *Courtesy Earl Palmer.*

work. High tractive effort of the M2s enabled them to handle heavier yard chores. The crews did not like them much because they were extremely rough riding on the road, and they were hard to fire and to keep the steam pressure up was difficult. Even with stokers, larger stacks and revised exhaust stands with increased drafting characteristics, the problem was never totally solved. The boiler was simply too big for the grate area.

A few changes were made during their service. Superheaters were added to the 1100 through 1149 from 1915 to 1919, and these remained classed as M2. Worthington BL feedwater heaters were added to some by the early forties. And a wide variety of tenders were used with these heavy 4-8-0s, but the 15,000 gallon N&W tenders were probably the only type still with them in the mid-fifties.

Except for number 1140, which was sold to the Durham and Southern in May 1939, the other sixty M2s remained in service until 1950. With the N&W purchase and building of seventy-five 0-8-0s from 1950-53, forty-four of the M2s had been relieved from service by the end of 1955. The last sixteen were used primarily for work trains and were retired by 1957. Dieselization had little effect on retiring these unpopular engines.

M2 Experimental Switcher

The M2s were basically the standard switcher for the N&W after World War II. The railway, in an effort to reduce the yard operating costs, set out to gain better utilization of its yard engines.

To do this required overhauling some power and testing some innovations that would improve the "yard goats."

M2 engine number 1100 went into the Roanoke Shops and emerged in April 1947 as a unit almost completely redone. Coal capacity of the tender was increased to twenty tons to permit continuous operation for twenty-four hours without refueling. The machinery, likewise, was given mechanical lubrication to make the engine available for round-the-clock operation. Stoker and water level controls were installed so that the engine could be left unattended for longer periods. And to gain more complete combustion, a combustion chamber was added, and a turbine-driven fan was mounted in the smokebox, thereby increasing the draft and reducing smoke and exhaust noise. The fan, stoker, damper and the standby water feed pump were tied into automatic control—the first such application as far as is known.

This rebuilt switcher had a look of its own. The running gear looked the same as before, but the boiler had no exposed piping, the smokebox was extended forward to accommodate the fan. The boiler top was enclosed with cowling for a stream-lined appearance, with the cab having a slightly slanted front. These improvements increased the engine weight to 279,530 pounds and the weight on drivers to 239,530 pounds. There was no change in tractive effort.

The 1100, in preliminary tests, was satisfactory except for the abrasive action of cinders on the induced draft fan blades. In September 1948 the Roanoke Shop modified another M2, number 1112, into a switcher with added improvements over the first one. The modifications were a new cinder collector, the addition of three circulators in the firebox, which increased the heating surface by 775 square feet, refractory walls in the firebox to return the cinders before emission and increased boiler pressure to 225 pounds per

In the 1950s thousands of rail fans rode N&W's "Virginia Creeper" on its passenger-mail-express-freight run between Abingdon, Virginia, and West Jefferson, North Carolina. It fought up a sustained 3% grade to reach the highest point attained by a passenger train east of the Rockies—3565 feet at White Top station. Engine 429 passes Green Cove, three rail miles—but only a mile as the hawk flies—from the summit. *Photo Courtesy Earl Palmer, Text N&W.*

A pair of Ms are pulling a heavy train for the Abingdon Branch across one of the numerous trestles and bridges along this picturesque line. The 55-mile branch and Class Ms are gone, and "we shall never see the likes of this again." (Quote from Earl Palmer.) *Courtesy Earl Palmer.*

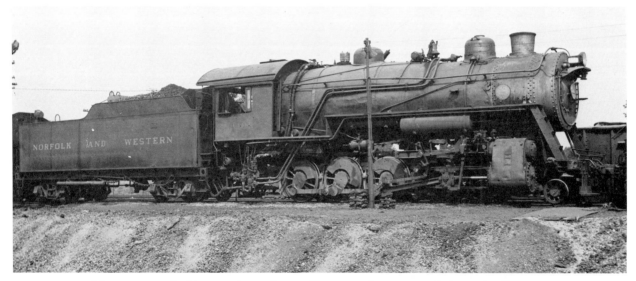

M2s were rough riders on the road according to engine crews. But in yards, they were stout, hard workers. With the arrival of 75 thoroughly modern 0-8-0 switchers, this fat-boilered class was finally eclipsed. 1106, with USRA tender, at Williamson, April 1950. *Courtesy Charles E. Winters.*

Most 1100s were retired in '50-'53 after more modern power took over yard chores. The remaining M2s were kept around primarily for work trains until dieselization. 1131 at Petersburg, Virginia, in November '52; retired October '53. *Courtesy C. W. Jernstrom.*

M2s were used mostly on the Norfolk Division during the late teens. 1130 awaits its next assignment at Norfolk terminal in February 1916. Note the oil lamp and old style slat pilot. *Courtesy Harold K. Vollrath.*

Ever mindful of its glorious past, N&W dressed up one of its old Ms to celebrate the founding of a predecessor line. Number 475 is refurbished to resemble a steamer of another era and stencilled with "Shenandoah Valley" on its tender flanks in 1957. *Courtesy Harold K. Vollrath.*

Of all man's creations, nothing he made captured and held the fancy as did the steam locomotive. We who grew up with and loved the faithful old iron horses, mourned their passing. We shall not behold their likes ever again. *Courtesy Earl Palmer, Photo and Text.*

Typical role of the Class M in its last decade of service—the mixed train. 475, at the head end of the "Huckleberry," passes Christiansburg after its run with the mixed consist on the Blacksburg Branch. Date is July 1954. *Courtesy Harold K. Vollrath.*

405 resting at Bristol, Virginia, in September 1955. The stack with a spark arrestor installed probably means this sturdy engine was being used on the Abingdon Branch. The spark arrestor was required on that line. *Courtesy Harold K. Vollrath.*

square inch for a better tractive effort.

The crews did not like the new 1112. The fire fly-ash that was ejected from the stack was very discomforting to the engine crews. The 1100 was used primarily at Lamberts Point, and the 1112 stayed at Roanoke. When the N&W purchased thirty 0-8-0 switchers in 1950, further experimentation was pointless. The railway had found the superior switcher it wanted. The two M2 improved switchers were retired and scrapped in 1951.

1100 experimental switcher working at Roanoke, July 1949. *Courtesy Charles E. Winters.*

Roanoke was the focal point of the system's passenger operations; a shifter was required to work the passenger terminal there. Number 464 awaits its next assignment at the old Roanoke passenger station in September 1946. *Courtesy Charles E. Winters.*

Class M 475, built in 1906 and rebuilt as a historical specimen for the railway, heads up a tripleheader of aged 4-8-0s to pull a rail fans' special to Blacksburg, Virginia in September 1957. *Courtesy Earl Palmer Photo and Text.*

Ms were ideal for light duties in late steam. Of sound design with a free-steaming boiler, the class was good for yard work and branch lines, lasting practically to steam's end. 457 resting at Roanoke 1934. *Courtesy N&W.*

Old-timer 396 pulling the long-lived "Huckleberry" from Christiansburg to Blacksburg, Virginia, in 1958. This is one of the last runs made before retirement of the engine and mixed train. *Courtesy Earl Palmer.*

4-6-0

TEN-WHEELERS

The newly formed N&W Railway first bought the 4-6-0 to update its passenger power. The 56-inch drivered Class V became mountain performers but were limited in speed. Number 956, like all other Class Vs, was rebuilt with 62-inch drivers and reclassed V1. With the arrival of 4-6-2 Pacifics, the 4-6-0s were soon relegated to secondary passenger work, in which they remained to their end. *Courtesy C. T. Felstead Collection.*

Class V

In 1896 when the new owners of the Norfolk and Western *Railway* assumed control of the company, the passenger service motive power was in the form of the 4-4-0, Class N, and the 4-6-0, Class U, from the predecessor Norfolk and Western *Railroad.* This older power had been good in its day, but was fast becoming obsolete in view of the more modern power the new owners had acquired in 1898 for freight work. The wheel arrangement, 4-6-0, was quite versatile, for it allowed good power and speed with one locomotive. With the varied profile of the N&W, a general purpose locomotive was desired for its passenger operations as well as for the high speed freights.

The N&W ordered two 4-6-0s from the Baldwin Locomotive Works, numbered 950 and 951, classed as V, which were delivered in May 1900. These locomotives were equipped with piston valves, which was one of the earliest applications of this feature on the railway. The cylinders were nineteen inches in diameter by twenty-eight-inch

Class A 89, new at Baldwin 1902. *Courtesy Harold K. Vollrath.*

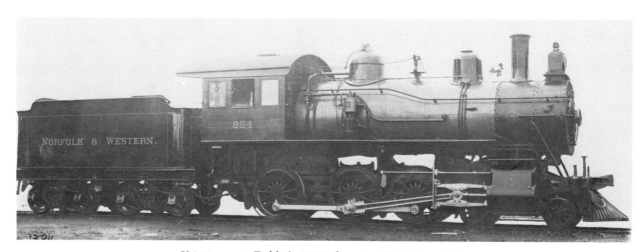

V 954, new at Baldwin 1900. *Courtesy H. L. Broadbelt.*

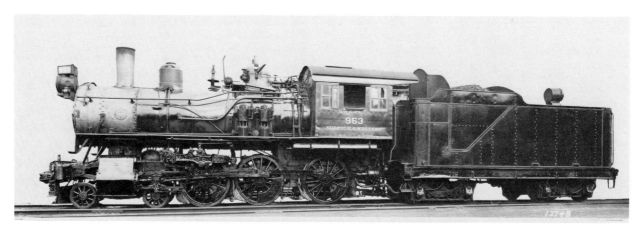

V1 953 (originally Class V, Baldwin 1900) with 9,000 gallon tender in 1934. *Courtesy N&W.*

stroke, boiler pressure was 200 pounds per square inch and the fifty-six-inch drivers developed 30,685 pounds tractive effort. The 32.6 square foot grate was placed between the drivers, and the grate and the boiler were almost identical to those used on the Class W, 2-8-0. The Class V total engine weight was 155,900 pounds with 121,650 pounds on the drivers. The tenders were 8.5 tons and 4,000 gallons capacity.

With fifty-six-inch drivers, the Class V was not for high speeds. In the initial runs over the hilly lines west from Roanoke to Bristol, they were found to be very good for the heavier passenger trains. The railway immediately sent another order to Baldwin for ten more, numbered 952 through 961. These ten were all delivered in November 1900 and had identical specifications to the original order.

The Class V1s were built as virtual duplicates of the Class V except for the substitution of a larger driver found to be more satisfactory. Since the wheel bases were the same for both classes, the entire class of Vs were rebuilt and reclassed as V1s by 1909, retaining their original numbers.

Class V1

In October 1902 the Richmond Locomotive Works built five new locomotives for the N&W.

Classed as V1 and numbered 962 through 966, they were identical to the Vs mechanically, except for a larger sixty-two-inch driver and a slightly larger cylinder with the bore enlarged to 19½ inches. The new tractive effort was 29,193 pounds. Also, the weight increased slightly, the engine weight being 162,350 pounds and the weight on drivers up to 128,025 pounds. All other specifications and data remained identical to those of the earlier Class V. This new power was better suited for passenger work, and that was what they were used for.

The original Class Vs were not as well suited to freight work as the superior wide firebox 2-8-0s then in use. Thus it was decided to alter the Vs by substituting the larger sixty-two-inch drivers and boring out the cylinders to 19½ inch diameter. Upon this rebuilding, the 950 through 961 were reclassed as V1. The 950 through 966 subsequently had the Stephenson valve gear replaced by the Baker gear.

The seventeen Class V1s were totally eclipsed by the numerous Pacific types in the early teens. But the sturdy little 4-6-0s were ideal secondary power for the many light-traffic branch lines and light passenger trains typical on these lines in that day. By 1920 most were on the Scioto and Pocahontas divisions, working their many coal

V1 954 shows that N&W maintained its power, including engines in secondary service, in first-class condition. *Courtesy C. T. Felstead Collection.*

feeder branches. It is thought that the decline of the branch line passenger business in the late twenties and the thirties was the downfall period for the V1s. The first seven were scrapped in 1929 and six more in 1931-35. The 950, 951, 954 and 956 all soldiered through World War II, and the last two (numbers 954 and 956) were not retired until 1950. The V1s remained practically unchanged throughout their career. The last four, at least, got the fourteen tons and 9,000 gallons tenders, and all were equipped with the electric headlight. The headlight position was changed on several occasions, but other than this, the V1 served the N&W faithfully for many years practically as built.

Class A

The Class V, 4-6-0, was built originally with fifty-six-inch drivers. It was soon evident that for faster service a larger driver type was required. The Baldwin Locomotive Works delivered four new ten-wheelers for passenger service classed as A, numbered 86 through 89, all built in February 1902. One additional A, number 90, was delivered in March 1904, and it was identical to the first four. Essentially, these As were a "slideruled" version of the V. The grate area was the same 32.6 square feet of the earlier V, but the boiler was slightly larger. The drivers were sixty-eight inches in diameter with the cylinders 20-by-28 inches. Boiler pressure was 200 pounds per square inch, developing a tractive effort of 28,000 pounds. The piston valves were provided along with the Stephenson valve gear, although the Baker valve gear was applied later. The engine weight was 166,300 pounds, and the 134,300 pounds on the drivers assured a good factor of adhesion. Diminutive 9.7 ton and 5,000 gallon tenders were supplied to the As.

The Class As were bought possibly as an experiment along with the Class V1 soon to be built. The A was not favored since the V1 was so similar to the V, the latter could be rebuilt into the V1. After the rebuilding of the Vs, the seventeen V1s fulfilled the requirements of the 4-6-0. The As remained mostly on the Shenandoah Division, as a class, and all were scrapped at the Roanoke Shops in August 1928.

4-4-2

PRELUDE TO BIGGER AND BETTER J'S

Because of 4-6-0 speed limitations, the Atlantic type was purchased for the faster flatland schedules. The 4-4-2 Js had the tallest drivers (79 inches) on a N&W engine bought new. In this 1916 photo, the Stephenson gear had been replaced by the Baker valve gear, and the electric headlight had been installed. The railway began the change from oil to electric headlights in 1913. *Courtesy Harold K. Vollrath.*

Class J

As the twentieth century was ushered in, the new owners of the N&W Railway had considerable numbers of former standard passenger power in the 4-4-0 and 4-6-0 types. After a brief fling with the 4-6-0 for passenger work, the railway officials wanted something with more speed on the flatter portions of the system. At this time the trailer truck was introduced in numbers to get greater size fireboxes than was possible with older power having the firebox between the drivers.

The Atlantic-type had been found ideally suited for the faster trains on many railroads, if the train weight was light. The N&W took stock of the situation and sent an order to the Baldwin Locomotive Works for six, trim, little Atlantic-types. These 4-4-2s were Class J, numbered 600 through 605, and were built between May and July 1903. The engines were designed for speed, and to see one gave that impression. The high seventy-nine-inch driving wheels were the largest the N&W was ever to order on a new locomotive. The nineteen-inch bore by twenty-eight-inch cylinders were capable of developing 21,750 pounds tractive effort with the boiler supplying 200 pounds pressure of steam. To provide a sufficient quantity of steam at speeds, the boiler had a grate area of forty-five square feet. The locomotive weight was 167,700 pounds with 85,340 pounds on the drivers. The tenders were of 13.8 tons and 6,000 gallons capacity. The Stephenson valve gear, the oil-burning headlight and the large cab were used,

as all were common equipment for both freight and passenger power at the time.

The J took to the road and performed admirably on the light trains. Whatever she could start, she could move along like the wind. In December 1904 the N&W received one more J, number 606, from Baldwin, bringing its total in this class to seven. The Js were used mostly on the Norfolk Division, although there are reports of occasional use on the Scioto. The biggest fault was their lack of tractive effort. This was not a design fault, just an inherent limitation of the type. They were most often seen on the N&Ws "Cannonball" that ran between Norfolk and the RF&P connection at Richmond via Petersburg. Some ran between Norfolk and Crewe, as well as between Portsmouth and Columbus.

The 600s were changed little in their day. Electric headlights replaced the old oil-burning type; the tenders were replaced by larger ones of 9,000 gallons and fourteen tons capacity. Five Js (numbers 600 through 602, 604 and 605) got superheaters in 1915. In 1931 number 600 was the first to go, and the last four were retired in 1935. The older Js, with light trains behind them, could "scorch the ballast" on the "racetrack" with relative ease in their day. What they did "back when" turned out to be a preview of exciting things to come. Later Class Js, 4-8-4s, also numbered in the 600s, were to "scorch the ballast" with much heavier trains and with equal ease some four decades later on the same "racetrack" between Petersburg and Norfolk.

J 606, new at Baldwin 1904. *Courtesy Harold K. Vollrath.*

Oddities

NONSTANDARD POWER

Over the years N&W developed an impressive roster of standard motive power. The railway had some nonstandard, or "odd" classes if you will, too! No comprehensive work could be complete without mentioning some unique types acquired and used over the years. This power included experimentals and that inherited from predecessors and other lines acquired by the N&W Railway. Narrow gauge no. 3 at N&W's Radford Tie Yard, December 1952. *Courtesy Harold K. Vollrath.*

Shay 56 (Lima 1907) at Bluefield about 1915. *Courtesy Harold K. Vollrath.*

VAC Ry 2 (Richmond 1904) became N&W Class 0-28 number 91. *Courtesy N&W.*

In 1896 when the present N&W Railway Company began operations, its motive power policy concentrated on developing standard designs. But there were a few nonstandard designs, too!

The new railway did inherit all of the old N&W Railroad's motive power in 1896. Likewise after 1896, the N&W took over several small short lines resulting in more nonstandard power being acquired. Most of the locomotives were 4-4-0, 4-6-0 and 2-8-0 wheel arrangements with a smattering of other types. These old engines will not be discussed except to say they continued in service for a number of years until more modern locomotives rendered them obsolete. Almost all of these "old-timers" were gone by 1920, with most being retired before 1913. However, there were some nonstandard engines worthy of mention.

When the N&W purchased the 8.8-mile Virginia Anthracite Coal (VAC) and Railway Company on August 29, 1911, a part of that deal included a camelback 2-6-2C locomotive, number 2. It was renumbered 91 and classed 0-28 by N&W. The engine was a June 1904 (c/n 29718) product of ALCO's Richmond works and had a large firebox to burn the anthracite coal produced at Merrimac Mines, Virginia. Its grate area of sixty-eight square feet was the largest used by nonarticulated power on the N&W up to that time. Other specifications: cylinders 18-by-24 inches, drivers fifty inches, weight of engine 140,000 pounds and tractive effort 23,794 pounds. This Prairie type served as a switcher until January 1916, when it was scrapped at Roanoke Shops. As a sidelight, the VAC rail line served primarily the previously mentioned coal mines at Merrimac, and this line became the N&Ws Blacksburg Branch on January 31, 1912.

One real oddity was the N&Ws Shay, purchased new from Lima in August 1907. The 300,000 pound locomotive (c/n 1893) had three 17-by-18 inch cylinders with forty-six-inch drivers. This geared engine worked the curved and heavy grade coal branch lines around Bluefield, West Virginia. It was hoped it could move heavier tonnage more economically. However, it tended to slow up all traffic. This adventure was dropped in December 1915 when the Shay, N&W number 56, was sold to Birmingham Rail and Locomotive Company for resale into logging service elsewhere in the south.

A narrow gauge group of nonstandard power was used at N&Ws Tie Treating Plant at east Radford, Virginia. All of the railway's ties, bridge and other structural timbers were creosote treated at this plant with some diminutive saddle tanks pushing and pulling mightily within that huge wood storage yard. There were three locomotives over the years—numbers 1, 2 and 3—all purchased used in the early twenties. Number 1 had been built by Pittsburgh in 1883 (c/n 700) as a

Narrow gauge number 1 at Radford Tie Plant about 1932. Originally a 2-6-0 with tender, this engine was reboilered at Roanoke Shops in 1932 and became a 2-6-0T at this shopping. *Courtesy N&W.*

Class G 237 was built by Roanoke Machine Works (c/n 99) in May 1890. This engine in her heyday was the mainstay of the predecessor N&W Railroad freight power roster. After forming the N&W Railway, this "horse" of another era worked for years with its new owners. *Courtesy N&W.*

2-6-0. Roanoke Shops applied a new boiler (c/n 265) in 1932 and converted number 1 to a 2-6-0T. Both numbers 2 and 3 were 0-4-0T Vulcan products. All three of these three-foot gauge saddle tanks performed their unglamorous jobs until 1955-57, when all were retired and scrapped as a result of a serious explosion closing the tie plant.

These "odd" classes of power did nothing to develop the N&Ws renown standard steam giants of the later steam era. But no N&W steam work could be complete without mentioning those obscure iron horses of this mighty steam railway.

4-6-2

STILL UNDER STEAM TODAY

In the early 1900s, passenger trains became heavier and new power was needed to supplant the 4-6-0 and 4-4-2. The Class E 4-6-2 was ushered in with its higher tractive effort and good speed capability. Soon eclipsed by the Mountain type, N&W Pacifics remained as secondary power until the decline of passenger service. Two worked almost to the end of steam on the Clinch Valley line for which they were ideally suited. 578, here preparing to leave Bluefield in March 1956, today is under steam at Ohio Railway Museum in Worthington, Ohio. *Courtesy Charles E. Winters.*

Class E and Class E1

Right after the turn of the century, the N&W had acquired some new passenger locomotives for its first-class trains. The 4-6-0 was being used on the slower trains and on the mountain grades, while the new 4-4-2s were speeding along on the level stretches of the N&W main. But the passenger train was becoming heavier, so larger power was needed. At the same time, the 4-6-2 was fast emerging as the new heavy passenger power to replace the 4-6-0 and to supplant the 4-4-2, hence higher tractive effort was needed.

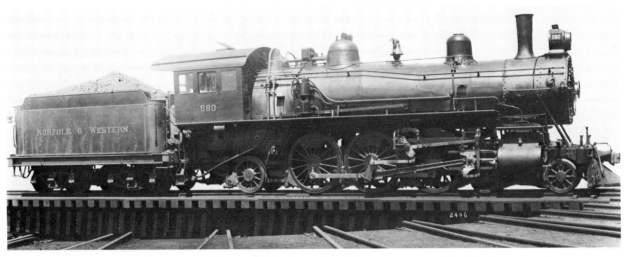

E1 580, new at Baldwin 1907. Class Es looked similar when new, except for Stephenson valve gear. *Courtesy H. L. Broadbelt.*

E 597 (Richmond 1905) with 9,000 gallon tender in 1934. Stephenson valve gear has been replaced by Baker type. *Courtesy N&W.*

The first five N&W Pacifics were delivered by Richmond Locomotive Works in December 1905 and January 1906. This new class of power was designated as E, numbered 595 through 599, and was at that time the largest N&W passenger power. The specifications were: twenty-inch bore by twenty-eight-inch stroke cylinders fed by a boiler with a forty-five square foot grate, boiler pressure of 200 pounds per square inch, total locomotive weight of 196,253 pounds with 130,618 pounds on the sixty-eight-inch drivers, tractive effort of 28,000 pounds and all were equipped with the Stephenson valve gear. The tender was of 13.8 tons coal and 6,000 gallons water capacity. The locomotive trailer truck was of the inboard bearing type as used on the earlier 4-4-2s.

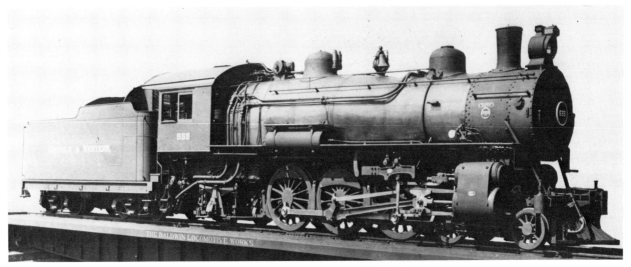

E2a 555, new at Baldwin 1912. *Courtesy Harold K. Vollrath.*

E2a 576 (originally Class E2, Richmond 1910) with USRA 12,000 gallon tender in 1934. *Courtesy N&W.*

E3 504 (originally PRR K3 8657, Baldwin 1913) with 15,000 gallon tender in 1943. *Courtesy N&W.*

With the increased capabilities of the engine clearly demonstrated, the railway decided it could use more of this proven power. Baldwin Locomotive Works delivered fifteen more 4-6-2s, numbered 580 through 594, in April and May 1907. These new locomotives were classed E1 and were identical to the E except for the use of the Walschaert valve gear. To give the E and E1 a mark of distinction, they had the piston valves to the inside of the cylinders, and the cabs were the same as used on the older Ws and Js (4-4-2).

The E and E1 remained virtually unchanged during the earlier years of their service. They all got electric headlights around 1913 when the oil lamps were removed, and a new stack was installed to improve drafting and exhaust characteristics. The Class E only got the Baker valve gear sometime prior to 1918, number 584 received a superheater in 1915, and later on, all the E and E1s received a second single air pump as well as larger tenders of fourteen tons and 9,000 gallons capacity.

When the 4-8-2s were built in larger numbers, the E and E1 types were relegated to secondary and branch line duties. Then, with the extended runs being performed by the newer power in the late twenties and the trimming of many branch line passenger schedules, the E1 locomotives, with their unpopular valve gear, started being retired in 1931. Most of them were scrapped in 1934-36, the last E1, number 584, in 1938. The Class E fared a little better since they were equipped with the Baker gear. Number 596 was scrapped in 1934, the other four going in 1938-39.

Class E2

The new Class E and E1 were so successful that it was decided to continue with the Pacific-type as the main passenger locomotive. But the train tonnage was increasing rapidly, and so the new power would have to be bigger. In February and March 1910 Richmond Locomotive Works delivered six new Pacifics, numbered 574 through 579 and classed as E2. Mechanically, the only similarity with the earlier N&W Pacifics was the grate area of forty-five square feet. The wheel base was longer, the drivers increased to seventy inches in diameter, and the boiler much larger—the first course of the E2 boiler was the same as the maximum diameter of the E and E1. The cylinders were 22½ inches in diameter by 28 inch stroke, the boiler pressure was 200 pounds per

556 awaits the call to leave Lynchburg, Virginia, in May 1950 with a local. E2s were good little engines in their day. However, by the fifties they were short on power and availability for N&W's needs. Except for three kept around until the mid to late fifties, all were retired by 1953. *Courtesy Charles E. Winters.*

Typical role played by the E2s in their later years—local secondary service. 557 at Bramwell, West Virginia, in 1947. *Courtesy C. W. Jernstrom.*

square inch, and the tractive effort was 34,425 pounds.

This locomotive weighed 247,000 pounds total and had 166,000 pounds on the drivers. The tenders were the standard fourteen tons and 9,000 gallons type, used on all the freight power purchased during this period. The engine trailer truck was a new outside bearing radial truck—the first to be used on the N&W. The railway was so pleased with these new locomotives that it immediately got Richmond to build ten more, numbers 564 through 573, during May and June of the same year. They were identical to the first six. All of the E2s were equipped with the Baker Pilliod valve gear.

In June 1912, six more Pacifics were built at Baldwin, numbers 553 through 558, Class E2a. These new locomotives were almost identical except for the use of the straight Baker valve gear then becoming popular, and the addition of superheaters—the first such application on N&W passenger power. Likewise, the Roanoke Shops constructed five E2as from July to September 1912, numbers 559 through 563 (c/n 193 through 197). To round out this building spree on Pacifics, the Roanoke Shops built 548 through 553 (c/n 198 through 202) in July through October 1913; then built five more, numbered 543 through 547 (c/n 203 through 207), in May and June 1914. These last ten were classed E2b since they had Hobart-Allfree cylinders installed. Everything else from the E2 and E2a remained the same.

Only minor alterations were made to the E2s. All were equipped with two 9½ inch air pumps that remained on this class throughout their service. New stacks and exhaust stands were installed that increased the draft and gave better exhausting characteristics. The headlight changed location several times during this class's career. Most significantly, the entire Class E2 received superheaters before 1920, got the standard Baker gear and were reclassed as E2a during 1925-27. Five of the E2bs, numbers 543, 544, 548, 550 and 552, had the ports sealed on the Hobart-Allfree cylinders, and these engines were reclassed as E2a during the mid-twenties. Several were later equipped with stokers around 1940.

The E2's reign as the primary passenger power was shortlived. The K1s and K2s took over all heavy passenger work, while the E2s (all thirty-seven) were used on other main line passenger duties until about 1929, when the passenger business, and therefore the number of passenger trains, declined. After this, they were assigned to less trafficked lines as primary passenger power. The Mountain-types got the nod on the extended passenger runs covering three districts in length, and the E2s became the power for local passenger operations.

With so many of the Pacific types in use, the

This clear photo vividly depicts the E2a in its last days. 562 at Petersburg, October 1952. *A. A. Thieme Photo, Courtesy C. T. Felstead Collection.*

In 1920 engine 596 with train crewmen is ready to pull a passenger train to Bristol. Location: Radford, Virginia. *Courtesy Earl Palmer.*

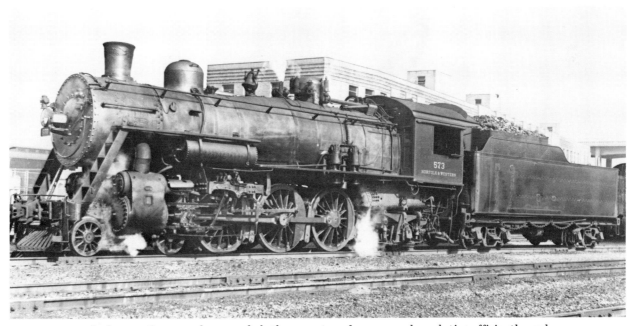

As locomotives are downgraded, they must perform secondary duties efficiently and reliably. The 4-6-2s filled secondary passenger duties well until after WW II, when the E2 and E3s became surplus. *R. J. Foster Photo, Courtesy C. T. Felstead Collection.*

Five 4-6-2s were purchased from "Pennsy" to replace aging N&W Class J 4-4-2s. The secondhand Pacifics first received USRA tenders. 502, ex-PRR 7095, at Crewe in November 1932. *Charles E. Winters Photo. Courtesy Harold K. Vollrath Collection.*

Lynchburg, on the main line, was busy with passenger traffic due to the Southern interchange and junction with N&W's Durham line. 504, at Lynchburg in 1946, shows its parentage with the Belpaire boiler, but the tender, pilot, headlight position, and smokebox front indicates N&W ownership. *Charles E. Winters Photo. Courtesy Harold K. Vollrath Collection.*

N&W 4-6-2 E2s were big passenger power when built. At Wytheville about 1910, new E2 575 has a long string of cars hooked to its drawbar and is taking on water at this station stop. *Courtesy N&W.*

older passenger power from the turn of the century was discarded. The reduction of secondary passenger work just prior to World War II led nine E2as and one E2b to be retired and scrapped between 1938 and 1940. The remaining twenty-seven E2s stayed on during the conflict, but as the K2s were modernized and upgraded, the old Pacifics' days were numbered.

The last E2b was number 547, which was retired in 1951, and the former E2b, now E2a, number 544, lasted until 1955. Numbers 563 and 578 (former E2) survived until 1958-59. They were used on the Clinch Valley line between Bluefield and Norton, where these locomotives were ideally suited to the operating conditions. Except for 563 and 578, the E2s were not affected by dieselization. In their latter years, they received the USRA and N&W 15,000 gallon tenders. Today, number 578 can be seen under steam at the Ohio Railway Museum at Worthington, Ohio.

One interesting sidelight on the Class E2a was that when the railway wanted a streamlined passenger locomotive for secondary service, the E2a was initially considered and a drawing was made

depicting the 576 in that all-familiar scheme applied to the K2s and Js.

Class E3

The Pennsylvania Railroad had surplus power in the form of its own Class K3 Pacifics. The N&W, possibly needing heavier power for the heavier passenger trains, purchased five of the PRR engines (numbers 8658, 7075, 7095, 7308 and 8657) and redesignated them E3, numbers 500 through 504. These Baldwin products of 1913 had been designed for high speed, and as one former official noted "they could not start much but once underway, they would run like hell."

A look at the general specifications helps to explain why. The drivers were eighty inches with the cylinders 26-by-26 inches. The tractive effort was 38,283 pounds with the boiler pressure set for 205 pounds per square inch. These features put them in the race horse category. Other general data: total engine weight was 293,600 pounds, weight on drivers was 196,300 pounds, Walschaert valve gear was installed and a grate

579 looks "fit as a fiddle" at Shenandoah, Virginia, on the Shenandoah Valley line in November 1932. By the early thirties, the 4-6-2s were mostly used in secondary passenger work, in which they remained to the end of their lengthy careers. This well-maintained engine has a N&W designed 12,000 gallon tender. *Courtesy N&W.*

area measured fifty-five square feet with no combustion chamber.

The E3 was not a popular locomotive type because of the Walschaert valve gear and overheating of the driving journal boxes. The class did receive some modifications, primarily the replacement of parts with standard N&W items such as headlight, boiler tube pilot, number plate and the

N&W 15,000 gallon tender. The E3s were used on the Scioto and Norfolk divisions, replacing primarily the older 4-4-2s. These Pacifics commonly worked the N&Ws "Cannonball"—between Norfolk and Petersburg then over the Atlantic Coast Line (ACL) tracks to Richmond for the Richmond, Fredericksburg and Potomac (RF&P) connection there. The entire class was retired in 1946-47.

4-8-2

"MIGHTY GOOD ENGINES"

The railway's 4-8-2s constituted one of the most widely used, utilitarian types on the system over the years. From 1916 to the end of steam, N&W's mountain types were used in all sorts of work. First they were primary passenger power with an occasional stint in manifest freight service, while later they handled all secondary passenger work and most way-freights. Number 112 was N&W designed. Built Class K1, it was used for decades in passenger service, then extensively upgraded after WW II for secondary freight work. However, it occasionally got the nod to haul passengers in place of the streamlined K2s. N&W 4-8-2s were jack-of-all-trades that ultimately led to the streamlined 600s. *Courtesy Charles E. Winters.*

K1 111 (Roanoke 1917) with N&W designed 12,000 gallon tender in the late twenties. Its original appearance was similar, except it had no feedwater heater, a 9,000 gallon tender, and a smaller diameter stack. *Courtesy N&W.*

Upgraded K1 100 (Roanoke 1916) with former C&O 22,000 gallon tender in 1955. *Courtesy N&W.*

K2 121 (Brooks 1919) with original USRA 10,000 gallon tender in early twenties. *Courtesy N&W.*

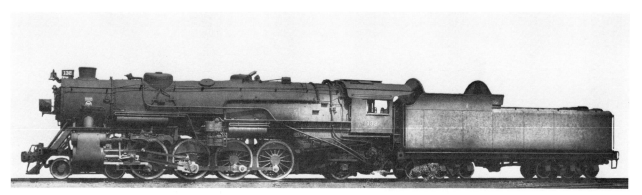

K2a 132 with 15,000 gallon tender, new at Baldwin 1923. *Courtesy H. L. Broadbelt.*

K2 120 (Brooks 1919) with 16,000 gallon tender in 1934. *Courtesy N&W.*

Streamlined K2 125 (Brooks 1919). All K2s were modernized from 1945-47. *Courtesy N&W.*

K3 203 (Roanoke 1926) in 1934. *Courtesy N&W.*

Class K1

The standard passenger locomotive, by the early teens, was the Pacific type. On the N&W, its Class E Pacifics held down all heavy passenger schedules system-wide. Even as the last N&W Pacifics were being built in 1914, passenger cars were increasing significantly in weight with a resulting increase in train tonnage. On the flat portions of the N&W system, the Class Es were performing well, but on the steep mountain grades, to keep the passenger trains on schedules, sectioning trains or doubleheading was becoming necessary. What was needed was a larger, more powerful locomotive with greater horsepower and more tractive effort. To do this, a larger boiler and grate area was required as well as more drivers.

The road's mechanical engineers then drew up a locomotive with a wheel arrangement new to the N&W. The mountain-type 4-8-2 had been tried on other railroads, but it had not been produced in quantity. The new 4-8-2 was being tried out as an experiment to some extent, for its wheel arrangement was relatively new. In size it was to eclipse the old passenger power then on N&W rails.

The first eight 4-8-2s, classed K1 and numbered 100 through 107, were built by the Roanoke Shops (c/n 208, 210-212, 209, 213-215) from June to August 1916. These impressive haulers had the unmistakable look of power. The big, long boiler with a maximum diameter of almost ninety-two inches was riding over two huge 29-by-28 inch cylinders connected to seventy-inch drivers. Interestingly, drivers of the same size and cylinder stroke had performed well on the Class E2s. Behind the drivers was an outside bearing radial trailing truck carrying the wide eighty square foot grate. The cab was very similar to the ones used on the Es. Likewise, the tenders were the same used by many classes of N&W power at the time—fourteen tons and 9,000 gallons capacity.

Although these engines looked like an enlarged version of the Class E2s, the similarity ended there. With thirty-five more square footage of grate area, and one and two-thirds times the tractive effort of the Pacifics, the K1s became the standard heavy passenger power for the mountain divisions. Its 57,200 pounds of tractive effort provided by the 200 pound pressure boiler enabled these locomotives to start heavy trains, even on the grades and, once underway, to move them at speeds that eliminated doubleheading and sectioning of the heavier passenger trains. As built, they weighed 347,000 pounds with 236,000 pounds on drivers.

At first, some problems were encountered with the running gear and there were combustion problems, but these were corrected. Soon another group of K1s were produced by Roanoke from October to December 1917. This second group of eight were numbered 108 through 115 (c/n 216 through 223). The sixteen K1s were the primary passenger power along with the newer USRA Class K2s until the streamlined 4-8-4s arrived in the early forties.

The class was upgraded and improved throughout its career. Larger stacks and redesigned exhaust stands licked the drafting problems previously mentioned. The original two 9½ inch air pumps on the left side were replaced by two cross-compound air pumps. When the feedwater heaters were being applied, the K1s received the Worthington number 4 BL heaters on the left side, the two air pumps being moved to the right. At first, a large style headlight was mounted at the top of the smokebox front. Later, the light was moved to the center of the smokebox front, and the bell was placed at the light's original location. The boiler pressure was increased to 220 pounds per square inch with a new tractive effort of 62,920 pounds. By the early thirties, all had been assigned the N&W-designed 16,000 gallon tender.

K1 with train 14 surrounded by snow-covered land west of Glenvar, Virginia, in January 1940. Roanoke-built K1s were used along with K2s in primary passenger service until the coming of sleek 4-8-4s in the forties. *Courtesy N&W.*

The most extensive rebuilding of the K1s was at the end of World War II. The K1s were totally stripped down and modernized. The frames were renewed and strengthened; a steel pilot beam replaced the old oak beam; new cast steel cylinders were installed; a new sandbox, like those applied to the streamlined K2, was placed on the boiler that had been totally overhauled; pressure and mechanical lubrication was applied; lagging was applied to the firebox sides; and a modern-looking cab replaced the old oversized one. Eight of the class received 22,000 gallon, twenty-three ton tenders purchased from the C&O (ex-Pere Marquette). One K1 had a 22,000 gallon, twenty-eight ton tender that had been acquired from the Bessemer and Lake Erie. The other seven re-

Upgrading the K1s changed their appearance considerably, such as square sandbox, steel pilot beam, cab, and firebox lagging. Other improvements included strengthened frames, new cast-steel cylinders, renewed fireboxes on many, and extended mechanical lubrication. Compare 114 with number 111. *Courtesy Charles E. Winters.*

Streamlined K2a 130 in front of K1. *Courtesy Charles E. Winters.*

ceived the N&W 18,000 gallon, cast steel, water bottom tenders.

Thus rebuilt, the K1s were used throughout the system on local freights. The crews thought very well of them after rebuilding, for the K1s were the ideal locomotive for local freights of light to medium weight. The K1s were the oldest class of N&W power to remain intact to dieselization. They all lasted until 1957 when the first two were withdrawn from service. All were gone by October 1958, with number 104 being the last one retired.

Class K2

With America's entry into World War I, the U.S. railroads were placed under federal control to alleviate the bottlenecks stemming from this country's economic unpreparedness for war. To run the railroads, the government set up the United States Railway Administration (USRA) and likewise it set up a Motive Power Committee to design standard locomotives for all of the railroads. The N&W was assigned ten of the USRA mountain-types, classed as K2, in May 1919 from the Brooks Plant of ALCO. Being a standard design, the K2 had a look of its own with the USRA

characteristic cab, sandbox and boiler front. The specifications were: the maximum boiler diameter was ninety-six inches, the boiler pressure was 200 pounds per square inch, the cylinder had a twenty-eight-inch bore and thirty-inch stroke, the grate area was seventy-six square feet, the drivers were sixty-nine inches with a tractive effort of 58,000 pounds, and the engine weight was 352,000 pounds with 243,000 pounds on the drivers. They were numbered 116 to 125.

The K2s were assigned along with the older K1s as the primary heavy passenger power for the mountain districts. After the N&W was released from USRA control, the railway decided that more mountain power could be used. Since the K2s were superior to the K1s in performance, the N&W wanted more of these USRA types. The Baldwin Locomotive Works built numbers 126 through 137 from April to July 1923. These new 4-8-2s were classed as K2a since they incorporated common boiler fittings and other parts used by the N&W, and they were built with an enlarged stack and exhaust stand. Likewise, a couple of minor improvements were made, such as the boiler inspection hatch to the left front of the steam dome and using the new N&W tender design of twenty tons and 15,000 gallons capacity.

Modernized K2s were more reliable than when first built 25 years before. Improvements that increased availability were new cast-steel cylinders and bar frames, complete mechanical and pressure lubrication, driver journal lubricators, roller bearings on all engine truck and tender journals, and high capacity tenders. *R. J. Foster Photo, Courtesy C. T. Felstead Collection.*

In May 1955 this engine was repainted and stencilled for the role of a C&O locomotive in the motion picture *Giant.* Thus K1 100 became the star of her class, and of the N&W as well. *Courtesy N&W.*

4-8-2s were versatile performers. K1 and K2s were at first primary passenger power, while some were used in fast freight service until the K3s were built. After being upgraded and modernized, only dieselization ended the K1 and K2s long, useful careers. *R. J. Foster Photo, Courtesy C. T. Felstead Collection.*

Streamlined Ks visited Norfolk regularly hauling trains from Roanoke and the "Cannonball" between Norfolk and Richmond. K2a 126 at Norfolk servicing facilities June 1953. *Courtesy C. W. Jernstrom.*

Eight of the K1s received ex-Pere Marquette 22,000 gallon tenders in the early fifties. Number 108 sports a tender that first belonged to a PM Berkshire. *A. A. Thieme Photo, Courtesy C. T. Felstead Collection.*

Soon after the delivery of the K2as, experiments were started on extended engine runs. Initially, the tests covered two divisions, but it was found that mountain-types with large 15,000 gallon tenders could run between Roanoke and Portsmouth, Ohio, without engine change. This was possible because of the increased power the 4-8-2 possessed and because of the large tenders. This marked the beginning of what would be carried out further with the beautiful 4-8-4s two decades later.

The K2s all got improvements to increase both serviceability and operating economies. The most significant changes were the addition of the Worthington number 4 BL feedwater heater to the left side, and moving the left side air pump to join the right side pump for better weight distribution. The original K2 had but one air pump, but they all received a second pump as well as an enlarged stack and exhaust stand. Around 1930 the entire class received larger tenders to include the twenty-six ton, 18,000 gallon, cast steel, water bottom type. By the late thirties, many had the boiler pressure increased to 220 pounds with a new 63,800 pounds tractive effort rating.

With the building of the 4-8-4s, the K2s were reassigned to secondary passenger work. By the

end of World War II, the N&W was keenly interested in maintaining a first-rate passenger service. Although it had a streamlined 4-8-4 for the heavy passenger duties, the railway wanted a flashy locomotive for the lighter trafficked lines and secondary passenger trains. It was decided to use the K2s, but first a streamlining scheme was needed to dress up these sturdy steeds.

Mr. Frank Noel, who had originated the streamlining effect on the beautiful 4-8-4, was asked to draw up another plan for the K2s. The question was whether to streamline the K2 like the J, or to do it less so. Noel drew two basic schemes. One was a K2 with the solid pilot and skirting of the J, with the boiler top unchanged. The second was a K2 as described before, but with an abbreviated boiler top cowling to break the engine top outline. These two ideas were proposed in two color schemes each: either a tuscan red and gold strip along the skirting as with the J, or a black and gold strip. After considering the proposals, it was decided to streamline the K2s in the same style as the Js.

Since the twenty-two K2s were to hold down all passenger duties that the Js did not, these USRA mountain-types were to be modernized for high availability and for greater reliability. Starting in

142

Near Waverly, Virginia, K1 107 rolling along the "racetrack"—a straight 52 miles between Suffolk and Petersburg. Date: March 1940. *Courtesy N&W.*

1945, the K2s were sent to the Roanoke Shops for an extensive rebuilding. The specific improvements consisted of applying a smooth-faced pilot with a retractable coupler, installing new cast steel cylinders and bar frames, application of complete mechanical and pressure lubrication to include oil lubricators to the driver journals and

increasing boiler pressure to 220 pounds on those not already converted. In addition, the company replaced the stokers with a newer type, renewed the fireboxes, applied roller bearings to the engine, trailer and tender truck journals, added streamlining, and assigned thirty ton and 22,000 gallon tenders.

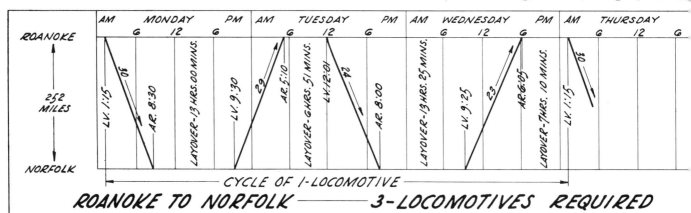

ROANOKE — 252 MILES — NORFOLK

CYCLE OF 1-LOCOMOTIVE

ROANOKE TO NORFOLK ———— 3-LOCOMOTIVES REQUIRED

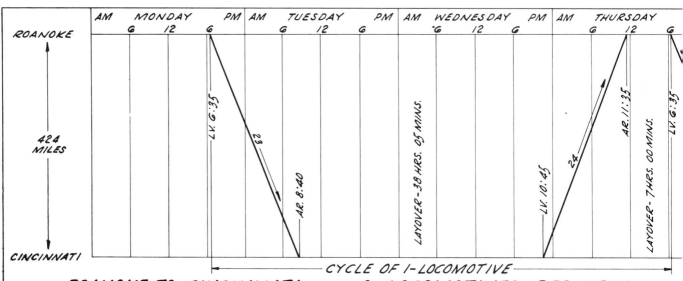

ROANOKE — 424 MILES — CINCINNATI

CYCLE OF 1-LOCOMOTIVE

ROANOKE TO CINCINNATI ———— 3-LOCOMOTIVES REQUIRED

(LOCOMOTIVES IN THIS POOL ALTERNATE AT CINCINNATI TO PROVIDE PROTECTION)
(FOR OTHER PASSENGER TRAINS OPERATING OUT OF THIS TERMINAL.)

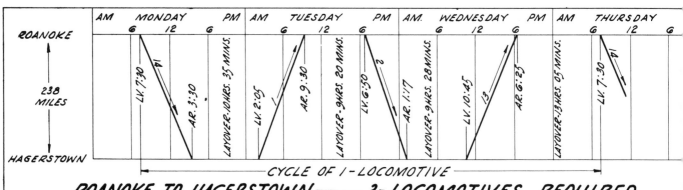

ROANOKE — 238 MILES — HAGERSTOWN

CYCLE OF 1-LOCOMOTIVE

ROANOKE TO HAGERSTOWN ———— 3-LOCOMOTIVES REQUIRED

BLUEFIELD — 100 MILES — WILLIAMSON

CYCLE OF 1-LOCO. — CYCLE OF 1-LOCO.

BLUEFIELD TO WILLIAMSON ———— 2-LOCOMOTIVES REQUIRED

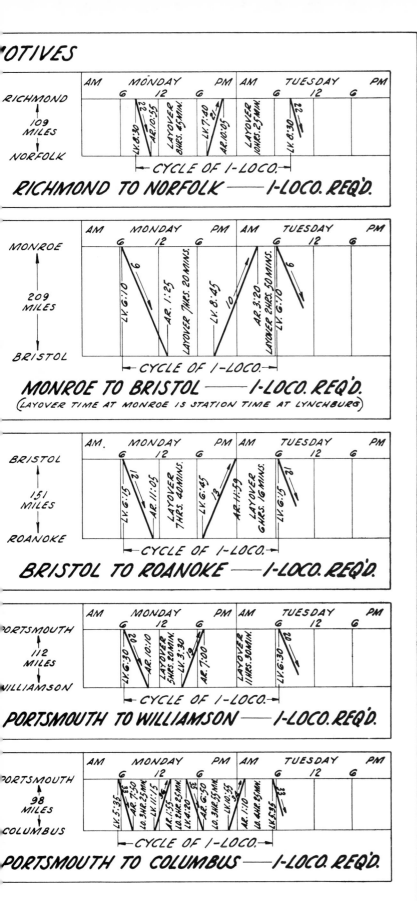

RICHMOND ← 109 MILES → **NORFOLK**

RICHMOND TO NORFOLK —— 1-LOCO. REQ'D.

MONROE ← 209 MILES → **BRISTOL**

MONROE TO BRISTOL —— 1-LOCO. REQ'D.
(LAYOVER TIME AT MONROE IS STATION TIME AT LYNCHBURG)

BRISTOL ← 151 MILES → **ROANOKE**

BRISTOL TO ROANOKE —— 1-LOCO. REQ'D.

PORTSMOUTH ← 112 MILES → **WILLIAMSON**

PORTSMOUTH TO WILLIAMSON —— 1-LOCO. REQ'D.

PORTSMOUTH ← 98 MILES → **COLUMBUS**

PORTSMOUTH TO COLUMBUS —— 1-LOCO. REQ'D.

N.&W. RY.   ROANOKE, VA.
M.P. DEPT.   MAY 16, 1947
SKETCH NO. 126 C.&G.

After modernization and streamlining of K2 class 4-8-2s, these upgraded and high utilization engines were assigned to most secondary passenger runs. The 4-8-2s performed this role from the mid-forties to the end of N&W steam. *Courtesy N&W.*

USRA 4-8-2s were superior performers in passenger service. After the delivery in 1923 of the second batch of K2s with larger tenders, these new Mountains were used on extended engine runs out of Roanoke over two, then three divisions without engine change. Larger tenders were subsequently used on all 4-8-2s for longer runs. *R. J. Foster Photo, Courtesy C. T. Felstead Collection.*

The angle of this shot does justice to the fat-boilered 202 and accents the massiveness of the class. Designed for power in manifest freight service, 63-inch drivers with a long main rod connected to the third driver created counterbalance problems. The K3s full potential was never achieved because of speed restrictions. *Courtesy Harold K. Vollrath.*

146

This K1 is speeding along with train 15 near Prichard, West Virginia, in 1939. *Courtesy N&W.*

The tenders were identical to the Class A tenders except that they did not have the cupola. The color scheme was like the J with the glossy jet black finish and the tuscan red strip with gold trim along the skirting and across the tender side. The rods of the running gear were all zinc plated. On the left side, the Worthington number 4 BL feedwater heater remained partially hidden behind the skirting and the lower portion behind the shield.

As rebuilt, the K2 was greatly admired both in service and in looks. The streamlined K2 was the primary passenger power on the Shenandoah Division, which ran between Winston-Salem,

North Carolina, and Hagerstown, Maryland. They were used on the N&Ws "Cannonball"—between Norfolk and Petersburg and over the ACL tracks to Richmond, Virginia. On the Portsmouth to Columbus District, and the Durham District, the K2 ruled supreme as well as being used on the secondary passenger runs throughout the system. And to see one of these engines at a distance, one would think he was viewing a Class J—thus the N&W folks referred to them as the "J-Junior." As the passenger business waned in the later years of steam, a few of these smart-looking locomotives were used in local freight operations. By late 1957, the diesel started crowding the

The superb K2s were mainstay passenger motive power until the coming of streamlined 600s. It was only natural that the superior performing K2 class were modernized at the end of World War II. Number 134 near Elliston, Virginia, in summer 1930. *Courtesy N&W.*

N&W rails and the K2s started being retired in December of that year. Almost all were gone by the end of 1958, with the last three being retired in July 1959. Numbers 124 and 137 were the last K2 and K2a, respectively, in service. One former engine foreman said the K2s and K2as were "mighty good engines." Indeed, they were!

Class K3

With a stable full of 111 compound Mallets of the 2-8-8-2 type, the railway had THE type of locomotive for its mountain districts and its heavy coal traffic. But the compound Mallet was a relatively slow machine, and what the N&W wanted was an engine to be used on the flatter portions of the system for the faster manifest freights. In the early to mid-twenties, K1s and K2s were given a hand at this manifest freight business, but they lacked the power to handle the normal time freight train on schedule. This resulted in doubleheading, usually with a 4-8-0, M.

The N&W designed a mountain-type engine specifically for freight service. This engine had a genuine look of power; indeed it was designed for its service role with exactly that in mind. Most noticeable was the extremely large boiler of 104 inches maximum diameter, with the large eighty-four square feet grate carried by the Delta trailer truck.

This was the only Delta truck application on the N&W. The large twenty-eight-inch bore by thirty-inch stroke cylinders were connected by a ponderous main rod to the third set of drivers, which was quite unusual for the mountain-type. To gain power the drivers were only sixty-three inches. The tractive effort was 68,880 pounds with the boiler pressure set at 225 pounds. Two cross-compound air pumps were mounted on the right side to offset the new Worthington number 4 BL feedwater heater, which made these the first N&W locomotives to be built new with a feedwater heater. The cab was a slant-front style, and

Appearance of the K1s changed little until the mid-forties, except for larger tenders and the use of specialty items. Compare this photo with the picture of 111 in the twenties. *R. J. Foster Photo, Courtesy C. T. Felstead Collection.*

Train 4, the "Pocahontas" with K2 119 at the head end, races through Salem, near Roanoke, in 1934. *Courtesy N&W.*

N&W wanted flashy passenger locomotives to haul secondary trains and with adequate power to back up those beautiful 600s. The 22 K2s had all the prerequisites, so they were streamlined and modernized between '45 and '47. The K2 modernization increased availability and reliability to the extent that almost all older passenger power was retired. *Courtesy Charles E. Winters.*

It's a Class J at first glance, but a second look reveals a 4-8-2 Class K2 modernized to resemble the renowned 600s. Operating men referred to the streamlined K2s as "J-juniors" because of operating and appearance similarities to the pride of N&W steam—the J. Number 134 highballing near Obetz, Ohio, on July 3, 1947. *Courtesy C. W. Jernstrom.*

Right side view of K1 101 in 1920 after first shopping. As built, the stack was smaller resulting in drafting problems that were licked by redesigning the stack and exhaust stand. Here the 9,000 gallon tender has a built-up coal bunker, otherwise the locomotive looks as it did new. *Courtesy N&W.*

the tender was a newly N&W-designed twenty-three ton, 16,000 gallon type with two three-axle trucks. The total engine weight was 401,900 pounds with 275,400 pounds on drivers, making this class of power one of the heaviest mountain-types ever built.

The Roanoke Shops built ten, numbers 200 through 209 (c/n 235 through 244) between June and October 1926. The new locomotives were classed K3. In service, it was soon discovered that the K3s had a superior boiler, but the small drivers with the heavy rods prevented fast running. The heavy main rod connected to the third driver caused severe counterbalance problems, and there was trouble with overheating of the driving journal boxes as a result. Likewise, they rode extremely rough and were particularly hard on the track. On the other hand, the boiler was of a good sound design and free steaming. As one former fireman said, the K3 was so free steaming, that "they steamed like a house afire." Unfortunately, the boiler was too much for the running gear.

The K3 was assigned duties on the Norfolk and Scioto divisions during most of its career. When the Radford Arsenal of Hercules Powder Company was constructed about 1940, some K3s were used to power special commuter trains from Roanoke over the Allegheny to the new plant near Radford, and return. Five trains daily with twelve to fourteen passenger cars each was typical. The K3 handled this assignment nicely, for the running speed was relatively low on the mountain grade and the boiler power was used fully.

With the construction of six Class J 4-8-4s and twenty-five Class A 2-6-6-4s in World War II, the K3s were surplus power. Some railroads were not as fortunate as the N&W in meeting their power needs. One of these, the Richmond, Fredericksburg and Potomac, bought six of the K3s, numbers 200 through 205, in February and in April 1944. The Denver and Rio Grande Western bought the other K3s, numbered 206 through 209, in May 1945. All ten of the former K3s were subsequently purchased by the Wheeling and Lake Erie, which eventually merged with the Nickel Plate Road, where the K3s served until retired.

2-6-6-2

"ENGINES THAT MADE THE RAILROAD"

Class Z 2-6-6-2s were the locomotives that literally "made the railroad." The class was N&W's first successful compound Mallet, a type ideally suited to motive power needs of the railway and a power principal that lasted to steam's end. In fact, Class Zs remained in large numbers until dieselization. Number 1442 was one of many 2-6-6-2s rebuilt and upgraded into Class Z1b. Lynchburg, April 1950. *D. W. Johnson Photo, Courtesy C. T. Felstead Collection.*

Z1a 1380, new at Baldwin 1914. *H. L. Broadbelt.*

Z1a 1467 (Schenectady 1917) with 16,000 gallon tender in 1948. *A. A. Thieme Photo, Courtesy C. T. Felstead Collection.*

Z1b 1409 (originally Z1a Baldwin 1914, rebuilt at Roanoke Shops 1928) with 16,000 gallon tender in 1934. *Courtesy N&W.*

The Z1b incorporated changes that substantially upgraded the Mallet 2-6-6-2, with most improvements made to the front low-pressure cylinders. Rebuilding Z1as into Z1bs, the slide valve low-pressure cylinders were replaced with inside admission piston valve cylinders, the exhaust passages and stack were enlarged, and a feedwater heater was installed above the left high-pressure cylinder. *Courtesy N&W.*

Single expansion Z2 1399 (originally Z1a Baldwin 1914) with 16,000 gallon tender in 1928. *Courtesy N&W.*

154

The first 15 2-6-6-2s, 1300-1314, had Walschaert valve gear installed, while all future Class Zs got the N&W favorite Baker gear. Here 1303 is seen near Bluefield in 1926. By the mid-twenties, the boiler tube pilot had replaced the original "cow-catcher." *Courtesy N&W.*

Class Z1

By 1910 the N&W was much interested in the development of the compound Mallet on the other roads. In that year the railway was delivered ten new Mallets of two different wheel arrangements, 0-8-8-0 and 2-8-8-2, five of each type. These locomotives were quite similar in some respects. The basic running gear was almost identical and the grate area and boiler dimensions were the same. But these engines were in many respects a test since they incorporated features that the railway was eyeing to determine firsthand if they were good or not. One of these features was a chamber ahead of the boiler used as a feedwater heater. Another was a "reheater" mounted in the smokebox to add heat to steam from the high pressure cylinders. Both of these features were on the 2-8-8-2 engine, while neither locomotive had a superheater. It was soon discovered that the 0-8-8-0 was not a good road engine, thus leaving the 2-8-8-2 class for that duty.

Another Pocahontas coal hauler, the Chesapeake & Ohio (C&O) had purchased a new 2-6-6-2, ran some tests on it, and immediately acquired more with improvements. One of these locomotives from the second batch, numbered 773, was borrowed by the N&W to compare it with its own 2-8-8-2. Walter Budwell worked with both of these locomotives in the ensuing tests. He said, "the C&O engine literally ran circles around the Y1." The Y1 was the N&Ws 2-8-8-2, which will be discussed in the next chapter. The 2-6-6-2 was the same weight as the Y1, but the C&O locomotive had a higher capacity boiler with superheated steam. Even though the 2-6-6-2 had two less driving axles, it was significantly more powerful either in simple or compound operation. The N&W decided that it need not look further for a compound Mallet as a prototype for a fleet of heavy freight power, and the rail line proceeded to buy a large number of these 2-6-6-2s.

The Richmond Locomotive Works built the first group of fifteen engines numbered 1300 through 1314, Class Z1, which were received in April and May 1912. Mechanically, they were almost identical to the C&O engines with Walschaert valve gear; 56½ inch drivers;

N&W originates most southwestern Virginia coal along its Clinch Valley line between Bluefield and Norton, Virginia. Z1b 1478 between road assignments at Norton in August 1936. *Courtesy Harold K. Vollrath.*

Near Roanoke with a solid coal train in 1921, 1383's appearance has changed little except for substituting electric headlight for the original oil type lamp. Class Zs were primary freight power until the arrival of large numbers of 2-8-8-2s. *Courtesy N&W.*

cylinders 22-by-32 inches for the high pressure cylinders, and 35-by-32 inches for the low pressure engine; boiler pressure 200 pounds; grate area seventy-two square feet fed by a Street stoker, and boiler with a combustion chamber about eighty-two inches long; an outside bearing radial trailing truck was employed. The tractive effort rating was 86,250 pounds in simple, while in compound it could develop 71,875 pounds.

These 427,000 pound engines had 354,000 pounds on the drivers. The tenders were fourteen tons and 9,000 gallons capacity. Their appearance was typical of the locomotives of that time with a large oil-style headlight just behind the slat pilot, and the cab a large style similar to the ones used on the recently built M2s. One 9½ inch air pump and one 8½ inch cross-compound air pump were hung on the left side of the boiler above the high pressure cylinder. And the low pressure cylinders were equipped with the D-slide valves housed in the characteristic flat-top steam chest.

The new Z1s were an immediate hit with the railway's officials, for one of these new Mallets could do the work of two older Ms or M1s. On the Elkhorn grade of the Pocahontas Division, with its long 3,000-foot-plus tunnel, the engine crews complained about the smoke and fumes in the tunnel due to doubleheading. With the Zs, doubleheading was eliminated and operating costs reduced. One M was rated at 590 tons for the slow freight while the Z1s could lug 1,100 tons on the Elkhorn "hill."

The railway decided that this was to be the standard heavy freight power, so it immediately went back to Richmond for twenty-five more. Numbers 1315 through 1339 were built between September and November 1912, and these locomotives were identical to those of the original order except for the application of the Baker valve gear. This last order was classed as Z1a. Still another order was placed with Richmond for forty more Z1as, numbers 1340 through 1379, and these began arriving in June 1913 with the last one delivered in August of that year.

Next, the railway had Baldwin Locomotive Works build forty Z1as, also exact copies of the earlier types. These were delivered July and August 1914, and numbered 1380 through 1419. Again, the N&W changed builders. Between January and March 1916, numbers 1420 through 1449 were delivered by the Schenectady Plant of the American Locomotive Company. Schenectady continued to build new Z1as, for during January and February 1917, and during July and August 1918, it built forty more in two groups of twenty each. These last two orders were identical to the earlier orders except that they were delivered with two, 8½ inch cross-compound air pumps. Thus, the N&W acquired 190 Z1 and Z1a engines in a period of six years.

Each of these locomotives replaced more than one other in the process. The railway's first successful Mallet was to start the N&W on a road that led to the use of the compound expansion of

In September 1926, 1445 is ready for its next assignment. Although the 2-8-8-2 Mallet became the standard freight type, the Class Zs were later improved, extending their longevity. Number 1445 was rebuilt and upgraded to a Z1b in March 1929. *Courtesy N&W.*

At Bluefield in July 1953, one of those unassuming Z1bs. *Courtesy Charles E. Winters.*

steam—a power principle that lasted to the end of the conventional steam locomotive era and a concept that remained synonymous with N&W steam. These 2-6-6-2 Mallets "were the locomotives that made the railroad," declared Walter Budwell. They were the first motive power acquired by the N&W that was ideally suited to the profile and traffic of this coal hauler.

The Zs received many improvements through the years. Some were minor, such as the changing of headlights to newer types and the replacement of the 9½ inch air pump with an 8½ inch cross-compound air pump on the first 150 engines. This last feature change was completed prior to 1920. More significantly, all of the original tenders were displaced by the USRA and the larger N&W standard tenders. Very significantly, the boiler pressure was raised to 225 pounds with a resulting tractive effort of 90,996 pounds in simple, and 75,830 pounds in compound. This was done by the early thirties.

The most significant improvement was the upgrading accomplished by redesigning the front low pressure cylinder steam distribution and exhaust system. As built, the low pressure cylinders were equipped with the D-type slide valves, which in service required considerable maintenance. Also, it was decided to effect some im-

provements to one Z1a as an experiment for later Z1as and for the new Y5s then being designed.

Number 1398 was outshopped in March 1927 with some valuable improvements. The front low pressure cylinders received inside admission fourteen inch piston valves to replace the slide valves. The larger fourteen inch valve was used, instead of the twelve inch used on the high pressure cylinders, to allow the greater volume of expanded steam to enter and exhaust from the low pressure cylinders. Furthermore, the exhaust passages were enlarged. These improvements were accomplished by the Roanoke Shops' foundry casting steel cylinders, and this casting was applied to the old engine frame. Other changes and additions: a Worthington number 4 ¼ BL feedwater heater was installed to the left side above and back of the high pressure cylinder; the two cross-compound air pumps were moved to the right side for better weight distribution, and to accommodate the increased volume of exhaust steam from the enlarged exhaust passages, a new larger stack was installed. Evidently, the changes were satisfactory because, starting in November 1928 and continuing through May 1931, seventy-three more Z1as were modernized with the aforementioned improvements at both the Roanoke and Portsmouth shops. The seventy-four modified

Close-up of a Z1 showing the compact, powerful appearance of N&W's first successful class of Mallets. The compound Mallet was a concept that lasted to the end of N&W steam, and the Mallet added efficiency and economy to the railway's operation. *Courtesy N&W.*

Practically all N&W steam power had steel pilot beams in the mid-fifties. One notable exception was the Class Zs, most of which retained oak pilot beams throughout their long lives. 1470 at Crewe in 1957. *A. A. Thieme Photo, Courtesy C. T. Felstead Collection.*

The last Class Z1b in service was 1438 at Portsmouth. This photo was made on April 23, 1958, and exactly one week later this last of a breed was scrapped. Unfortunately, none were saved from the torch. *Courtesy N&W.*

Z1as were reclassified as Z1bs, and all received the N&W 15,000 or 16,000 gallon tender at the rebuilding.

Some Z1as received the piston valve low pressure cylinders as replacement for cracked and worn out original slide valve cylinders. These Z1as did not receive the other improvements applied to the Z1bs, so the classification did not change. The "piston valve" 2-6-6-2 did not automatically mean it was a Z1b!

The Zs were the primary heavy freight power until the coming of large numbers of the 2-8-8-2s starting in 1919. By 1928, the ninety Y3s and Y4s, along with thirty-one Y2s, discharged the primary main line duties. The Zs were being pushed back into secondary service on the main line and in heavy yard and mine work. With the building of the Y5s, the older Ys began working in "Z-territory," and so in 1934 the first large group of Zs was retired. All of the Z1s were scrapped, and by the end of 1936, thirty-six of the Z1as and one Z1b had been removed from service and dismantled. The Z1bs remained in large number, but the Z1as were retired at regular intervals, until by 1953 the last thirteen were scrapped. Thus the Z1as were not affected by dieselization, for "taps" had been sounded before the diesels hit.

The Z1bs were much in evidence at the start of dieselization. At the end of 1955, fifty-three of this fine old breed were working the coal tipples, branch lines or at heavy switching chores. The Z could handle well anything that the smaller 0-8-0 switchers could not in yard work but were unsuitable for the hump with the heaviest trains. Their short driving wheel base was ideal for moving into and out of yard tracks, and on the sharp curves of the mountain lines. In addition, in yard work they had very good acceleration. The only other modifications employed to the Z1bs were the substitution of some 18,000 gallon N&W-designed tenders on some and increasing the driver tires to fifty-seven inches on all by increasing the tire thickness.

With the coming of dieselization, the older Z1bs were the first Mallets to succumb. Most were retired in 1957, and the last eight were scrapped the following year. They were called "baby Malley's" by the engine crews, but the term should be viewed in relation to the larger Ys. They were the N&Ws first successful Mallet, and they were the locomotives "that made the railroad" by serving the company well for forty-five years. It would have been longer except for the diesel.

Class Z2

The railway was very pleased with the fleet of compound Mallets for the heavy drag work, but for high speed freight it looked for a better, faster locomotive. The K3s were built in an effort to in-

160

"Locomotive that made the railroad" was the claim of N&W's 2-6-6-2. The compound Mallet had been experimented with earlier on the railway, but the Zs were the road's first successful Mallets. This early usage of the compound became a trademark of N&W for years to come. *Courtesy Harold K. Vollrath.*

Number 1460 at Roanoke between assignments in heavy switching service. Note spark retarder mounted to stack. Date: July 24, 1953. *Courtesy Charles E. Winters.*

Back in mountain hollows were many coal branches twisting and turning through the hills. The 2-6-6-2s were ideal for these lines, since they were easier on the curves and closer to needed capacity than a 2-8-8-2. Z1a 1411 on one such branch near Ciatto, West Virginia, in 1947. *Courtesy C. W. Jernstrom.*

Z1b 1482, with boiler tube pilot, indicates it is being used in road service. Williamson, West Virginia, in July 1953. *Courtesy C. W. Jernstrom.*

crease speed. But running gear on this engine was so ponderous for the smaller drivers, that it ended up a speed restricted engine. As an experiment, the road decided to take one of the numerous Z1as and convert it into a four cylinder simple articulated locomotive. So into the shop went 1399. Its front low pressure cylinders were replaced by high pressure 22-by-32 inch cylinders identical in size to the rear cylinders. The boiler was modified somewhat by increasing the total heating surface to 6,019 square feet, the smokebox had a double stack added and the pressure was set for 225 pounds. As modified and rebuilt, the engine weighed 441,000 pounds with 377,825 pounds on the drivers. The tractive effort was

93,342 pounds. The 1399 was reclassed as Z2 when outshopped in September 1928.

In service, it was found that the Z2 could run faster than its compound counterpart. But it used a much larger quantity of steam and thus was an uneconomical venture. The Z1a boiler was designed for and capable of sustaining two 22-by-32 inch cylinders. It is small wonder that a similar boiler, with four such cylinders to charge, did have problems. The 1399 was used until 1934 when it was retired and scrapped. The most important aspect of this experiment was that much useful data was gained to help in designing the Class A 2-6-6-4.

2-8-8-2

SIRE OF THE "WORKHORSE"

N&W championed the 2-8-8-2 Mallet for heavy-duty freight service. USRA 2-8-8-2s performed so well that Y3s, such as 2003, became the basis for future Mallet development leading to the "workhorse" Y6. In the late steam era, older Class Ys were found on yard, branch, and road assignments requiring brute power at lower speeds. These Mallets were sure-footed "horses," and they served well until dieselization. *A. A. Thieme Photo, Courtesy C. T. Felstead Collection.*

X1 990 new at Schenectady 1910. *Courtesy Harold K. Vollrath.*

Y1 999 new at Baldwin 1910. *Courtesy Harold K. Vollrath.*

Y2 1700 with N&W designed 12,000 gallon tender, new at Roanoke Shops 1918. The 20 Baldwin Y2s had 9,000 gallon tenders when built. *Courtesy Harold K. Vollrath.*

Y3 2009 (Schenectady 1919) in 1920. *Courtesy N&W.*

Y3a 2063 with 15,000 gallon tender, new at Richmond 1923. *Courtesy N&W.*

Y3a 2058 (Richmond 1923) with 18,000 gallon tender in 1942. Y3's appearance was very similar. *Courtesy Harold K. Vollrath.*

Y4 (then Y3b) 2080 with 16,000 gallon tender, new at Richmond 1927. *Courtesy N&W.*

Y5 2100 new at Roanoke Shops 1931. Note the Bradford throttle ahead of stack and bridgepipe on low-pressure cylinders. *Courtesy N&W.*

Class X1 and Class Y1

The first Mallet articulated locomotive for U.S. service was built in 1904. This initial U.S. Mallet, an 0-6-6-0 for the Baltimore and Ohio (B&O), had some faults, and after its experience in service, more Mallets were built incorporating the lessons learned. Starting in 1906, large numbers of the compound Mallets were placed in road service and were an immediate hit with railroad officials because these locomotives allowed the movement of maximum tonnage per train. These articulateds doubled almost overnight the tractive effort of the nonarticulated then used and eliminated doubleheading that was customary even on the level portions of railroads.

The N&W watched the development of the Mallet on other roads and immediately saw that it could use this power on the heavy coal drags. But there were some problems with the Mallets.

Innovations were being tried and tested yet were not always successful. So when the N&W purchased its first Mallets, it bought two classes of power evidently as an experiment to test various devices and items of equipment. Possibly, the railway planned to "take the best of both worlds," and purchase in quantity a resulting class of Mallets.

The two experimental classes were of two wheel arrangements: the 0-8-8-0, Class X1; and the 2-8-8-2, Class Y1. Both classes were purchased in 1910, with the X1s built by the Schenectady plant of ALCO and the Y1s by the Baldwin Locomotive Works. The X1s, numbered 990 through 994, and the Y1s, numbered 995 through 999, had many similarities. The grate areas were each seventy-five square feet; the boilers including the firebox, tubes and tube length were similar; the running gear and the 24½-inch and 39-by-30 inch cylinders coupled to the 56-inch drivers were the

In 1927 road power began receiving feedwater heaters after the success of the device on new Y4s. Here 2026 has had its air pumps relocated to the right side before installation of the feedwater heater. Clearing of air pumps from the engine's front improved the Mallet's appearance and facilitated pump maintenance. Date: September 28, 1928. *Courtesy N&W.*

Roanoke Shops built 1705-1710 as Y2a's in 1924, incorporating improvements from Y2 and Y3 experience. Principal modifications were a second steam dome, improved running gear components, increased diameter rear cylinders, redesigned front low-pressure cylinders (reduced 18-inch piston valves to 14 inches), and extended mechanical lubrication. The 25 Y2s were modified and reclassed Y2as by 1925. Number 1705, the first Y2a, at Roanoke in January 1924. *Courtesy N&W.*

same in both cases, except the low pressure cylinders of the Y1s had piston valves and those of the X1s had slide valves.

Furthermore, both classes employed the large style cab used on the earlier Class Ms, and the two types had the same fourteen tons and 9,000 gallons capacity tenders. As delivered, each type had 200 pounds boiler pressure developing 83,615 pounds tractive effort in simple, and 66,892 pounds in compound. One major difference, in addition to the wheel arrangement, was that Y1 had a front boiler feedwater heater section and a smokebox located "reheater." The feedwater heater was a second set of the boiler tubes running through a chamber between the front boiler sheet and the smokebox, where the chamber water was preheated before being fed into the boiler proper. There was a short space between the two sets of flues. The Y1s also had a device that reheated the once expanded steam on the way to the front low pressure cylinders.

The Class X1s were found to be no good for road service without the lead and trailing trucks.

The Y1s were poor performers because of the feedwater heater and reheater. The short space and front set of flues continually got clogged up with cinders. A subsequent test of the Class Y1 with a borrowed C&O Railway 2-6-6-2 locomotive indicated the superiority of the 2-6-6-2 using a larger boiler with Schmidt superheater. As a result, the N&W Class Z1s were acquired in large numbers for main line freight work. The unsuccessful Y1s were never found useful except as pushers, and they were all retired in 1924. The X1s, a little more successful, were used until 1934. The X1s appeared most efficient in yard work, and in 1930, the boiler pressure was increased to 230 pounds with an increase in tractive effort to 108,211 pounds simple and 90,176 pounds compound. The X1s were equipped with superheaters in 1914.

Class Y2

The first successful Mallets on the N&W were the 2-6-6-2, Class Z1. These locomotives had eliminated the usual doubleheading of the heavy trains and were doing a creditable job on the mountain grades. With a sizeable fleet of these Class Zs in service, the railway wanted to increase still further the Mallet concept by making a larger locomotive to haul heavier trains than even the Zs could pull.

The 2-8-8-2 had proven popular and successful on other roads, although it was built in very limited quantities. The N&W then set out to design and build a 2-8-8-2 of its own. What emerged was a machine that made quite an impact on the U.S. locomotive market. This engine's basic design was used far beyond the limits of the N&Ws own realm.

In March 1918, number 1700 (c/n 224), Class Y2, rolled from the Roanoke Shops and was immediately placed in service to see what type of performer it was. On the westbound run out of Roanoke up the steep 1.3 percent Allegheny climb, a lone Y2 could haul 1,600 tons as compared with the 1,200 tons of the Class Z. On the easier eastbound Allegheny grade, a loaded coal train of 5,500 tons was the rating of the Y2, with pusher, while the Class Z had been 4,400 tons with a pusher. Mechanically, the Y2 employed the equipment proven successful on the earlier Mallets, the Class Zs. It could be said that the Class Y2 was an evolution of the Class Z into a larger, more powerful locomotive with several improvements. Specifically, it had fifty-six-inch drivers that were connected to 24½-inch diameter

Number 2107 leaving east Roanoke yards with a long coal train in May 1939. This engine was one of 20 Y5s whose design was a milestone in N&W Mallet development. The later designed Y6 was essentially a Y5 with minor improvements. *Courtesy N&W.*

Test rigging is installed on Y1 998 when comparing this engine to a borrowed C&O 2-6-6-2. The C&O locomotive "literally ran circles around the Y1" and, as a result, N&W ushered in its own Class Z1s, a copy of the C&O Mallets tested. *Courtesy Walter Budwell.*

by 32-inch stroke, high pressure cylinders, and low pressure cylinders with the same stroke and a 39-inch bore. The grate area was ninety-six square feet with a huge 109-inch maximum diameter boiler charged with 240 pounds of steam. The low pressure cylinders had piston valves as a departure from earlier 2-6-6-2s, but the Baker valve gear was used as with the Z1as.

With the U.S. entry into World War I, the railroads were placed under Federal control through the United States Railroad Administration. A committee of motive power officials, mechanical engineers and locomotive builders set out to build a 2-8-8-2 Mallet for the U.S. railroads, and this committee used the N&Ws Class Y2 as the basis for the proposed locomotive. The resulting USRA 2-8-8-2 was widely used by some railroads during and after the USRA era.

The N&W received fifty of these new USRA 2-8-8-2s with the classification of Y3. Meanwhile, the USRA allowed the N&W to continue building new Y2s that were already started at Roanoke, and it released the Baldwin Locomotive Works to deliver an order for twenty more of the Y2s to the N&W. Between January 1919 and April 1921, the

Roanoke Shops built 1701 through 1704 (c/n 225 through 228) and Baldwin completed 1711 through 1730 between February and December 1919. Also, the Roanoke Shops had constructed six Y2 boilers in addition to those used on 1700 through 1704, and it was decided to complete these last six, numbers 1705 through 1710 (c/n 229 through 234).

Completed between January and March 1924, these new locomotives, Class Y2a, incorporated features from the experience gained from the older Y2s and the USRA Y3s. The improvements embodied in the Y2as were principally in the running gear and cylinder components to give better utilization and increase serviceability. Likewise, the high pressure cylinders were increased by one-half inch in diameter (to twenty-five inches), and modifications were made to the steam delivery system and exhaust nozzles. Evidently, these improvements were well received, because by 1925 all of the Y2s had been upgraded and reclassified as Y2as. The Y2as weighed the same as the Y2s.

Y2as were not as satisfactory or as serviceable as the offspring Y3s. Although the Y2s were used

The 2-6-6-2 Mallet was a good performer, yet more power was needed for mountain work. This resulted in Class Y2 2-8-8-2 getting the added power. The Y2 became the design basis for USRA 2-8-8-2 Mallets, and this USRA type made an impact on the remainder of the N&W steam policy. Here a Y2a is in road service on the Radford Division in 1936. *Courtesy N&W.*

in road service initially along with the Y3s, the Y2s with the smaller fifty-six-inch drivers could not operate at as high a speed and had counterbalance problems. The engine crews generally considered them inferior to the USRA engines.

With the coming of the Y5s in 1930, the Y2s began to be downgraded to pusher service, yard work and mine runs. Where slow work was the order of the day, the Y2as were very good for hard work since their tractive effort was a little greater than the Y3s and Y4s of like boiler pressure. Numbers 1702, 1706 and 1714 were fitted with two Franklin tender boosters each, and numbers 1717 and 1720 were each equipped with a Bethlehem tender booster for yard work. The Franklin booster-equipped locomotives produced 158,660 pounds total tractive effort at 240

pounds boiler pressure, while the Bethlehem-fitted engines with a boiler pressure of 270 pounds per square inch obtained 158,894 pounds total tractive effort.

Most Y2as had an increase in boiler pressure—some to 270 pounds—by the mid-forties, and those that remained after World War II all got a one-inch driver size increase by adding one-half inch to tire thickness. Eventually all the Y2as received various larger capacity tenders.

During World War II, many roads needed more power for the increased wartime tonnage. The Denver and Rio Grande Western was one such road, and the N&W had surplus power now that its new home-produced Class As and Y6as were handling increased tonnage with a vengeance. The D&RGW bought fifteen of the old Y2as be-

Y5s were built at the height of the Depression, and this homebuilt construction helped stabilize shop forces. A new Mallet 2098 is being shown to employees and to interested people along the N&W way. This fostered great pride in N&W's great homebuilt engines. *Author's Collection*

Ten huge 27-ton, 24,000 gallon tenders were purchased from the former ACL in 1953. These unique (for N&W) four-axle truck tenders were all assigned to Y4s, which increased the massive appearance of the class. *Courtesy N&W.*

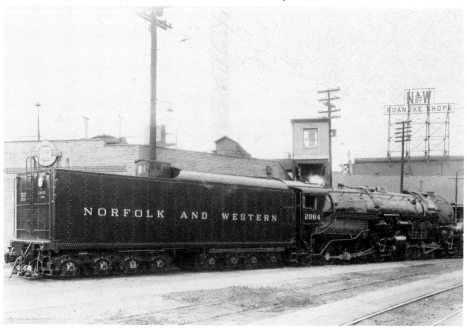

tween 1943 and 1945. Two additional Y2as had been sold to the Utah Copper Company in 1943. Except for 1702, which was retired in 1946, the last thirteen remained in service until the coming of the Class Y6bs. By the end of 1951, all of these tired old Y2a "horses" had been "put out to pasture."

Although the Y2s were not as popular as the USRA Y3s, it must be remembered that the N&W Y2 was the sire of the USRA 2-8-8-2s, and the descendents of the Y3s (USRA Mallets) were to be known as the "workhorses of the N&W"—a term synonymous with N&W steam.

Class Y3

When the N&W was placed under federal control, the USRA designed standard locomotives to be built by all the major builders, and then assigned these engines to the particular railroads. The N&W, after testing its own home-built Y2 (2-8-8-2), decided it could use some of this power. The USRA allocated to the railway fifty of its 2-8-8-2 compound Mallets. These locomotives were Class Y3s, numbered 2000 through 2049, with the first forty-five delivered out of Schenectady from March to June 1919, and the last five were built by Baldwin in September of the same year.

Although USRA Mallets had been based on the N&Ws Y2 in design, these Y3s were to be mechanically different in some ways and were to have a distinctive look of their very own. The driving wheels were fifty-seven inches in diameter and the cylinders had a thirty-two-inch stroke with the high pressure cylinders having a twenty-five-inch bore and the low pressure cylinders thirty-nine inches in diameter. The boiler pressure was set for 240 pounds, the grate area was ninety-six square feet, the boiler had a maximum outside diameter of 104 inches, and the Baker valve gear was used. These locomotives had standardized features characteristic of their USRA heritage such as the cab, sandboxes and tender. The Y3s as delivered had air pumps mounted on the smokebox front, weighed in at 531,000 pounds with 474,000 pounds on the drivers, and the tender had sixteen tons and 12,000 gallons capacity.

The Y3s were first assigned to the Radford and Norfolk divisions, and were well-liked by the engine crews. These USRA Mallets had tonnage ratings the same as the Y2s, but in service were

Near historic Appomattox, Virginia, in May 1941, 2021 looks like a "workhorse" with a coal train in tow. It was at Appomattox Court House that General Robert E. Lee surrendered the Confederate Army of Northern Virginia to General U. S. Grant in April 1865. *Courtesy N&W.*

Y4s were assigned mostly to the Pocahontas and Radford divisions during the early years of the class. Number 2082 on the Elkhorn in June 1930. *Courtesy N&W.*

superior to the Y2s in maintenance requirements and serviceability. The railway was so pleased with the Y3s, that after the N&W returned to private management from the USRA, the company bought thirty more of these Mallets, numbered 2050 through 2079, and they were classified as Y3as. They were built by the Richmond Locomotive Works from March to June 1923 and were initially used on the Scioto and Pocahontas divisions.

The Y3as were virtual duplicates of the Y3s, except for minor changes through the substitution of standard boiler fittings and other standard parts common to other locomotives on the Norfolk and Western. Furthermore, an inspection manhole was placed on the boiler to the left front of the steam dome and a newly designed tender of twenty tons and 15,000 gallons capacity was attached.

The Y3 and Y3as composed the bulk of the main line heavy freight power used until the coming of the Y6s and the modernization of the Y5s. To the end of steam, all of the Y3s received improvements and additions to upgrade them.

After the Class Y4s with the feedwater heater

A small, modern engine facility at Pulaski, Virginia, serviced power that worked the surrounding yard and the North Carolina Branch to Galax, Virginia. Y3a 2072 over inspection pit beside the small machine shop. *Courtesy N&W.*

installed were delivered, it was soon realized that these devices increased operating efficiencies. All eighty of the Y3s then received a Worthington number 4 ½ BL feedwater heater mounted on the left side, and the air pumps were removed from the smokebox front and placed on the right side for better weight distribution. The smokebox front was modified to look similar to the Y4s, except the bell was hung at the top of the smokebox front on the Y3 and Y3as.

The Y3 and Y3as received a variety of standard N&W tenders during their service. Eight of the Class Y3as received 22,000 gallon, twenty-three ton capacity tenders purchased from the Bessemer and Lake Erie in the early 1950s. By the end of World War II, all the Y3s and Y3as had the boiler pressure increased to 270 pounds, and this increased the tractive effort from 121,764 to 136,985 pounds in simple, and from 101,470 to 114,154 pounds in compound. Furthermore, the driving wheels were enlarged to fifty-eight inches in the 1940s by increasing the tire thickness one-half inch. Since the Mallet was extremely hard on the driving wheel tires, this allowed the tires more wear before they required replacement.

Five Y2as and one Y3 received boosters to gain additional starting power. Evidently these were not totally successful, since the boosters were later removed. Number 1714 at Portsmouth in January 1931. *Courtesy N&W.*

Prior to the late-era A and Y6s, the Y3 and Y4s were the mainstay for freight operations. Here is Y3 2015, near Chillicothe, Ohio, on October 13, 1932, barreling along with a long string of coal-laden cars. Note the semaphore signal used, since replaced by position light signals and CTC. *Courtesy N&W.*

The Class Y3s were downgraded to secondary service with the coming of the Y6s and As. In World War II, nineteen of the class were declared surplus by the railway and these locomotives were sold to other railroads desperately in need of additional power. Six were sold to the Pennsylvania Railroad in May 1943, eight to the Santa Fe Railway in July and October 1943 and October 1944 (seven of these subsequently sold to the Virginian Railway), and five to the Union Pacific Railroad in June 1945. The thirty-one remaining Y3s lasted until 1957-58, when dieselization forced their retirement. The Y3as held out until 1958-59 when all were retired with the downgrading of the Y5 and Y6s from main line duties.

In the latter years, the Y3 and Y3as were used in heavy yard and hump duty, on coal branches and mine runs and on heavy secondary work. The engine crews thought well of the Y3 and Y3as since the dome throttles were easier to work in yards and on the secondary lines where the throttle setting was being changed continually. These older locomotives did not receive many of the engineering improvements of the newer Y6s, for they were used in slow speed work only.

Class Y4

In January 1927 the N&W received from Richmond ten more compound Mallets of the basic

This super shot reflects the personality of Class Y4. This class was the latest word in Mallet development when built: feedwater heater, improved running gear features, redesigned steam admission and exhaust passages, and strengthened low-pressure main frame assembly. Smokebox door shape was unique to Y4s; later a round door was installed. Number 2086 in West Virginia, June 1930. *Courtesy N&W.*

Almost brand new Y5 2098 at Roanoke in the summer of '31. The principal improvement over the Y4 was the higher capacity boiler. Most noticeable improvement was the bridge pipe connecting the front cylinders with the enlarged exhaust passages. Y6s got all of these improvements, too! *Courtesy C. W. Jernstrom.*

Mallets worked the coal trains on level districts prior to the development of single expansion articulateds. Between Portsmouth and Columbus, Y3 2018 heads north with a coal drag in 1932. *Courtesy N&W.*

At first look, one thinks this is a Y5, but a glance at the road number indicates a Y3a. Large bridgepipe connecting front low-pressure cylinders reveals that 2068 received Y5 front engine frame and cylinders when that class got roller bearings and bed castings. *Courtesy C. W. Jernstrom.*

USRA design. The 2080 through 2089, Class Y3b, were essentially the Class Y3a with improvements. The most noticeable changes were the addition of a Worthington number 4 ½ BL feedwater heater on the left side of the boiler and the two air pumps on the right side for better weight balance. The altered smokebox front arrangement looked very similar to the smokebox door feature established on the USRA mountain-type, Class K2. The bell was placed near the top of the boiler just forward of the new slant-front cab. The tender was a modified design built on the same tender frame used on the Y3as, except the water cistern was higher and the coal bunker larger. This meant a new tender capacity of

twenty-three tons and 16,000 gallons.

Mechanically the Y3bs were identical to the earlier USRA Mallets, except the boiler had an additional 113 square feet of heating surface and the side and connecting rods were of a new design with floating bushings. These floating bushings both facilitated lubrication and increased availability. All of the older USRA Mallets were to receive this new type of rod and bushing as well as all subsequent steam power other than those equipped with roller bearing rods. The two main engine frames were of new construction, each incorporating two cast steel side frames bolted together by a crosstie casting between each set of axles. In service, the crosstie castings became

After modernization of 19 Y5s and the building of 16 Y6as from '40 to '42, some Y2as were declared surplus and sold to roads needing extra power. D&RGW was one of these roads, receiving 15 Y2as and 2 Z1as. Number 3559 is ex-N&W 1709 at Denver in August 1946. *Courtesy Charles E. Winters.*

gradually twisted and bent due to the tremendous piston thrusts. These main frames were subsequently modified by casting all of the crosstie castings as one unit for the front main frame. There were no further major frame problems after this alteration. The shop classification of the Y3b was changed to Y4 in 1928.

As built, the Y4s had a boiler pressure of 240 pounds, and by the mid-forties, all had been modified to 270 pounds pressure. The engine weight was 567,000 pounds with 508,500 pounds on the drivers. The tractive effort for the Class Y4s was the same as the Y3s and Y3as. The original fifty-seven-inch drivers were increased to fifty-eight inches by the late forties. Also, the Y4s used all of the standard N&W tenders at one time or another. In 1953, all ten of this class were assigned a tender unique to the N&W that gave the Y4s a mark of distinction. The tenders, acquired second-hand from the Atlantic Coast Line, were a huge 24,000 gallons, twenty-seven tons capacity type that rode on two four-axle trucks. These tenders remained with the Y4s until the class was retired.

The Class Y4 engines were used along with the other older Mallets initially in road service and finally ended their distinguished careers in heavy secondary work. The entire class remained intact until 1958, when all were sent to the scrap lines.

In the modern steam era of the N&W Y6, the Y4s were the newest of the older compound Mallets after the upgrading and modernizing of the Y5s in the early forties.

Class Y5

After 1927 the Norfolk and Western produced in its Roanoke Shops all of the reciprocating steam locomotives it was to acquire to the end of steam, other than the 0-8-0 switchers purchased from the C&O in 1950. The first type of locomotives the Roanoke Shops delivered in this final, fading phase of N&W steam were the Y5s. Again, the railway was to continue upgrading and improving the USRA Mallets for heavy freight service. The Y5 was nothing more than the Y4 with improvements. When being built, these new locomotives were to be designated as Y4as, but when completed all were classed as Y5s.

The Class Y5 was to be the forerunner of the famous Y6, and many of the features first to appear on the Y5 became standard for the ensuing Y6s. The first major improvement was the steam and exhaust distribution systems on the low pressure cylinders. One of the major limitations of the Mallets was inherent slow speed. To obtain a higher speed, it was necessary to get freer exhaust passages and a larger distribution system for the once expanded steam from the high pressure to the low pressure cylinders. To gain better delivery into and exhaust from the low pressure cylinders, the eighteen-inch piston valve replaced the fourteen-inch valve. And, to make freer exhaust passages to the stack, a newly designed bridge pipe connected the two low pressure cylinders in front of the lower portion of the smokebox. This bridge pipe allowed a larger exhaust pipe to be mounted above the frames instead of constricting an exhaust pipe down between the frames, as was the case with older Ys.

The second major improvement was increasing the boiler capacity by enlarging the grate area to 106 square feet simply by widening the firebox by ten inches. Originally the boiler pressure was to be 280 pounds per square inch, but it was changed to 300 pounds pressure as built. At first, the firebox had no lagging, but it was added later prior to their rebuilding in the early forties.

The twenty locomotives of this class were delivered between April 1930 and February 1932. The inclusive numbers were 2090 through 2109 (c/n 245 through 264), with the first ten built in 1930, nine in 1931, and the last one (2109) in 1932. This new class had a total engine weight of 582,900 pounds with 522,850 pounds on drivers. The tender was a new design featuring a water bottom, cast steel frame—the first such feature on new N&W power. The tender capacity was twenty-six tons and 22,000 gallons.

Individual Y5s had special items of equipment applied, evidently for testing purposes. Number 2092 had a Nicholson thermic syphon installed that added 124 square feet of heating surface. Number 2094 received the new American multiple throttle, while 2093 and 2100 through 2109 each had a single valve Bradford front-end throttle mounted just ahead of the stack. This was the only application of the Bradford throttle on the N&W. All other Y5s had the long-established dome throttles and all had the type "A" superheater, except the 2094, which was equipped with a type "E" superheater.

The Y5s became the frontline heavy freight power throughout the N&W system. With the

Y3s were used around large terminals in heavy switching service. Number 2047, sporting footboards, is on the ready track at Roanoke's Shaffers Crossing in October 1953. *Courtesy Harold K. Vollrath.*

A Y5 gathers speed as it approaches the foot of the westbound Alleghany climb at Elliston, Virginia. One can see the locomotive is moving at higher speed and can imagine hearing the characteristic deep roaring exhaust as the engine rolls by. *Courtesy N&W.*

After receiving a round smokebox door and covered sandpipes, the Y4s looked very similar to their descendents Y5. The 24,000 gallon tenders, however, gave this class a mark of distinction in its last five years. Here 2083 is standing by on the ready track beneath Roanoke's coal dock. *Courtesy C. W. Jernstrom.*

coming of the Y6s, the Y5s continued to be used on the main line interchangeably with the newer power. Many of the features tried on the Y5s became standard later on the newer power, such as the American multiple throttle, the larger capacity boiler with higher pressure and an increased grate area and the redesigned steam distribution and exhaust system of the low pressure cylinders.

The Y5s were as powerful as the Y6s with a tractive effort of 152,206 pounds in simple, and 126,838 pounds while working in compound. When the Y6s appeared in 1936, the major improvements incorporated in them were the addition of cast steel locomotive frames with the cylinders cast integral, and the application of roller bearings to all axles. These refinements increased the availability of the Y6s significantly and reduced maintenance.

Since the Y5s had all of the other major im-

provements used so successfully on the new Y6s, it was decided to upgrade the Y5s by replacing the bar frames with new cast steel beds with integral cylinders, and by installing roller bearings on the engine axles. When the Y5s were being designed, it was contemplated equipping them with roller bearings; but in 1930 it was felt that this feature was too costly. In 1940-41, the Y5s were shopped and received these improvements. Many, if not all, of the original Y5 frames were applied to the Y3 and Y3as needing extensive frame repairs. (For a discussion of the modernized Y5, see chapter on the modern 2-8-8-2.)

One Y5 did not undergo the modernization. Number 2092 had a boiler explosion and plunged to destruction as a result of a wreck on June 30, 1937, at Maybeury, West Virginia. This locomotive was retired and never rebuilt.

THE N&W GIANTS OF STEAM

Opposite Page: These three types represented road power used in the last two decades of N&W steam. The stream-lined Class J 4-8-4 was one of 14 built for passenger service. The 43 Class A 2-6-6-4s, numbered in the 1200s, were powerful dual-service engines. The 2100s were 100 classes Y5 and Y6 2-8-8-2 heavy freight locomotives, ideally suited for mountain operations and the "work-horse" of the N&W fleet. All 157 of these road engines were built in the company's own Roanoke Shops. Also Roanoke built 45 new Class S1a 0-8-0 switchers, which were almost identical to 30 practically new shifters the N&W purchased secondhand. All of these road and yard engines were truly the N&W giants of steam! *Courtesy N&W.*

Part 3

Modern Steam

There are few words that can adequately describe the modern steam locomotives of the N&W. But to tell of the N&W steam giants' performance leaves little doubt as to their capabilities and accomplishments when compared to other types of power. For example, in 1947 the Roanoke Shop-built Class A 2-6-6-4 handled an average train something more than twice as large as the average for the road freight diesels in the U.S. as a whole, and handled this train at a considerably higher average speed. Furthermore, the As averaged more miles of service per engine, per day than did the average U.S. road diesel.

Also, the home-built Class J 4-8-4 passenger locomotives averaged more mileage per engine, per day than the road passenger diesel did for the nation as a whole. The N&W passenger power did

this on a rather short and very hilly railroad with many curves and on relatively short passenger engine runs. The railway also built Class Y6 2-8-8-2 heavy-duty freight power that piled up 6,000 miles per month in drag service. Even though the main line was not favorable to heavy trains or high speeds, in 1953 the modern, home-produced, steam motive power accounted for ninety-four percent of the N&Ws gross ton-miles per freight train-hour and eighty-four percent of the passenger train-miles.

Thus, the As, Js and Y6s were the most productive trio of power ever in the age of steam. Finally, in the early fifties, Roanoke produced the last and most modern steam switching fleet in the nation during the steam era. These N&W steam giants shall never be forgotten!

2-6-6-4

"THE FINEST STEAM ENGINE EVER BUILT"

Those who knew and operated N&W's 2-6-6-4s put this phrase on the Class As. The 1200s could do any assigned job well—heavy passenger and time or slow freight alike in hilly or flat country. The long, smooth lines of the handsome As gives one the impression of a speedy, all-powerful engine. That is what it was—a real worker. *Courtesy N&W.*

Class A 1200, new at Roanoke Shops 1936. *Courtesy N&W.*

Class A 1212, new at Roanoke Shops 1943. *Courtesy N&W.*

Class A 1212 (Roanoke 1943) with solid steel pilot and streamlined tender in mid-forties. The original 10 As looked similar in the same era. *Courtesy N&W.*

Class A 1238 with unique improvements new at Roanoke Shops 1949. *Courtesy N&W.*

In the mid-1920s the Norfolk and Western possessed a large fleet of compound Mallet locomotives for its heavy freight work. These Mallets were well suited for their slow mountainous duty and the inherently heavy coal drags encountered throughout the system. However, there was something lacking for the manifest freight or merchandise trains. That something was speed. The Mallet had many pluses, but speed was not one of them. To whip its time freights over the road faster, a simple expansion locomotive was needed. In essence the N&W started seeking a locomotive with both power and speed shortly after World War I.

With the delivery of the second batch of USRA Mountains, designated as Class K2a, the railway usually assigned some 4-8-2s to time-freight operations on the more level stretches of the system. The K2 did a creditable job on the "flat lands" with a light to medium weight train; however, it did lack power to move the heavier trains at the desired speeds. In the quest to gain more power, the 4-8-2, Class K3, emerged from the Roanoke Shops in 1926. These locomotives were designed for dual service with a considerable increase in power potential. In actual service, though, they were not wholly satisfactory because of running

gear and counterbalancing problems. These engines still lacked power to handle time freights in the mountains and, with speed limitations inherent in their sixty-three-inch driving wheels, fell short of speeds on the level portions of the main line. They still were not what the N&W was looking for.

In a vain attempt to upgrade some existing power, a 2-6-6-2 compound Mallet was shopped and converted to a four cylinder single expansion locomotive and classified as a Class Z2. Although the starting tractive effort was higher, this locomotive essentially had too much running gear for the boiler—a reversal of the K3 problem. It was decided to go to the drawing boards and with experience gained from these earlier models and experimentals, to come up with a radically new locomotive design to fulfill the desired tasks.

Class A

What the railway wanted was a locomotive expanded out to almost the maximum allowed by clearances and track curvature. To attain the higher speed and to lick the counterbalance problems of small drivers, a driving wheel in the seventy-inch range was required. To insure that the locomotive was "big enough" in tractive effort and horsepower, about six axles of drivers

Over the years, the early As got some modifications: smooth steel pilot, covered sand-pipes, and streamlined tender. Number 1201 portrays clean lines and an all-powerful appearance accented by the aforementioned modifications. *H. Stirton Photo, Courtesy C. T. Felstead Collection.*

and a very large boiler were essential. To keep the locomotive within the clearances with the desired boiler and driving wheels, the firebox had to be placed behind the drivers to attain good combustion characteristics. And to negotiate the track curvature, the locomotive would have to be an articulated type if it was to have more than four driving axles.

Within these parameters, the mechanical engineers of motive power started drawings for a locomotive that was to be totally different from anything previously produced or used by the Roanoke-based N&W. It was to be a 2-6-6-4 four cylinder, single expansion articulated with seventy-inch drivers and a wheel base that was just about as long as was feasible for the driver size, turntables and track curvatures to be encountered. The boiler was of phenomenal size.

Opposite Page: 1200s developed maximum drawbar horsepower in the 40-45 mph range. In flat country, As reached speeds in excess of 70 mph when operating conditions permitted. *Courtesy N&W.*

In May 1936 the first locomotive of the new type was outshopped from the Roanoke Shops for service. The engine was numbered 1200 and designated as Class A. This locomotive also marked the beginning of what the railway termed the era of the modern coal-burning steam locomotives. From this point on, the railway produced locomotives that held the dike against the flood of dieselization longer and better than any other railroad.

This new class of locomotives had a look of power, yet with clean lines and larger drivers it transmitted the feeling of speed. The Class A gave the impression of being "everything business," and this was just what this locomotive was—by design a dual service type, in action a real worker.

The Class A pilot was the N&W standard boiler tube type, which immediately preceded the cast steel, outside bearing lead truck that was a first on the N&W. The front cylinders were connected with a ball-jointed steam distribution pipe extending from the smokebox side. The smokebox front was of the typical N&W design as established on the earlier Class Y. Mounted in front of the large single stack was a new Worthington

Officially rated at 114,000 pounds tractive effort, 1200s approached 124,000 pounds in dynamometer car tests. Pound for pound, for a 12-drivered engine the A was tops in power for starts and while running. *Courtesy N&W.*

When the last five As were built, they incorporated improvements that had proven mechanically superior on the streamlined Js. Improvements, installed on 1238-42, were namely roller-bearing equipped lightweight rods and reciprocating parts. Super articulated 1241 is speeding time freight 77 on the Norfolk Division. *Courtesy N&W.*

type 6 SA feedwater heater, which was also another first for a N&W locomotive. The boiler top had two sandboxes, and a steam dome was placed just ahead of the rear sandbox. Two cross-compound air compressors were hung, one on each side of the boiler, for good distribution of weight and were just in front of the rear cylinders. The main rods were connected to the rear set of drivers on both the front and rear engines. The 122-square foot grate was carried entirely behind the driving wheels over a cast steel, four-wheel trailer truck, which was another first for the N&W. There was no lagging over the firebox sides. Behind the boiler was the standard N&W cab with the slanted front that had been used on the earlier Y4 and Y5s. The locomotive road number appeared on the cab side with the name "Norfolk & Western" stencilled beneath it. The tenders were cast steel, water bottom types similar to those used on the earlier Y5s with a capacity of twenty-six tons of coal and 22,000 gallons of water.

Mechanically, the Class A was in a league by itself, since it was equipped with the most up-to-date features in U.S. railroading. Such features would become standard items for all future N&W road power. The As employed two huge steel castings as locomotive beds with the cylinders cast integral into the main frame. All locomotive and tender axles were equipped with roller bearings and, starting with 1206, the valve gear was installed using needle roller bearings. Tenders on 1201 through 1209 originally had Buckeye trucks, but these were replaced in the mid-1940s with Commonwealth trucks like those used on all other tenders of the Class As. American multiple front-end throttles were used and adopted following the experiment conducted on 2094. Initially the 1200 through 1209's boiler pressure was set for 275 pounds per square inch with a tractive effort of 104,500 pounds from the twenty-four-inch diameter and thirty-inch stroke cylinders. In the late thirties this boiler pressure was increased to 300 pounds per square inch with a corresponding tractive effort of 114,000 pounds. The total engine weight was 570,000 pounds with 430,100 pounds on drivers. The boilers were the longest and heaviest made or used by the Norfolk and

1200s were constructed for system-wide use. Yet, most of the A's mileage was compiled on flat portions of the railway in manifest as well as heavy coal traffic. *Courtesy Harold K. Vollrath.*

Western. They employed welded construction of the firebox, had flues of twenty-four feet in length and a combustion chamber of 114 inches. To round out these superb locomotives, they were equipped with pressure and mechanical lubricators and employed the N&W favorite Baker valve gear.

Locomotives 1200 and 1201 (c/n 266, 267) were built in May and June 1936. Whatever doubts the officials had at first, if any, were put aside after the initial tests. The new As were so successful that the railway immediately built eight more, numbers 1202 through 1209 (c/n 273 through 280), in the Roanoke Shops in 1937. The As wheeled 10,950 ton coal trains out of Williamson, West Virginia, to Portsmouth, Ohio, on a nearly level track profile. One of these new As handled a 7,500-ton train on level tangent track at sixty-four miles per hour, and given an occasional heavy passenger train, could meet passenger train schedules without the need of doubleheading. This class became known as the N&Ws most versatile performer, and to the operating men,

there was no finer locomotive. N&W men described the Class A as "the best engine ever by the N&W," or "the Class A was tops," or that they were "one of the best locomotives in operating efficiency" or they were a "real engine." It was only fitting that one of this great class, number 1206, was sent to the 1939 New York World's Fair for public display in 1939-40.

With the coming of World War II, the use of troop trains for the transportation of the armed forces became widespread. One former official of the railway stated that an "'A' was good for almost any job needed" and one such job was the long, heavy troop trains. With twenty-eight pullmans, or a consist of both Pullmans and flatcars, the troop trains were handled by an A like regular passenger trains of half that size using older power.

Prior to the coming of the new 4-8-4s in 1941-42, 1200s were regularly assigned to the joint N&W-Southern Railway's trains number 41 and 42, "The Pelican," between Roanoke and Bristol over N&W tracks. The railway liked the fruits of

Front view of 1232, in the Columbus roundhouse, shows vividly the steam pipe connecting the front cylinders. Steam behind the stack vent is from a released safety valve, meaning it was deafening in the "house." A Class M and auxiliary tenders are on either side. Date: April 1958. *Courtesy C. W. Jernstrom.*

One of a class of real workers at Crewe on the ready track. These 12-drivered engines pulled 18,000 ton coal trains, truly making the 573,000 pound As a superior performer. *A. A. Thieme Photo, Courtesy C. T. Felstead Collection.*

Handling 190-car coal trains, about 18,000 tons, became routine for the 1200s in the last few years of steam. No wonder N&W operating men thought the Class As could not be improved upon for level district steam freight power. *Courtesy C. W. Jernstrom.*

Number 1220 highballing time freight 78, east of Lynchburg near Nottoway in March 1956. The powerful, swift As could wheel manifest freights at near passenger train speeds. *Courtesy N&W.*

its investment in this new power and decided to produce more of it for the numerous duties these engines could accomplish. So, in 1943-44 the Roanoke Shops built twenty-five more of the locomotives, numbered 1210 through 1234 (c/n 332 through 346, 353 through 362). The first fifteen were delivered in 1943.

These new engines were essentially the same as the earlier models except for use of the Alligator crossheads instead of the multibearing type, which had caused some difficulties on the original models. All were built with 300 pounds boiler pressure and had lagging applied to the firebox sides. The new tenders were similar to the earlier type used on the initial 1200s, except the coal capacity was increased to thirty tons. With a total of thirty-five modern, high speed articulateds, the N&W was capable of handling increased coal traffic and merchandise freight, heavy passenger trains and troop movements with ease. During the war the majority of the class were assigned to the Roanoke Terminal, and a lesser number handled wartime traffic on the Scioto Division.

These earlier thirty-five locomotives did receive some modifications and improvements at the end

of World War II. The most notable was that the boiler tube pilot was replaced with a streamlined retractable coupler pilot like those used on the Js in 1941. This new pilot provided more safety for the locomotive and its crew when operating on the faster schedules. Also, the sand pipes were covered by the boiler jacket to hide piping hitherto exposed. Engine weight increased slightly. All the tenders were modified by raising the round top water cistern of the earlier models up to the flat top version usually associated with N&W steam in its later days. The tenders of 1200 through 1209 were also increased to thirty tons coal capacity by extending the coal bunker and applying a longer stoker trough, with all the tenders of the first thirty-five Class As acquiring a "streamlined" look in this shopping.

Troop movements and passenger patronage waned with the end of World War II, but coal traffic for the Port of Norfolk was increased in 1946, resulting in continuation of the export coal traffic via N&W rails. Although used to handle time freights and heavy passenger trains on all grade districts, the As were doubly suited to haul heavy tonnage coal trains over the flatter portions of the system. To alleviate the shortage of

The Class A was once described as a "real engine." Although designed and built primarily for manifest freight and heavy passenger service, 1200s were soon discovered to be ideally suited for heavy coal trains in flat country. There were no weak points with this class. Number 1204 speeds time freight 86 through the Blue Ridge in January '46. *Courtesy N&W.*

Most of Class A's mileage was in freight service, although the 1200s were used occasionally on passenger assignments. 2-6-6-4s were standard power on heavy passenger trains and on troop movements through WW II. In 1939, number 1200 wheeling train 41, the "Pelican," west of Wytheville, Virginia. *Courtesy N&W.*

This photo reflects the personality of a 1200 in action: working at speed. For all-around performance, most operating men preferred the A with its ability to start heavy trains and work them at higher speeds. *Courtesy N&W.*

this fast, heavy power, the railway constructed eight more Class As in 1949-50. These eight, numbered 1235 through 1242 (c/n 380 through 387), incorporated all the improvements the earlier models had received at the end of the war. The tenders, though, were constructed as streamlined types of thirty tons and 22,000 gallons.

The 1238 through 1242 had unique improvements made during their construction. These fast moving and powerful articulateds were equipped with roller bearings on the main and side rod connections and had lightweight reciprocating parts. The roller bearings were placed on the crank and wrist pins of the main rods and the crank pins of the side rods. Use of the Timken reciprocating parts resulted in a weight reduction of thirty-eight percent from the earlier, conventional parts used. The advantages of these last improvements were greater reliability, increased availability, lower roundhouse maintenance cost, reduction in hammer blow on the rails and longer locomotive runs without lubrication. The lightweight rods with roller bearings were so successful that many officials felt that if additional As had been built,

these As too would have been equipped with the new rods with bearings.

In the 1950s after the addition of auxiliary tenders for through freight service, the 1200s were worked to their capacity on the Norfolk and Scioto divisions. Out of Williamson, the "order of the day" was to haul 190 loaded hoppers, about 16,000 to 18,000 tons, to Portsmouth by one lone "A." This was the maximum tonnage assigned. Their continuous drawbar horsepower rating was 5,300 at forty miles per hour, although they could occasionally reach 6,300. In passenger and manifest freight service, they were capable of sustained speeds in excess of seventy miles per hour. No wonder that engineers thought there were no faults in this engine! As far as they were concerned the railway could not build a better one than the Class A.

With the coming of dieselization, the Class As were not affected at first, for the N&W philosophy was to dieselize certain light districts to release heavy power for main line freight work. Since the As were competitive with the diesel when working at capacity, they continued to haul

While 1213 is heading west with a solid train of coal at Williamson, the "Powhatan Arrow" pauses before continuing its speedy run from Cincinnati to Norfolk in 1953. After adding auxiliary water tenders, As routinely pulled 190 loaded hoppers west to Portsmouth. This was the A's, perhaps steam's, finest hour. *Courtesy N&W.*

Whatever doubts existed were put aside after the initial runs and tests. Here eight-day old 1200 showing its mettle with a reefer train east of Roanoke on May 16, 1936. To many N&W men, there were no finer steam engines, and these locomotives were declared N&W's most versatile performer. *Courtesy N&W.*

New 1200 working a time freight east of Roanoke in May 1936. The class was impressive in looks and performance. *Courtesy N&W.*

In July 1942, 1208 has time freight 85 in tow at 60 mph near Montvale, Virginia. Because of the outstanding performance of the first 10 1200s, 25 more were built during WW II. *Courtesy N&W.*

the heavy coal trains west from Williamson and east from Roanoke.

In 1958 with the decision to dieselize in total, the 1200s began to be retired since, unlike the Y6s, they were not suited for tipple work on the coal branches. By fall of 1959 all were gone. There is one lone Class A survivor, 1218, which is on display at the Roanoke Transportation Museum. Of those who designed, ran, maintained and operated N&W steam power, the 1200s were the prime favorites.

2-8-8-2

"WORKHORSE OF THE N&W"

For heavy-duty freight service, 2100s were the mainstay. The classes Y5 and Y6 2-8-8-2s were ideally suited for utilitarian duties—main-line power, heavy branch-line work, and yard hump operations. For brute power they were unsurpassed and were commonly referred to as "workhorses." Designed for highest possible drawbar pull, the modern 2-8-8-2s used every pound of engine weight to gain high adhesion. Also the running gear and steam distribution system improvements made possible more power at higher speeds for these compound Mallets. They were indeed the "workhorses of the N&W." *Courtesy Harold K. Vollrath.*

Y6 2130, new at Roanoke Shops 1938. *Courtesy N&W.*

Y6a 2156, new at Roanoke Shops 1942. *Courtesy N&W.*

Y6a 2156 with streamlined tender in the mid-forties. All Y5 and Y6s received streamlined tenders and later had standpipes covered. *Courtesy N&W.*

Y6b 2171 with overhanging smokebox front, new at Roanoke Shops 1948. *Courtesy N&W.*

Y6b 2197 with conventional looking smokebox, new at Roanoke Shops 1952. *Courtesy N&W.*

Y5 2114 (originally 2095, Roanoke Shops 1930) modernized with bed castings and engine axle roller bearings in 1940. *Courtesy Harold K. Vollrath.*

Numbers 2171-2194 were built with an unusual smokebox front arrangement. These 24 Y6bs subsequently received a more conventional looking front end like that on 2175. *Courtesy N&W.*

Class Y6

The compound Mallet articulated had been a standard type used by the N&W as its heavy-duty fleet of steam power since 1912. First operating with the 2-6-6-2 and then the 2-8-8-2 to gain more power, the railway used basically two types of the latter from the beginning of World War I. Its own home-designed Class Y2 had been a basis for the well-known USRA 2-8-8-2 produced during the First World War, some of which the N&W had acquired. Since the USRA design proved superior, the company set out to upgrade it, for the type was ideally suited to heavy mountain work.

As a result of this effort to improve the basic design, the Class Y4 and Class Y5 locomotives appeared in 1927 and 1930-32, respectively. The latter engines were built in the company's Roanoke Shops. In 1936, the railway started producing its own version of the modern coal-burning steam locomotive. The first two locomotives produced were the 1200 and 1201 of the Class A mentioned earlier. In September 1936, the first of the modern Mallets, number 2120 Class Y6, rolled from Roanoke Erecting Shop to start the breed that would represent the epitome of compound Mallet development.

Many of the improvements incorporated in the new Y6s had been tried on the Y5s earlier, such as the higher capacity boiler of 106 square feet grate area. The Y6 continued to use the larger eighteen-inch piston valves on the front low pressure cylinders to improve the steam distribution to and exhaust from the cylinders. The superior American multiple front-end throttle was placed in the smokebox just behind the large single stack of improved drafting characteristics. The arched bridge pipe connecting the two front low pressure cylinders was again employed as established on the Class Y5. Superior design and performance of this exhaust system had been proven. This new

The Y6's exhaust had a characteristic deep roar, leaving no doubt as to the capabilities of these "workhorses." *Courtesy C. W. Jernstrom.*

Road tests revealed that power could be increased on the existing Y6 fleet. In 1953-55, modification of the Y5 and Y6s resulted in an increase of more than 1,000 maximum drawbar horsepower attained at a higher speed of 25 mph. *Courtesy C. W. Jernstrom.*

class was equipped with the Worthington number 4 ½ BL feedwater heater on the left side of the boiler with two cross-compound air compressors hung on the right side for improved weight distribution. The Y6s also continued to be equipped with the favorite Baker valve gear and Alligator type crossheads. To give a new look, this class got a slanted stack resulting from slanting the stack forward eight degrees to make room for the new front-end throttle. The exhaust stand in the smokebox floor stayed put. It was simply a

matter of taking advantage of available space within the smokebox. Also, the locomotives were built with lagging applied to the firebox sides.

As with the first Class As, the outside bearing, cast steel lead truck was employed on the Y6. This same type of truck was also used as the trailer truck. The engine bed frames were all cast steel with the cylinders cast integral as one unit. Roller bearings were equipped on all locomotive and tender axles and, starting with 2125, the valve gear also had needle roller bearings. The

For a steam locomotive of such power and capacity, Y6s had a relatively light driving axle load of roughly 69,000 pounds. This added versatility enabled their use on many branch lines, too. *Courtesy N&W.*

Y6s were originally built with fifty-seven-inch drivers, had 300 pounds of boiler pressure; the cylinder had a thirty-two-inch stroke and twenty-five-inch bore for the rear, high pressure engine and a thirty-nine-inch bore for the front, low pressure engine. In simple operation, the starting tractive effort was 152,206 pounds and in compound operation 126,838 pounds. The total engine weight was 582,900 pounds, with 522,850 pounds on the drivers. All Class Y6 engines were equipped with either the Standard Modified type "B" or Berkley stoker. To increase the power potential and output, the valve settings were modified from that used on the earlier Mallet locomotives. The new valve settings were found to be very satisfactory after some initial tests in 1937 with locomotive 2124.

In actual operation, the Y6 did not have to prove a great deal, since this class was an upgraded version of that already in service. With the roller bearings and cast steel locomotive beds,

the availability was greatly increased. Although designed for road work, the Class Y6 was used in all types of freight work, even yard switching on the hump.

The Y6 was particularly well suited to mountain terrain with its heavy grades and sharp curvatures, so they were at home in the N&Ws coalfields. With the inherent slow speed and wide range of work, this type of power became known as "the workhorse of the N&W." And workhorses they really were! To hear one of these giants laboring on a grade gave an impression of brute power. The deep, roaring exhaust could be heard for miles when "slugging it out" on the grade, but there was no stopping her. One engineer and a fireman declared, "when a Y6 got down to six miles per hour, just pull that throttle wide open and you couldn't stop her."

If a better locomotive could have been produced as a "workhorse," it is hard to visualize. And these locomotives could be used on more

Rated officially 152,206 pounds starting tractive effort, improved Y6s reached 160,000 pounds in actual service. For power and economy, these Mallets were unbeatable in mountain work. *Courtesy C. W. Jernstrom.*

During World War II, petroleum products for the northeast were frequently shipped via railroads instead of the treacherous submarine-infested Atlantic route. N&W moved solid blocks of tank cars. *Courtesy N&W.*

On a dreary April day, two mighty steam giants are all glory and thunder on their eastbound Blue Ridge climb. Doubleheading east of Roanoke over the last mountain barrier to port was common procedure in late steam. *Courtesy C. W. Jernstrom.*

level portions of the road also. They were so well counterbalanced that speeds of fifty miles per hour were obtained. To see the old workhorses plodding along at thirty miles per hour with heavy trains on near-level track was commonplace. The maximum horsepower output was reached at twenty-five miles per hour, which certainly is not slow for this type of engine. Therefore, it could be used in a wide range of work. Good on the road or in the yard, for time freights or for coal traffic, on the level or the grade districts, for slow or moderate speed requirements, the Y6 was at home and wore her title well as "the workhorse." This term was applied to the Y6 affectionately by those who knew her best.

The first group of these modern 2-8-8-2s were Class Y6 and numbered 2120 through 2154 (c/n

268 through 272, 281 through 310) and were built between 1936 and 1940. The tenders were all cast steel, waterbottom types carrying twenty-six or thirty tons of coal and 22,000 gallons of water. Most of these tenders were equipped with the Buckeye trucks, although twelve had Commonwealth trucks originally. All of the Commonwealth trucks were exchanged later for Buckeye trucks tried on the Class As. The railway was so pleased with the performance of these modern compounds that it continued to build new ones at the beginning of World War II for the anticipated increase of wartime tonnage.

In 1942 the Roanoke Shops produced more of the 2-8-8-2s, Class Y6as, numbered 2155 through 2170 (c/n 316 through 331). The Y6a was a virtual copy of the Class Y6 except for the stokers, which

Y6bs were the desired Mallet for time, or manifest, freights until upgrading of older Y5 and Y6s. On May 14, 1950, 2187 is rolling a time freight north of Portsmouth, Ohio. *Courtesy C. W. Jernstrom.*

were the Standard Type "HT"; the feedwater heater was a Worthington number 4 ½ BL-2, a newer version of the number 4 ½ BL heater, and the tender axles had plain bearings.

The Y6 and Y6as did get some minor improvements. Shortly after World War II the driver size was enlarged to fifty-eight inches in diameter by increasing the tire thickness by one-half inch, which allowed much longer tire life before replacement was required. Also, the sandpipes were covered but the most noticeable change was the streamlining of the tender. The coal bunker was increased to thirty tons capacity after applying a long stoker trough on the tenders of 2120 through 2144, and the round top water cistern was raised to a flat top with the water capacity remaining at 22,000 gallons. All of the tenders of Y6 and Y6as received the flat top cistern.

Beginning in the early forties, a number of these earlier Y6s were modified with an extended combustion chamber. The original Y6 had a tube length of twenty-four feet and a very short combustion chamber. It was discovered that the tubes were so long in the Y6 for its grate area that little benefit was gained from the tubes near the smokebox area. Nor was combustion quite complete. On the modified Y6s with an extended combustion chamber, the tubes were reduced to twenty feet in length and four feet added to the combustion chamber. The results were most favorable. Even with a reduction of over 1,000 square feet of heating surface, the modified boilers were better steamers, and the locomotive could work with a near clear stack because of better combustion characteristics.

At the end of World War II, the Norfolk and Western continued to modernize its freight locomotive fleet by retiring the older and more costly

210

All eastbound N&W coal crossed the Alleghanies at Christiansburg, until the merger with Virginian. Heavy tonnage trains required a pusher on the 1% maximum eastbound climb from Walton to the summit, a distance of seven miles. Under the Blacksburg Branch overpass, an eastbound coal drag with 2150 at the head end approaches the summit with the enginemen coaxing every bit of power possible to keep the train moving. *Courtesy C. W. Jernstrom.*

.... A few minutes later, the front of the coal drag has begun its descent down the eastside of the Alleghanies, and the pusher cuts off from the rear as it nears the summit. Here 2170 is halting within sight of the overpass and will return to Walton to assist the next 10,300 ton coal train. Date: June 2, 1954. *Courtesy C. W. Jernstrom.*

The 2-8-8-2 Mallet was the backbone of the N&W steam fleet. Because of its utilitarian qualities, it was the most numerous homebuilt giant and became known as "workhorse of the N&W." Number 2127 performing that all-familiar task of pulling a coal train through the mountains. *Courtesy N&W.*

to maintain locomotives. It upgraded the main line freight power by building more of its standard locomotives. From 1948 to 1952, thirty (c/n 363 through 379, 391 through 397, 414 through 419) of the compound Mallets left the erecting shop for heavy freight service. Many of these had been built to replace the discontinued electrification on the Elkhorn grade. The new power, designated Class Y6b, incorporated all the latest modifications applied to the earlier Y6. The most important improvements applied to the new Y6bs were redesigned valve events and larger stacks with lower back pressure producing exhaust nozzles. These last design improvements increased maximum drawbar horsepower by more than 1,000 horsepower over that of the first Y6s.

Also, the Y6bs were constructed with the extended combustion chamber as standard equipment. They came equipped with the fifty-eight-inch drivers, the sandpipes covered and the

tenders of cast steel, waterbottom construction built new in a streamlined style to look similar to the earlier rebuilt streamlined versions of the Y6 and Y6as.

New to the Mallet compound was the Worthington type 6 SA feedwater heater placed in the smokebox just ahead of the slanted stack. This feedwater heater presented a new, if not peculiar, look to the Mallets. To make room for the heater, the upper smokebox portion was extended forward while the lower portion was not, thus providing for clearance of the large low pressure cylinders and for placement of the feedwater pump. This produced a large overhanging boiler front. The large round smokebox door of earlier Y6s was replaced with a smaller oblong door. This fearsome looking front end was applied to locomotives 2171 through 2194.

The 2195 through 2200, as built, received a more conventional looking smokebox front. The large round smokebox door of earlier models returned. So that the extended smokebox would clear the big low pressure cylinders, the front below the door sloped back gently with the feedwater pump being relocated beneath the left front running board. This new arrangement gave a pleasing appearance and the impression of an all-powerful locomotive of extremely clean lines. The 2171 through 2194 were subsequently modified with the round smokebox door arrangement starting in 1951 at normally scheduled shoppings at Roanoke.

Two cross-compound air compressors were mounted, one on each side of the boiler, for better weight balance. The Y6bs, like the earlier Y6s, had cast steel beds, roller bearings on all axles, pressure and mechanical lubrication and Baker valve gear with needle roller bearings throughout the valve gear. The Y6bs represented the zenith

of the compound Mallet in American railroading and were certainly prize winners of the "workhorse" class. At terminals serving the mountain districts, locomotive dispatchers always tried to save a Y6b for the time freights, since the on-time record was slightly better with these, the most modern Mallets.

The veteran Y6 and Y6as received major improvements to bring them up to the Y6b standards. These older "workhorses" got the redesigned valve events and new stacks with larger exhaust nozzles so successful on the new Y6bs. All eighty-one Y6s received the external reducing and booster operating valves. To take advantage of the increased power when the booster valve was in operation, some fourteen tons of lead was added to the front engine frames, thus increasing total locomotive weight. These same improvements were also applied to the older Y5s. The Y5s

Number 2145 gives the impression of a powerful locomotive hard at work. Feel the ground tremble as this giant passes by on the eastbound Alleghany climb to Christiansburg on June 12, 1955. *Courtesy C. W. Jernstrom.*

Y6a 2159 at Bluefield, March 1956. All Y6 and Y6as received larger stacks when external reducing valves were installed from 1953-55. Compare difference of stack appearance here with that of 2139. *Courtesy Charles E. Winters.*

Y5 and Y6s were used as pushers on the Blue Ridge and doubleheaded with Class A 1200s across this formidable obstacle. 2100s assisted the As east to Phoebe, near Lynchburg, and then would doublehead back to Roanoke with another train westbound over this mountain barrier. *Courtesy C. W. Jernstrom.*

N&W placed the road name and number on the cab side as seen on 2139 in December 1939. Beginning in mid-1941, locomotives received "Norfolk and Western" stencilled across the tender flanks. *Courtesy Charles E. Winters.*

and Y6s equipped with these improvements were referred to officially as the Improved Y5/Y6. After all one hundred locomotives had received these modifications in 1953-55, the "improved" reference was discarded. (For a discussion of the booster valve, *see* the section on locomotive engineering—covering the improvements of the compound Mallet.)

The Improved Y5/Y6 performed as well as any sixteen-driver articulated ever built up to thirty miles per hour. These compound Mallets were used primarily in the very expensive mountain operations, where operating speeds are relatively low. Modern Mallets, they developed tremendous power at the lower speeds, too, and were unbeatable in slow, heavy work. Interestingly, these magnificent machines did their trudging labors by using their steam more efficiently. It is perhaps impossible to visualize a better conventional steam locomotive for mountain work. On the tough Radford Division, an eastbound coal train on the Allegheny climb of one percent was rated at 10,300 tons for two improved Y5 and/or Y6s. Just *two* locomotives for 10,300 tons! With this kind of ability, no wonder the Y5 and Y6s were called "the workhorses." These modern compounds were used throughout the N&W system, but they were the mainstay on the Shenandoah, Radford and Pocahontas divisions for freight operations.

With the coming of dieselization, they were not affected at first, since the old Class Z1bs and old Class Ys were being retired. But the N&W had a stable full of capable "workhorses," which could fill in nicely on the mine runs and similar unglamorous jobs. While other modern power got bumped from main line operations and retired, the Y5 and Y6s were well suited for other duties. When the main line steam operations ceased in the late summer of 1959, there were still some fifty modern Class Y6s in the N&W coalfields on mine runs, running out serviceable miles and awaiting the final order of diesels. The last Class Y6s were retired at Williamson in the spring and summer of 1960. One Class Y6a, 2156, has been donated to the National Museum of Transport in St. Louis, Missouri, and is on public display there.

Modernized Class Y5

The Class Y5s were constructed by the Roanoke Shops in 1930-32. These locomotives when new had been fitted with a number of innovations that were later adopted as standard equipment on the newer Class Y6. Among these were the eighteen-inch piston valves on the front low pressure cylinders, the arched bridge pipe connecting the two low pressure cylinders for better exhaust characteristics, and the then new higher capacity

215

This great engine is a symphony of steel and sound on a heavy grade district near Bluefield. Circa 1955. *Courtesy Harold K. Vollrath.*

Y5 and Y6s were heavy-duty freight locomotives of the N&W steam roster and were the "workhorses" of the steam era. Number 2117 performing the heaviest duties of the Roanoke hump. *Courtesy C. W. Jernstrom.*

Y6 2136 takes on water at Wilcoe, West Virginia, late in steam. N&W's last steam citadels were in the coalfields where giant Y5 and Y6s, and little giant S1as, were the last survivors. Almost all main-line steam operations were over in this December 1959 photo. *Courtesy C. W. Jernstrom.*

One usually thinks of N&W's modern Mallets as used only on coal drags in the mountains. On Radford, Pocahontas, and Shenandoah divisions, Y5 and Y6s were used between major terminals on all through-freight service—manifest and coal traffic. *Courtesy N&W.*

This photo clearly shows the advantage of double tracking the main line for the heavy-trafficked N&W. As an eastbound time freight, powered by Y6a 2167, roars by Dry Branch, Virginia, an empty coal train is rolling back to the coalfields in June 1946. *Courtesy N&W.*

Modernized Y5 2102 at the head end of tank car train ready to proceed westbound from Roanoke in June 1943. Note Bradford throttle prevalent on this "workhorse" class. *Courtesy N&W.*

boiler of 300 pounds pressure and a grate area of 106 square feet.

As originally built, the Y5s had bar frames bolted together by crosstie castings like Y4s, with conventional lubrication and friction bearings on the axle journals. Even with these improvements, the Y5 still fell behind the newer Y6s in performance. Mainly, it required more servicing, and in general had greater nonavailability time due to the lack of roller bearings and having problems with the frames. Although the Y6s had cost more to build, a considerable savings was gained through greater availability and less maintenance. So between 1940 and 1941, the Y5s were shopped and upgraded to the Y6 standards. These older Y5s got one-piece steel locomotive bed castings with the cylinders casted integral with the frames. Roller bearings were installed on

engine axles only with pressure and mechanical lubrication provided throughout. Tender axles retained plain bearings. Numbers 2101 through 2109 remained numbered the same with the shopping but the 2090 through 2100 (minus 2092) were renumbered in a haphazard manner so that the entire class was numbered 2101 through 2119, inclusively. The old and new numbers for this renumbering were: 2094/2110, 2090/2111, 2098/2112, 2096/2113, 2095/2114, 2100/2115, 2091/2116, 2097/2117, 2099/2118 and 2093/2119.

As rebuilt, the modernized Y5s became totally interchangeable with the newer Y6s. As the Y6s were modified with improvements, so were the Y5s. At the end of World War II, the Y5s had the sandpipes covered, received the fifty-eight-inch drivers by increasing the tire by one-half inch in thickness, received new stokers, and the tenders

Stout 2133 barreling along east of Bluefield on June 25, 1943. This eastbound coal train will proceed along the gradually ascending New River line to Walton, where a pusher will assist the heavy drag over the Alleghany summit before the consist reaches Roanoke. *Courtesy N&W.*

Rolling down the east slope of the Blue Ridge Mountains near Montvale on July 15, 1941. Y5 and Y6 engines had a maximum speed of 45 to 50 mph when operating conditions permitted. *Courtesy N&W.*

Within sight of the Blue Ridge summit, 2137 blasts westbound upgrade with a long, time freight in tow on January 5, 1946. One cannot but notice the well-maintained track, a tribute to the maintenance of way forces. *Courtesy N&W.*

The Y5 and Y6s were essentially the same capacity, but the main differences were that the latter had bed castings and axle roller bearings. In 1940-41, Y5s received the Y6 refinements. Modernized 2114 powering a coal train west of Chillecothe, Ohio, on July 17, 1942. *Courtesy N&W.*

Two steam giants, a Y6 and an A, are struggling to keep a loaded coal drag moving eastbound on the steep Blue Ridge grade. Both of these powerful articulateds are being assisted by a pusher, another Y6. After crossing the Blue Ridge, the 1200 will get more hoppers and then proceed on alone eastward on a mostly descending grade. Date: September 1956. *Courtesy N&W.*

were streamlined after increasing the coal bunker to thirty tons capacity and raising the water cistern to a flat top.

The number 2110 had its type "E" superheater replaced with a type "A." In 1951, the 2114 received a new boiler (c/n 413) as a result of a boiler explosion. This new boiler had a front-end multiple throttle, BL feedwater heater, a slanted stack, and it was outfitted with an extended combustion chamber. That was the only application of a slanted stack and extended combustion chamber to a Y5. In 1953 this class began receiving the external reducing and booster operating valves, redesigned valve gear settings and had

lead added to the front engine as the Y6s did. Eventually all Y5s were fitted with such modifications, which upgraded these tireless "workhorses" to the standards of the Y6s. The Y5s all retained the inboard bearing lead and trailer trucks, which was a distinguishing characteristic of the entire class.

The Y5s survived to the end of the steam along with the newer Y6s. When main line steam operations ended, at least ten of the class were still working in the coalfields. It is regrettable that none of this mighty breed was spared the torch. All were retired by June 1960.

4-8-4

"THE LAST FINE STEAM TRAIN"

Streamlined 600s were superior in every way and these superb engines pulled crack N&W passenger trains in a grand style. Among the renowned "named" trains that graced N&W rails, Class Js were probably best known for their role of pulling the railway's "Powhatan Arrow." The "Arrow" was an all-passenger train with no head-end baggage cars, and it turned out to be America's "last fine steam train." But the 4-8-4's performance was just as impressive on other passenger trains rolling through mountains or flatlands. As for dependability, Js often went from one monthly shopping to the next never missing an assignment. Mechanically, there were no finer reciprocating steam engines! *Courtesy N&W.*

Class J 600 new at Roanoke Shops 1941. *Courtesy N&W.*

Numbers 605-610, classed as J1, were built in 1943 without the streamlined cowling and lightweight rods to conserve vital war materials. After considerable running gear trouble, J1s were shopped in 1944 being refitted with streamlined cowl, lightweight rods, and reclassed as J. *Courtesy Harold K. Vollrath.*

In the June 1950 *N&W Magazine*, the railway said of its newly built 611, and her Class J sisters: "At normal passenger train operating speeds of from 40 to 60 miles an hour, these coal-burning, steam locomotives develop more tractive power than even giant 6,000-horsepower diesels, a great advantage on the Norfolk and Western which traverses mountainous territory." To the motive power people, this was reason enough to continue steam passenger operations. *Courtesy N&W.*

N&W employees became more and more excited as the first J took form in 1941. Just a few days before 600 was completed, it is being "wheeled" in the erecting shop at Roanoke. One marvels at this sight and wonders if there is anything comparing with this today. *Courtesy N&W.*

Number 600 rolls from Roanoke Shops into sunlight for the first time on October 20, 1941. This sleek beauty was in a class by itself in looks and performance. Could there be a more beautiful streamlined steam engine retaining all characteristic contours and shape of steam power? For the reciprocating steam locomotive, they were unsurpassed mechanically. *Courtesy N&W.*

The area served by the N&W did not have a great passenger traffic potential. Yet, the railway was never unmindful of the people along its tracks. The competitive role of the railroad in the people transportation industry, and in general its motto of "Precision Transportation" bespoke its desire to do everything in a first class manner. Thus, the N&W had top-notch passenger trains for the long hauls and numerous locals for the shorter passenger work. As the Great Depression abated in the late 1930s, passenger business started picking up. This brought about longer and heavier passenger trains for the long distance runs.

Much of the passenger equipment had been acquired in the late twenties and the thirties. The last new heavy passenger power, Class K2a, had been purchased in 1923; and, after a major upgrading to higher capacity in the late twenties, the units were capable of the main line work required with the ever heavier equipment then in use. When the passenger business took an upswing in the late 1930s, it became apparent that the K2 and K2as were reaching their limit.

The railway decided to embark on producing a locomotive that was second-to-none for passenger service. With the heavy grades on the N&W system, four driving axles were essential. Likewise, to cut down on the overhead, better utilization of the locomotives was a paramount call. This could only be done with longer engine runs and fewer stops for servicing. Also in the late thirties many railroads were streamlining the passenger power on their crack trains. Subsequently, the N&W wanted a flashy locomotive that would catch the public's eye. With this in mind, the N&W employees designed, built, streamlined and operated one of the most fantastic passenger locomotives of all time. Those who saw and watched them at work will never forget them.

Ground-level camera snaps 603 rolling up passenger train-miles near Roanoke in late steam. In 1953, the 14 homebuilt J "racehorses" accounted for 84% of the system's passenger train-miles. *Courtesy Harold K. Vollrath.*

On a fall day in 1950, 608 glides into Roanoke passenger terminal with one of the joint N&W–Southern Railway name trains. These joint trains operated over N&W tracks from Lynchburg to Bristol. *Charles E. Winters Photo. Courtesy Harold K. Vollrath Collection.*

Class J

The railway's design engineers decided on seventy-inch drivers, since the older 4-8-2s and 4-6-2s had used this size very successfully. Furthermore, the new Class As outshopped in 1936-37 had employed this wheel with improved counterbalancing in an exemplary performance. A large capacity boiler with a larger furnace required a four-wheel trailer truck to support the very heavy weight of the firebox. Roller bearings were to be supplied to all engine and tender axles for increased availability and reliability that were hallmarks of the modern articulateds, the Class As and Y6s. As for streamlining, a proposed scheme was drawn, but it first needed some touching up before it could be presented to the railroad's hierarchy for approval.

Frank C. Noel of the railway's Passenger Car Department touched up this first sketch. What he saw was a large 4-8-4 engine with a typical N&W boiler tube pilot, a pointed smokebox front very similar to the Southern Pacific's GS engines,

a boiler top cowling from the stack to the cab, the running boards with no skirting and a new streamlined tender like the ones actually produced later. The officials rejected this first sketch as not fancy enough.

At this point, Noel became even more keenly interested in the streamlining project. He then drew a second scheme that was almost identical to that of the New York Central's Hudson elongated out to the 4-8-4 configuration. This scheme was rejected as "too fancy." Now Noel made a third sketch, and this was the scheme used by the railway for what is considered by many the most beautiful streamlined steam locomotive ever. It was not gaudy but had very simple, clean lines that give a "racey" look. Yet, the streamlining was not excessive to the point that it would significantly hinder either maintenance or servicing.

The employees in the Roanoke Shops began to get excited as the new 4-8-4, Class J, took form. As the first one, number 600, rolled from the erecting shop into the sunlight, all of the people of

Number 605 working out on heavy grade district near Bluestone, West Virginia, under N&W's catenary west of Bluefield. This close-up shot puts in proper perspective these massive, sleek beauties. *Courtesy J. W. Jernstrom.*

the N&W "family" showed pride in their product. Just to see this magnificent machine was exciting, for it was truly something to behold. It sported a new streamlined pilot with a retractable coupler, a bullet shaped shell with an enclosed headlight installed over the smokebox front, a boiler top cowling that encased the large stack, sandbox, steam dome with whistle, bell and safety valves. Along the running boards a broad skirting was applied from the cab and firebox sides forward over the cylinders, then narrowing as it turned down and into the pilot. This skirting was painted tuscan red, trimmed in gold, and this tuscan red stripe extended under the cab and along the streamlined tender's side.

Mechanically, the Class Js were superior—and more. They had roller bearings on all engine and tender axles and were equipped with needle roller bearings on the Baker valve gear. They had Timken lightweight reciprocating parts, and roller bearings were installed on the crank and crosshead pins. This application of roller bearings and lightweight reciprocating parts was the first such undertaking to an entire class of power in the U.S. American multiple front-end throttles were used, a Worthington type 6 SA feedwater heater was placed in the cowling in front of the stack, and it had pressure and mechanical lubrication equipment to 200 points. The mechanical lubricators had a capacity sufficient to operate

1,300 miles without replenishment. Roller bearings on the crank and wrist pins had sufficient lubrication capacity to operate 500 miles without replenishment. The seventy-inch drivers were propelled by the twenty-seven-inch bore and thirty-two-inch stroke cylinders charged with 275 pounds pressure of steam. The locomotive weighed in at 494,000 pounds with 288,000 pounds on the drivers, and could develop 73,300 pounds starting tractive effort. Its grate area was 108 square feet. The tenders were cast steel, waterbottom type with the exterior surfaces sleek and smooth with welded construction instead of the usual rivets. The tender capacity was twenty-six tons and 22,000 gallons.

Numbers 600 through 604 (c/n 311 through 315) rolled from the Roanoke Shops from October 1941 to January 1942. All of this first group were identical except for 602, which was equipped with a trailer booster rated at 12,500 pounds tractive effort with total engine tractive effort of 85,800 pounds. The total engine weight of 602 was 505,300 pounds.

These locomotives were unique in appearance and performance. As they were being broken in it became evident that here was a real winner. There just were not any faults! One engineer opened one up to 110 miles per hour on a straight and level section of track just to see what it could do. It could thunder up Christiansburg Mountain to the summit of the eastern continental divide with a heavy passenger train at forty-five to fifty miles

The first of a fast breed, 600, is ready at Roanoke to start its run to Norfolk. This setting was an all-familiar one during the steam era at Roanoke: beautiful streamlined engines in view of the railway's own Hotel Roanoke (in background) and Roanoke Shops (to right of photo). *Courtesy Harold K. Vollrath.*

Above and Below: Proposed color and semistreamlining schemes considered for modernization of 4-8-2s. The streamlining scheme adopted for the K2 upgrading was that of the sleek Class J 4-8-4s. *Courtesy Frank C. Noel.*

Initial drawing received by Frank Noel for touching up. The diagram was "not fancy enough." *Courtesy Frank C. Noel.*

"Too fancy" was labelled this second drawing. Noel then developed the streamlining scheme actually used on the Js. *Courtesy Frank C. Noel.*

First two Js, 600 and 601, pose at Roanoke's Shaffers Crossing engine terminal on February 18, 1954. These two "racehorses" have just completed 2,000,000 miles service each since built in 1941. High availability and dependability made the Js a favorite with operating men. *Courtesy N&W.*

N&W and Southern jointly operated passenger trains over N&W rails. SR inaugurated a streamlined train for service between Memphis and Washington, D.C., in the early forties. New 600 is shown making its first run with a streamlined train, then new, all silver "Tennessean" on October 30, 1941, at Elliston, Virginia. *Courtesy N&W.*

Number 600, the first J, is speeding a long string of passenger coaches west of Glenvar, Virginia on August 10, 1945. This shot accents the large size, speed, power, and personality of this superior class. *Courtesy N&W.*

The graceful lines and beautiful color scheme of N&W's streamlined Js are truly evident in this pose of 602 at Roanoke's Shaffers Crossing. Viewing this immaculate engine, one cannot help but realize the magnificent 600s were an elegant class. *N&W Photo, Courtesy C. W. Jernstrom.*

236

per hour. West of Bluefield, West Virginia, where the speed limit was forty-five miles per hour, and thirty on many severe curves, the Class Js could slow down for the curves, then quickly accelerate to the speed limit on the straighter stretches. As one engineer said, "They (the Js) could run like the devil." One official said for the Class J engine to get to 100 miles per hour "was the easiest thing in the world." They simply could wheel a heavy passenger train at a "smart clip" up a mountain and then turn around and "run like a scared rabbit" on the flat lands. And their acceleration was second to none. To hear one roaring out of a station with twelve to fourteen cars in tow left no doubt as to its capabilities.

World War II hit the N&W passenger service with a vengeance. More modern passenger power was needed—and needed fast—so in 1943 six more 4-8-4s were constructed, numbered 605 through 610 (c/n 347 through 352). But these locomotives, classed as J1s, embodied some notable changes because of the wartime shortages. To conserve vital war materials, the streamlined cowling was left off and the rods were not equipped with roller bearings. In addition, the Alligator crosshead was found more satisfactory

than the multibearing type installed on the first group of Class Js, so the J1s were equipped with the Alligator type. All other mechanical aspects of the J1s were the same as the earlier Js.

These eleven J and J1s performed yeoman service with the swollen wartime passenger traffic, for with their roller bearing-equipped axles, these engines were dispatched frequently seventy minutes after arriving at the terminal. This amounted to superior utilization of power and equipment. For example, the N&W hauled 374 percent more passengers in 1943 than in 1939, and did this with the same amount of equipment because of its inability to acquire new passenger cars. Thus these Class J and J1 engines played a vital role in the nation's war effort. Their availability and reliability truly stood out.

Some minor changes were made on these first eleven engines. In 1944, the J1s were shopped and the streamlined shroud was applied along with the roller bearings for the newly applied lightweight rods and valve gear. The J1s were reclassed as Class J upon this shopping. All of the Js got higher boiler pressures of 300 pounds per square inch with a resulting boost in tractive effort to 80,000 pounds, thus becoming the most

This J was built with a booster installed, and 602 still has it in June 1945. The booster was removed late the following December since increased maintenance costs were not justified for the high tractive effort 4-8-4s. *Courtesy C. W. Jernstrom.*

J 608 thundering upgrade on the Blue Ridge with train 4, the "Pocahontas." The 600s were at home in the mountains as well as on the flatlands. Date: October 12, 1955. *Courtesy N&W.*

powerful 4-8-4 ever produced. Likewise, the tenders were modified to carry thirty-five tons of coal by lengthening the bunker space, and this reduced the water capacity to 20,000 gallons. And because of the trouble experienced with the trailer booster, it was removed in December 1945 from number 602.

After World War II, passenger traffic on the railroads started declining sharply, and the N&W was no exception. The Norfolk and Western made a determined effort to keep passengers riding the rails. One thrust was to provide the best possible service and equipment. To provide the finest service, the railway inaugurated its streamlined all-coach train, "The Powhatan Arrows," for a predominately daylight run between Norfolk and Cincinnati. The equipment, ordered in the late

forties, was of the highest quality to the best specifications possible. The locomotives were of unsurpassed quality for the service intended, and so the railway built three more Class Js in 1950, numbered 611 through 613 (c/n 388 through 390), to pull "the Arrow." These engines were identical to the first eleven and embodied all modifications of the earlier models such as 300 pounds boiler pressure and the tender with coal capacity of thirty-five tons.

All of the Class Js were assigned to the pool of streamlined passenger locomotives based in Roanoke. The 600s were such tireless greyhounds that they hauled the main line passenger trains from Roanoke to Cincinnati without engine change—a distance of 423 miles. They took on water at regularly scheduled station stops where standpipes were located. If they should run low on coal, they often stopped at one of the three on-line coaling stations.

The Southern Railway and Norfolk and Western jointly had three crack passenger trains that ran each way behind N&W steam power over N&W rails between Kinney, Virginia, near Lynchburg, and Bristol. A number of Class Js, for these joint trains, were pooled and serviced at the N&W's facilities at Bristol and the Southern's terminal at Monroe (near Lynchburg). This eliminated a changeover of power at Roanoke; thus the same locomotive could run through—a distance of some 212 miles. These extended runs were how the Class Js achieved 15,000 miles of service a month. Locomotive number 600 ran 1,200,000 plus miles in its first eight years of service. When the last three Js were constructed in 1950, they were identical to number 600. This is testimony enough to their reliability and soundness of design. Remember, they were designed and built by the employees of the N&W. These employees had a right to be proud!

The 600s held on during the early stages of dieselization. But the diesels bumped them from their customary passenger duties in the summer of 1958. One was retired shortly after, while the others were used in local freight work to complete their serviceable miles. By the end of October 1959, all were without work. One of these sleek beauties that graced the N&W rails is on public display at the Roanoke Transportation Museum. She is 611, which happened to be the last J in service.

The Powhatan Arrow

What became the N&Ws last bid to keep rail passenger service going turned into America's "last fine steam train." But what a show it was while it lasted! Even by today's standard, it was the epitome of the most modern, comfortable and safe means of travel possible. And with the unsurpassed N&W roadbed it traversed, the train provided superior comfort and service to the railway passenger riding in "top-drawer" quality cars. The Norfolk and Western's president, R. H. "Racehorse" Smith, was the one primarily responsible for the upgraded passenger service. His attitude was that to win back the passenger, top quality service must be provided. And, in Smith's view, a passenger could be an actual or potential shipper or receiver of freight who would be impressed by the passenger service and the railway's efficiency as well.

The following article was published in the December 1949 issue of N&Ws monthly magazine.

It gives a vivid description of the typical seven-car, all coach train that graced the N&W rails and provided the finest possible rail travel.

Our New Powhatan Arrow

The new Powhatan Arrows are on our rails! Delivery of new equipment for two complete, beautiful trains, embodying the latest features in safety, riding comfort and luxury, began on November 22 and both trains were expected to be in regular service by the time this MAGAZINE is in circulation.

Already the pride of the Norfolk and Western, the colorful, ultra modern streamlined cars, manufactured by the Pullman-Standard Car Manufacturing Company, of Chicago, will add new lustre to the shining reputation of The Powhatan Arrow, which made its first run on April 28, 1946. From the start, patrons have praised the Arrow's reputation for on-time dependability, the solid comfort of its coaches and lounge cars, the fine food served on its diners, and especially the courteous and obliging service of the men who operate it. (The equipment, formerly used on The Arrow, is modern and in excellent condition and will be used in other trains, notably The Pocahontas.)

All of these attractions, plus the finest in equipment, convenience and service will be enjoyed by our patrons on the new trains.

First of the new trains to be received made its debut to the press and radio in a special run on November 30, from Roanoke to Bluefield and return. Then came an exhibition run, December 4-11, when thousands inspected and acclaimed the trains at stations where The Arrow makes regular stops.

These are more than just new trains. They are new conceptions of travel comfort, safety and convenience—all the way from the train crew's compartments and lockers in the head coach to the exciting and luxurious lounge-tavern-observation car on the rear.

Here are a few distinctive features of the new cars that make The Powhatan Arrow one of the truly fine trains of America:

. . . large, fog-proof picture windows.

. . . interiors beautiful in color, decoration and furnishings.

. . . coach sets of foam rubber, seats that are really restful, seats that rotate and recline.

. . . automatic, thermostat-controlled heating and air conditioning, insuring temperatures that are just right, always.

. . . "feather touch" doors, that open with finger-tip pressure, that close automatically.

A Completely NEW Powhatan Arrow — Connecting the MIDWEST with the VIRGINIA SEASHORE

SCHEDULE

	Train 25 Daily (Read Down)				Train 26 Daily (Read Up)	
AM 7 00	Lv.	Norfolk (Terminal Sta. [E. T.])	.N. & W....	Ar.	11 55	PM
7 23	"	Suffolk......................	"	Lv.	11 27	
8 20	Ar.	Petersburg....................	"	"	10 30	
9 00	Ar.	Richmond......................	.A. C. L....	Lv.	9 25	
7 20	Lv.	Richmond......................	.A. C. L....	Ar.	11 10	
8 20	Lv.	Petersburg....................	.N. & W....	Ar.	10 30	
B 9 01	"	Blackstone....................	"	Lv.	B 9 44	
9 20	"	Crewe........................	"	"	9 30	
9 46	"	Farmville.....................	"	"	8 59	
10 50	Lv.	Lynchburg.....................	"	Ar.	8 00	
12 05	Ar.	Roanoke......................	"	Lv.	6 55	
12 15	Lv.	Roanoke......................	"	Ar.	6 45	
12 59	"	Christiansburg................	"	Lv.	5 59	
A 1 47	"	Pearisburg....................	"	"	A 5 08	
2 45	"	Bluefield.....................	"	"	4 20	
3 50	"	Welch........................	"	"	3 03	
5 35	"	Williamson....................	"	"	1 25	
7 17	"	Kenova.......................	"	"	11 35	
7 32	"	Ironton......................	"	"	11 20	
8 10	"	Portsmouth....................	"	"	10 50	
10 45	Ar.	Cincinnati....................	.N. & W....	Lv.	8 20	
6 40	Ar.	Chicago (C. T.)...............	.P. R. R....	Lv.	11 30	
7 30	"	Chicago (C. T.)...............	.N. Y. C....	"	11 45	
8 00	"	St. Louis (C. T.).............	"	"	10 30	
7 00	"	Detroit (E. T.)..............	"	"	11 30	
7 40	"	St. Louis (C. T.).............	.B. & O....	"	11 20	
7 20	"	Detroit (E. T.)..............	"	"	11 40	
8 15	Lv.	Portsmouth....................	.N. & W....	Ar.	10 40	
10 45	Ar.	Columbus.....................	"	Lv.	8 00	
6 55	"	Cleveland (E. T.).............	.N. Y. C....	Lv.	11 50	
7 30	"	Chicago (C. T.)...............	.P. R. R....	"	10 45	
7 00	"	Pittsburgh (E. T.)...........	"	"	11 00	
AM 8 10	Ar.	St. Louis....................	.P. R. R....	Lv.	6 30	PM

A and B—Conditional Stops.
Seats reserved without extra charge. No checked baggage handled.
Light Type Indicates "AM"
Heavy " " "PM"

PASSENGER DEPARTMENT

REPRESENTATIVES

	Telephone

CHATTANOOGA 2, TENN.—1124 Volunteer State Life Building
J. H. Davis, General Agent, Passenger Department...........6-5355

CHICAGO 4, ILL.—Room 602, 208 South La Salle Street Building
J. W. Ryan, Western Passenger Agent.............RAndolph 6-2715

CINCINNATI 2, OHIO—116 Dixie Terminal Arcade
B. C. Farfsing, District Passenger Agent........MAin 0575 or 1825

COLUMBUS 15, OHIO—716 Huntington Bank Building
N. A. Hyatt, Traveling Passenger Agent................ADams 1332

LYNCHBURG, VA.—Virginian Hotel Building, 726 Church Street
R. A. Safrit, City Passenger Agent.....................2-7531

MEMPHIS 3, TENN.—822 Exchange Building
A. E. Hughett, Traveling Passenger Agent.................8-3351

NEW YORK 18, N. Y.—Room 908, 500 Fifth Avenue
J. V. Fagan, General Eastern Passenger Agent...PEnnsylvania 6-0032

NORFOLK 10, VA.—145 Granby Street
W. B. Plaine, Passenger Agent..............................25679

PETERSBURG, VA.—N. & W. Freight Station
J. C. Dellinger, Traveling Passenger Agent....................4442

RICHMOND 15, VA.—801 East Main Street
F. B. Henretta, District Passenger Agent...................2-3616

ROANOKE 3, VA.—507 South Jefferson Street
W. A. Thurman, City Ticket Agent........................3-4728

ROANOKE 17, VA.—General Office Building
A. O. English, Traveling Passenger Agent.................4-1451

WASHINGTON 5, D. C.—924 Fifteenth Street, N. W.
J. B. Ragland, General Agent........................NAtional 7856

WINSTON-SALEM 3, N. C.—105 Reynolds Building
S. E. Fort, Traveling Passenger Agent.........................7851

C. B. Perkins
General Passenger Agent
Roanoke, Va.

E. L. Repass
Passenger Traffic Manager
Roanoke, Va.

Courtesy N&W.

THE *Powhatan Arrow*

THE *Powhatan Arrow*

NEW *Luxury* EQUIPMENT

Between the **MIDWEST** and the **VIRGINIA SEASHORE**

Norfolk and Western **RAILWAY**

241

. . . wire-recorded music, assuring a wide selection of favorite melodies.

. . . quiet riding due to sound insulation . . . smooth riding on roller bearing trucks, equipped with shock absorbers, bolster roll stabilizers and other devices.

. . . inviting and hospitable dining cars, furnished with the most attractive appointments . . . dining car kitchens with frozen food lockers, electric dish washers, garbage disposal units, plate warmers, etc.

. . . unusual and striking observation-lounge-tavern cars, with rounded observation end, where passengers may enjoy music and refreshments, read, write letters, play cards and have a sweeping view from the Vista-Vue windows of the scenic panorama along the Norfolk and Western.

Yes, our new Powhatan Arrows are really brilliant trains in which every member of the Norfolk and Western Family may take genuine pride and boost to their friends and neighbors.

Now let's take a tour of the train. Starting with the sleek and powerful "600"-type locomotive, which pulls The Arrow comfortably and speedily over its 676-mile run between Norfolk and Cincinnati, we come next to the combination coach and locker car, which seats 40 passengers and includes a comfortable lounge, lockers and toilets for members of the dining car crew. The coach section of this car features a smoking room with individual chairs for eight persons.

The decorative treatment of the main coach compartment of the head end car includes ceilings of light tan and wall tones in a medium green. The window shades are a gold tone textured material and seat coverings are in a deep brown with a Chevron pattern. Floor covering is mahogany brown rubber tile under the seats, with the main aisle strip in a green marbleized tile, inlaid with cream marbleized rubber tile. The bulkheads of this car are covered in a beige corded synthetic leather and large gold tone mirrors are placed on

The Powhatan Arrow, seemingly with little effort, gliding along the New River in southwestern Virginia. In this well-known photo, 602 is heading west with the all-coach "Arrow" on the daily daylight run between Norfolk and Cincinnati. Although this train began in 1946, the lightweight steel cars shown were not acquired until late 1949. America's "last fine steam train" was unsurpassed in quality, and it will be long remembered. *Courtesy N&W.*

This is the inaugural run of the "Powhatan Arrow" on April 28, 1946. The new, crack streamliner is waiting at Roanoke to begin what would become America's "last fine steam train." In 1949, new ultra-modern streamlined cars were delivered for service providing the best possible riding comfort, luxury, and safety. *Courtesy N&W.*

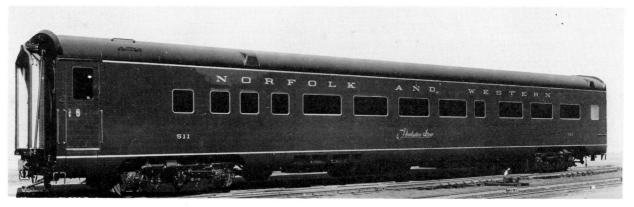

Two-compartment coach, Class P2. *Courtesy N&W.*

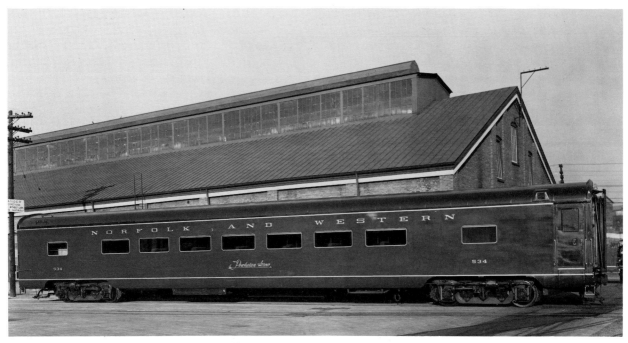

Full coach, Class P3. *Courtesy N&W.*

either side of the door openings.

The next car in the train is the two-compartment coach, with offices in the front compartment for the conductor and train passenger representative. In this coach, which seats 42 persons in one section and 24 persons in a second section, the general color scheme is tan and brown. Ceilings are light tan, walls are medium tan. The window shades, made of horizontally striped, textured material are in a slightly darker tan than the wall colors. Coach seats are upholstered in a brown Chevron pattern. The floor is covered with red marbleized tile under the seats, with mahogany brown for the aisle and passageway floors.

On either side of the main entrance doors in the two-compartment coach there are photomurals, worked out in gold tones. The murals are unusually interesting pictures of scenes along the Norfolk and Western.

In the men's and women's rooms of this car, blue is used with tan to contrast with the main body of the coach. Ceilings are light blue, walls medium blue, window shades in tan, seat coverings in blue and the floor in mahogany marbleized rubber tile.

Coming next to the full coaches in the train, each of which has a seating capacity of 58, we find the color scheme divided into three different treatments. One car is in the tan and brown color scheme, identical to the two-compartment cars.

Another is done in gray and cedar combinations, with the main coach compartment having ceilings of light gray, walls of medium gray and window shades of a two-tone cedar material. Coach seats are upholstered in a gray super needlepoint. Flooring under the seats is a gray tile and the aisle is in a cedar red rubber tiling.

The aisle coverings in each car feature an arrow design to harmonize with the name of the train.

Bulkheads in the main body of these cars feature photomurals in gold tones. On the bulkheads at the men's and women's rooms, and visible from the main compartment, are round bevelled edge gold mirrors further complementing the gold tones of the photomurals.

The remaining coach is done in a blue and brown combination, with lounge rooms in tan and blue.

The new dining cars on the train, which are identical to those which have been in service on Trains 3 and 4 for about a month, seat 36 passengers and are arranged and decorated so as to be convenient for operation and service, friendly and colorful in atmosphere.

Ceilings of the diners are a light yellow to give warmth and to enhance light reflections. A very striking effect is introduced into the dining room by the use of flesh-tinted mirrors on the backs of which are etched designs in gold. Colorful venetian blinds add to the over-all decorative scheme.

The kitchen of the dining car is a housewife's

dream come true. Unusually large, this well-arranged kitchen is an impressive study in stainless steel—used throughout for cleanliness and general appearance. Every modern facility is built in for the proper storage, preparation and serving of food. The kitchen is equipped with ranges, steam tables, broiler, electric dish washer and garbage disposal unit, frozen food lockers, and cup and plate warmers.

Lighting throughout the diner as well as all other cars of the train is fluorescent.

The most unusual and striking car on the new Powhatan Arrow is the observation-lounge-tavern car. This 85-foot car, with rounded observation end, is divided into three sections—a lounge, tavern-lounge and observation room.

Color schemes for the three sections, while related, differ in detail, making each portion of the car an interesting individual section. Venetian blinds are used throughout the car.

Featuring a lower ceiling, the lounge section is divided from the tavern-lounge section in the middle of the car by wing partitions. The ceiling is done in light apricot and the walls in gray Rift oak. Wall covering on the bulkheads is a synthetic leather in a corded design. Bulkheads at the forward end have framed illuminated transparencies of typical Norfolk and Western country and full color treatment makes them very effective.

An open bar features the tavern section and the bar front is worked out in a diamond design of red leather with a yellow leather piping. The bar top is in yellow Formica and flesh tint mirrors are used at the back bar creating interesting reflections. A photomural is used on the back bar central portion and the subject is an unusual and beautiful waterfall picture showing the Norfolk and Western territory.

The lounge section, which seats 28 passengers,

Observation–lounge–tavern car, Class P4. *Courtesy N&W.*

Observation room interior of the lounge tavern car is shown prior to installation of furniture and fixtures. This room was designed to provide passenger comfort, relaxation, and enjoyment of the scenic panorama along the N&W. A vaulted ceiling and extra wide Vista-Vue fog-proof windows were also featured. *Courtesy N&W.*

In the tavern section, passengers may enjoy refreshments and congenial companionship in colorful and luxurious surroundings. *Photo and Text Courtesy N&W.*

Shiny 604 is underway with the all-coach—no baggage cars—"Powhatan Arrow" from Roanoke on October 8, 1950. *Courtesy Charles E. Winters.*

has ceilings of light apricot, walls of medium blue and has draperies of a two-tone horizontal striped cedar rose material. Table tops at the card sections are done in a pearl type of Formica while the tables in the other sections are done in a blond maple type Formica.

The observation-lounge seats 16 persons in individual chairs, has ceilings of light apricot and walls of medium blue. The bulkhead at the forward end of the lounge has two beautiful water color paintings with the sea as the subject matter. Flesh tint mirrors are used at the pier panels and create interesting reflections in the room.

Lighting is of the direct, indirect type, giving both direct light for reading and indirect light for general illumination. This section also features a writing desk and magazine racks.

Each car in the new Powhatan Arrows is equipped for wire-recorded music which will assure passengers a wide selection of favorite melodies. Conveniently and scientifically placed speakers will bring entertainment to passengers without blare or distortion.

Multi-channel reproducers are located in the cars to offer a selection of different types of music. One channel will pipe popular or luncheon music to the various cars, while the other will provide semi-classical or dinner music. To facilitate train announcements, the system is linked with a public address system which may be controlled from the steward's locker in the dining car or from the passenger representative's office in the two compartment coach.

Eight speakers are located in the ceilings of the combination coach and locker cars, nine in the compartment coach cars, ten in the regular coaches, six in the dining car, and eight in the observation-lounge-tavern car.

All cars have been wired for possible future installation of AM and FM radio reception.

There will be no struggle against hard-to-open doors on the new Powhatan Arrow because all end doors are electro-pneumatically controlled.

A slight touch of the door plate on the outside or a slight pull of the door handle on the inside will open doors automatically. Doors will close themselves without slamming.

Door action is timed to conserve conditioned air within all cars of the train.

0-8-0

"ENERGETIC AND HARD WORKING"

Most roads did not invest heavily in new yard power. N&W, likewise, did not acquire switchers designed for that purpose until 1950. When it did, the railway found a design that was ideally suited to N&W's needs and, according to the railway, was the best investment for new power in the late steam era. Thirty practically brand new switchers were bought from C&O in 1950, and 45 more, like 224, were built in Roanoke Shops from 1951-53. *Courtesy C. W. Jernstrom.*

Yard operations was an area that was often neglected by the railroads in terms of new power. The usual practice was to take old road power and, with a minimum of modification, press these into yard service. The Norfolk and Western customarily accomplished its yard chores with a conglomeration of older power; namely, the classes X, V, W, M, Z and older Ys.

In contrast, the competing Chesapeake and Ohio had a stable full of up-to-date switchers through the years to handle the light to medium work in its yards. In 1948, the C&O, still dedicated to steam motive power, ordered thirty locomotives, based on the USRA 0-8-0s. The thirty made up the most modern switcher fleet of its type in America. These locomotives, built by Baldwin and numbered 255 through 284, had all the latest equipment and design refinements expected of any locomotive. They had cast steel locomotive frames with the cylinders cast integrally, American multiple front-end throttles, superheater, pressure and mechanical lubrication and the Baker valve gear. The tenders held twelve tons of coal and 8,000 gallons of water, and these tenders were constructed with a low profile water cistern and a high, narrow coal bunker to facilitate engine crew vision when backing. The C-16s, as they were classed on the C&O, had 200 pounds boiler pressure, a grate area of forty-seven square feet, twenty-five-inch bore by twenty-eight-inch stroke cylinders connected to fifty-two-inch drivers developing 57,200 pounds tractive effort.

In 1949 the C&O launched its dieselization program, and the operations affected first were the yards. The new Baldwin switchers were without work, and their new paint had hardly been covered with grime. With these twenty-one-month old switchers offered at a rock bottom price, here was the chance the N&W wanted to replace its aging fleet of yard power.

C&O Class C-16, new at Baldwin 1948. *Courtesy N&W.*

S1a 201, new at Roanoke Shops 1951. *Courtesy N&W.*

S1 283 with modified tender of 15 tons, 9,100 gallons capacity at Crewe 1956. *A. A. Thieme Photo, Courtesy C. T. Felstead Collection.*

The railway announced in its July 1950 *N&W Magazine,* "High tractive effort of the new switchers, combined with the relatively small driving wheels, provides for quick acceleration and contributes to more efficient yard operation. The locomotives will have a lower maintenance cost, use less fuel, and have higher availability than the locomotives which they will replace." *Photo and Text Courtesy N&W.*

Class S1

In March 1950 the thirty practically new Baldwins, redesignated as Class S1, were placed in service on the N&W. This new yard power retained the C&O's old road numbers. Immediately the new locomotives made quite a hit with the yard crews and railway officials alike. The engines were very stout and could "wheel and deal" over the yards much faster than anything that had preceded them. Very surefooted, they could push or pull long strings of cars at relatively low speeds with ease. They had extremely good acceleration—as one engineer said, the S1s had better acceleration than a modern diesel. As received, the S1s had no design faults, but some minor improvements were made as a result of operating conditions on the N&W. Some of these were a new headlight, different type of over-fire air jets, added marker lamps and a second air compressor hung on the left side. The tenders were modified to carry fifteen tons of coal and 9,100 gallons of water by extending the coal bunker higher and raising the water cistern between the water hatch and coal bunker. To get more power from these "yard horses," the N&W raised the boiler pressure to 220 pounds per square inch, thereby increasing the tractive effort to 62,932 pounds.

Before the newly acquired S1s were on the N&W property a full year, the railway realized it could use more of this power. Therefore, the Roanoke Shops started a massive building program to make this the standard N&W yard engine. From 1951 to 1953, the company shops produced forty-five new switchers, fifteen each year. The locomotives were numbered 200 through 244 (c/n 398 through 412, 420 through 449), and the last one built, 244, completed in December 1953, had the unfortunate distinction of being the last reciprocating steam locomotive built in America for a Class I railroad.

These forty-five N&W-built 0-8-0s were designated as Class S1a. The 200 through 244 were virtual copies of the older S1s. As built, all incorporated the changes applied to the 255 through 284 with one exception, all-welded tenders with an increased water capacity to 13,000 gallons. These tenders were constructed using the frames and trucks from former 12,000 gallon USRA tenders the N&W had acquired in 1919. Each of the N&W 0-8-0s weighed 247,000 pounds, and they were distinctive in that the bell was hung from a cantilever bracket at the top of the smokebox front.

Although yard power performed an unglamorous job, yard operations were costly. The

N&W received the C&O swtichers with only one cross-compound air compressor. S1s, like 274, had an additional compressor installed while the S1as were built with two pumps. *Courtesy Harold K. Vollrath.*

N&W 0-8-0s were designed mechanically with features that significantly increased availability. With mechanical lubricators on driving axles and large tenders, these modern switchers worked around the clock with a minimum of servicing. *Courtesy C. T. Felstead Collection.*

The 75 0-8-0s acquired between '50 and '53 replaced more than one engine each—140 older locomotives, mostly in yard service, were retired. To show the impact of S1s on older power, all W2 2-8-0s were retired, only a handful of 4-8-0s remained, and many Class Z 2-6-6-2s were scrapped. *Courtesy C. W. Jernstrom.*

Surefooted "yard horses" could push or pull long strings of cars with relative ease. Yard crews thought well of them for their reliability, power, and acceleration. Number 276 at Roanoke in 1956. *Courtesy N&W.*

Sturdy S1 281 is switching at Norfolk passenger terminal in March 1955. S1s were good for all types of shifting and some branch-line work, too! *Courtesy Charles E. Winters.*

Having high tractive effort and good acceleration, these small engines were ideal for yard chores, and they trimmed away costly yard expenses. No wonder the railway thought the 0-8-0s were late steam's best new power investment. *Courtesy N&W.*

A stirring sight, the "shop train" was pulled by an energetic, hard-working S1 switcher through the passenger terminal from Roanoke Shops about 4:30 PM every day in late steam. The small engine working upgrade created quite a spectacle that won the admiration of spectators. Another reason for this train's popularity was that it paraded the production of that day's work from the Roanoke Shops. This day's consist was 32 cars. Date: March 7, 1956. *Courtesy N&W.*

"Shop train" being shifted at Roanoke Shops. There were three such trains—one brought in supplies and materials at 4:00 AM; the other two hauled out empties, new and rebuilt cars, scrap and storehouse material at 4:30 PM and at midnight. Notice the tenders, cabs, and other steam locomotive parts in the background. *Courtesy N&W.*

seventy-five new yard switchers on the N&W trimmed away many costs associated with older power not ideally suited for shifting work. These new 0-8-0s replaced many classes of power in the light to medium range. S1s accomplished this because each new shifter replaced more than one of the older engines. This was possible because of the S1s greater availability and very high tractive effort for a relatively small locomotive. The S1s 62,932 pounds tractive effort was substantially greater than the classes V1, W2, M and M2s had.

As for availability, the S1s could work around the clock by taking on coal once and water twice daily. With pressure and mechanical lubrication throughout, shoppings were few and far between for these low mileage machines. With the higher availability and greater power of the new S1s, the 4-6-0s and 2-8-0s were retired, and the only 4-8-0s left were used on branch lines and work trains where the speed of road service was too great for the low-driver shifters.

Likewise, the new Class S1s forced some of the old Class Z1s into retirement, since some of these Mallets were held for heavier tasks beyond the capabilities of the old 2-8-0 and 4-8-0s. The S1s were highly regarded by both yard crews and rail-

way officials alike. One former official stated that the 0-8-0s were the best investment in steam's closing days, and that it was unfortunate that this power was not acquired earlier. The reliability of this class and its economy in operation would have given it a longer useful life had steam survived.

As dieselization started, one of the objectives was to replace the older power used in the yards. This meant that old Mallets, classes Z and Y, were sent to scrap while the S1s remained intact as a class until mid-1958. In the summer of 1958, the final decision to dieselize all operations resulted in the practically new Class S1s going to the scrap lines in large numbers. Numbers 208, 215, 217, 231, 234 and 235 were renumbered 290 through 295 in 1959 to make room for electric power taken over in the Virginian merger. Along with a few of the class Y5/Y6s, some S1s lingered on until the very end of steam. The last steam stronghold on the system was at Williamson, where the renumbered Class S1as 290 through 295 were among the final N&W steamers in service and were retired in September 1960. These engines were not big road power, yet as modern yard shifters they were little giants of the N&W Steam Era.

256

Six S1as were renumbered 290-295 to free a block of road numbers for former Virginian electrics taken over in that merger. These six 0-8-0s were the last steam switchers in service. Here 295, ex-235, is stored at Williamson in June 1960, and she will never be recalled to steam again. Her sister 291, ex-215, on May 7, 1960, was the last N&W steamer ever dispatched. *Courtesy Harold K. Vollrath.*

Part 4

Other Power

THE SEARCH FOR NEW POWER

The reciprocating steam locomotive had a relatively low overall efficiency, and any substantial improvement was extremely difficult. Therefore N&W was keenly aware of other forms of motive power, particularly those using coal for fuel. First, there was electrification to relieve a steam bottleneck; subsequently, there were proposed and experimental types in the search for new revolutionary power. N&W's last bid for a coal-burning locomotive was the steam turbine electric, which could not be perfected before arrival of the diesel. The diesel meant a major change in motive power policy, and the decision to make this was not hastily or easily made. Before dieselization, turbine electric 2300, affectionately named "Jawn Henry," has a long coal train near the Alleghany summit at Christiansburg. *Courtesy N&W.*

259

Although steam ruled supreme for many years, the N&W was not unaware of other forms of motive power. Matter of fact, the Norfolk and Western had been an early user of electric motors to hoist eastbound coal up the tortuous Elkhorn grade. As technology advanced, the company became increasingly interested in more efficient forms of power than the reciprocating steam locomotive. Even while searching for this revolutionary power, the N&W was vitally concerned in promoting the coal industry, using only the coal-burning locomotive. Hence, all proposed and experimental types were to be coal-fired machines. Even the electric motors got electricity generated by coal-burning power stations. But the antiquated electrics gave way to greatly improved, modern steam power in 1950, and the N&Ws last bid for a coal-burning locomotive turned out to be the steam turbine electric.

This last endeavor combined the best of the coal-fired and electric drive principles; however, it came a little too late to be perfected before the final rush of dieselization. As for the diesel, this represented a major departure from previous motive power policies for the N&W. The increased availability and reduced servicing of the diesel made adoption of this new form of power inevitable. Not only did the motive power change, but also the size and character of the whole railway. First, the traffic flow changed, and second, the era of modern mergers commenced. Many would say that the Norfolk and Western was reaching its maturity and coming of age—as indeed it was.

Electrics

ELECTRICS FOR THE MOUNTAINS

N&W ventured twice into using electrics as a form of motive power. First, the tough Elkhorn grade created a real bottleneck that was largely overcome by electrification. Using two classes of jack-shaft electrics, these silent workers plodded the Elkhorn for more than 35 years. LC-2 2515 is seen west of Bluefield in June 1930 with a heavy-tonnage train. N&W's second stint with electrification was taking over the old Virginian line and operating its electric system for 2½ years. Never receiving the publicity that the steam giants did, electric locomotives were a very significant part of N&W's movement of coal to port or market for years. *Courtesy N&W.*

LC1 2511 built by Baldwin and Westinghouse in 1915. *Courtesy N&W.*

LC2 2512 built by ALCO and Westinghouse in 1924. *Courtesy Harold K. Vollrath.*

As the chapter on the background history of the N&W points out, the line west of Bluefield proceeded down the west side of Flat Top Mountain which, to the railroader, is known as the Elkhorn grade. On this grade is Flat Top, or Coaldale, Tunnel, 3,015 feet in length and built in 1888. Coal traffic had increased to such an extent that by the early nineteen hundreds, this tunnel and grade had created quite a bottleneck. The N&W main line was now double tracked to facilitate traffic flow, yet at some locations, usually tunnels, the main line was single tracked. One of these was the old Flat Top Tunnel, which created probably the worst traffic congestion ever on the N&W main.

What really complicated the problem was the two percent eastbound grade! With the heavy eastbound coal drags in the days of early steam, doubleheading Ws first, then Ms and finally single Zs fought the grade, and any of these engines on the head end required a pusher. When doubleheading, the smoke and fumes in the tunnel created a real hardship on the engine crews. Of the three types that toiled in the tunnels, the Zs could haul the most tonnage but at their same plodding seven miles per hour. The single-tracked tunnel and slow trains daily tied everything up for extended periods.

What was needed was bigger power and more efficiency in the operation at hand. The Class Z 2-6-6-2 was approximately five percent efficient,

maybe slightly more. It was determined that by generating electric power and using electric motors, the railway could just about double the thermal efficiency of the Elkhorn operation. In 1913-14, the N&W began erecting a catenary from Bluefield that ultimately reached Iaeger, West Virginia, a distance of fifty-six miles. The electric operation started in early 1915, and the economies of electrification were clearly shown from the outset. These electrics did have a thermal efficiency of about ten or eleven percent, double that of steam. Likewise, the train tonnage was increased by a time and a half, roughly, with the train speed doubled to fourteen miles per hour. No longer was there a problem from the smoke and fumes nuisance in the tunnel.

This electrification project used the best equipment and technology available at the time. There was no commercial source of power available to

EL-C 235 built by GE in 1956 for Virginian as number 135. *Courtesy N&W.*

Most powerful electrics to run on N&W were the Class EL-2B. Weighing more than a million pounds, these GE locomotives were considered the most powerful continuously rated motive power ever built. Its square, brutish look and eight trucks left no doubt of her capabilities. EL-2B 227, still in Virginian garb, working at Princeton, West Virginia, in March 1960. *Courtesy N&W.*

the railway in that area then, so it constructed a power station at Bluestone, West Virginia, to furnish the 11,000 volt, 25-cycle alternating current needed. As with electric power today, there were peak periods of power usage. The N&W did two things to alleviate this: one, regenerative braking, and two, in the mid-twenties it tied in with the Virginian Railway's power station. Regenerative braking means, of course, the electric motors being used as a generator to "brake" the descending train, and the motor placing power in the catenary instead of using power. In this way, a train being braked on the descending grade could supply much of the power needed for another train proceeding up a grade. This practice of regenerative braking was first employed by the Norfolk and Western, and this concept was widely used afterward in electric railroading. It differs from the dynamic braking of the diesel by returning power to the catenary to be used elsewhere.

Did the N&W electrics replace steam entirely on the Elkhorn? No. The "juicers" were used to haul the eastbound coal, originating in the Pocahontas field, to Bluefield for shipment farther east. The electrics would haul empties west. Steam continued to haul westbound coal down the Elkhorn grade for further shipment to Williamson. Eastbound empties were returned to the pick-up points by steam, and the lighter empty trains could make a faster schedule under steam on this steep grade. In this way, steam did not slow down the electric's operation. All passenger service in the district remained under

A few hundred yards west of the Alleghany summit on the old Virginian line was Merrimac. Virginian EL-C 140 is starting down the west slope of the Alleghanies beneath N&W's Blacksburg Branch, which served the Merrimac anthracite coal mine. Today, the electrics, N&W line, and mine are all gone. *Courtesy Earl Palmer.*

Steam power hauled heavy trains at 7 mph up the Elkhorn through a single-track tunnel that created a real bottleneck. Train speed was just about doubled with electric power alleviating most of the traffic jam through Coaldale Tunnel. Number 2508 at Maybeury, West Virginia, on June 12, 1930. *Courtesy N&W.*

steam power, except for the heavy passenger trains needing assistance from an electric through the Flat Top Tunnel to the summit.

As for Virginian electrification, this railroad strung its catenary in 1925-26 between Roanoke and Mullens, West Virginia. The Virginian's power station was located at Narrows, Virginia, on the New River. With both the N&W and the Virginian stations linked, each could accommodate the other in power needs or exchanges, for there was no 25-cycle commercial power available. The Narrows station was a little more efficient than the N&Ws Bluestone station, since the Virginian station was newer in design and con-

struction. The two plants had relatively low pressure boilers and turbines, which in their day were the best available but became obsolete and increasingly inefficient as the years rolled by.

At Bluestone, the thermal efficiency in the early years was so good that two or three pounds of coal would produce one kilowatt hour. By the end of World War II, some thirty years later, these old boilers and turbines had worn so much that it took in the neighborhood of four pounds of coal per kilowatt hour. Now the thermal efficiency had dropped from about eleven to less than eight percent.

Likewise, the Y6 and Y5 locomotives had been

refined and upgraded to such an extent from the World War I engines that these modern compound Mallets were about seven percent efficient. In the meantime, studies indicated that boring a new double-tracked tunnel and relocating the Elkhorn grade with a decrease in gradient, was economically desirable. This justification for the new tunnel and grade stemmed from the increased efficiency of the N&W compound Mallets and the mounting expense of electrification on the old grade.

According to studies made, train tonnage could be doubled on each train using the Class Y6 engines on the proposed new grade. Since the old electrification system, both power station and the motors, were by then worn out, N&W electrification came to an end in 1950 with the opening of the new Elkhorn Tunnel of 7,110 feet in length.

The new reduced grade of 1.4 percent was completed in 1952. With the opening of the new tunnel, the N&W went from a steam and electric railroad to an all-steam road again. One wonders if such a change back to all-steam power had ever before taken place.

In the late forties, roughly one-third of the coal hauled by the N&W went east to the market or to the port of exportation. Soon after completion of the tunnel and the new line, the "Tidewater Coal" started increasing until today more coal goes east than west. This is a result of the exporting of more coal than ever before. Since all of the coal is mined west of Bluefield, this eastbound coal must be hauled over three mountain ranges en route to port. With the increased movement of eastbound coal, the project paid for itself much sooner than was originally anticipated.

While electrics wrestled freights on the Elkhorn, steam continued to handle passenger trains. Occasionally passenger power was not capable of pulling heavier trains, so an electric would doublehead. LC1 2506 has the honors to help out. April 1929. *Courtesy N&W.*

LC1 2508 waiting at Bluefield for its next assignment in May 1940. *Courtesy Harold K. Vollrath.*

The N&Ws second venture into electrification was a result of its merger with the Virginian Railway on December 1, 1959. The electrified Roanoke to Mullens line of the Virginian paralleled the N&W main to Bluefield most of the way. The N&W used only the most modern Virginian electrics, those built after World War II. The power station at Narrows had been modernized, but the catenary still carried the 25-cycle current—a real limitation since it required the railway to make its own power. The power station, like the old Bluestone plant, had a low pressure boiler and turbine system that was getting more and more costly to operate.

Furthermore, after the merger, loaded coal trains were moved east by the electrics on the old Virginia line from West Virginia to Roanoke, but the electrics, too, had to return empties on the same line. This slowed down traffic on the single-tracked line when opposite moving trains met. After investigating the feasibility of extending electrification into Bluefield and Roanoke over connecting N&W tracks, the engineering study indicated the catenary would have to come down for the most economical operation. It must be remembered the old Virginian electrification line was an isolated system and an isolated operation.

It just was not economically feasible with a few electric locomotives tied to one restricted line.

Class LC1

For the new N&W electrified district between Bluefield and Farm, the railway bought the electric locomotives from the Baldwin Locomotive Works in conjunction with Westinghouse. These motors were actually twenty-four box-cab units (serial numbered 1 through 24) with two cabs (successively serial numbered) semipermanently attached together to form one locomotive unit called "locomotives" hereafter.

These electric locomotives were constructed between December 1914 and December 1915, numbered 2500 through 2511, and were classed as LC1. Each cab had four motors with two jack shafts placed between two driving axles each. The jack shafts were connected to the sixty-two-inch driving wheels by rods, and each shaft was in line with the wheel axles. The frame on each cab was articulated between each set of four drivers. The gear ratio was 85:18 between the motors and the driving wheel. Each cab had two-wheel lead and trailer trucks.

Two cabs forming one locomotive unit together weighed 600,000 pounds with 540,000 being

Superlative shot has 2514 on the head end, while a close look reveals another electric behind the caboose as a pusher. December 1929, west of Bluefield. *Courtesy N&W.*

carried on the drivers. The maximum 3,211 horsepower could be developed between fourteen and twenty-eight miles per hour for a one-hour rating. At fourteen miles per hour, the continuous horsepower rating was 2,464. The continuous tractive effort was 66,000 pounds, one-hour rating 84,000 pounds, and the maximum rating 125,000 pounds for five minutes. A continuous 2,875 horsepower rating was attained at twenty-eight miles per hour, while the continuous tractive effort was 38,500 pounds. Forty-three thousand pounds was the one-hour rating at twenty-eight miles per hour.

The eight three-phase motors in each of the LC1s were capable of hauling a train of 1,625 tons on the Elkhorn grade. These locomotives performed the herculean tasks in that quiet whine-like rhythm of the electric engine. After thirty-five years of continuous hard service, they were worn out, and with the opening of the new Elkhorn Tunnel in June 1950, the "juicers" were shortly retired.

Class LC2

The electrification of the district west of Bluefield (extended to Iaeger in 1923) having been quite successful in eliminating the bottleneck at Flat Top Tunnel and in solving the problems of using steam in the restricted tunnel, it was decided that more electric power was needed for this operation. In July 1924 American Locomotive Company and Westinghouse started delivering eight box-cab units, the last two completed in

The LC2 was newer and more powerful with a tonnage rating of 2,100 tons on the Elkhorn, whereas the LC1 could handle 1,625 tons. Jack-shaft electrics used by the Virginian were almost identical to N&W's LC2, except that VGN Class EL-3A had three units semipermanently attached instead of two like the 2512. Near Bluestone, West Virginia, on December 10, 1929. *Courtesy N&W.*

Two EL-Cs show past and present owners—235 N&W and 231 VGN—in May 1961. The 12 GE EL-Cs were the last word in electric locomotive technology when built in 1956-57. *Courtesy Harold K. Vollrath.*

May 1925. These box-cab units (serial numbered 25 through 32) were hooked together semipermanently in groups of two (each two cabs in successive serial numbers) to become a locomotive unit. The four resulting locomotives were numbered 2512 through 2515, Class LC2.

The LC2 had a different look than the LC1. This new power had a box-cab and each unit had four driving wheels of sixty-two inches each. There the similarity stopped. Each cab of the LC2 had two jack shafts, each driven by one large motor. The jack shafts were placed at each end of the driving wheel base, with each shaft three inches above the driving wheel centers. From each jack shaft, a main rod was connected to the second driving wheel, while a side rod joined the first and second driver to each other. The gear ratio was 100:21.

The LC2s were shorter in length but heavier than the LC1s, with 600,000 pounds on drivers and 832,000 pounds total. Each cab had a rigid frame, and a single axle truck was on each end,

giving the LC2 a 2-8-2 + 2-8-2 wheel arrangement. Each locomotive, although shorter in length and with four less motors, was more powerful, with a tractive effort of 90,000 pounds at fourteen miles per hour and 52,500 pounds at twenty-eight miles per hour. At the slower speed, the one-hour tractive effort rating was 108,000 pounds, while the maximum accelerating effort was 162,000 pounds. At twenty-eight miles per hour, the one-hour rating was 63,000 pounds. The continuous and one-hour horsepower ratings were 3,330 and 4,000, respectively, at fourteen miles per hour, while at twenty-eight miles per hour these were increased to 3,880 and 4,660 horsepower.

The LC2s worked alongside the LC1s, but the new electrics had a higher tonnage rating of 2,100 tons. At the time of scrapping N&W electrification, the LC2s were in reasonably better shape than the older electrics. This somewhat newer electric power was scrapped in 1950.

271

As a sidelight, this VGN 2-6-6-6 Class AG was not sold for scrap until after the N&W and VGN merger. A total of 15 steamers and all of the jack-shaft electrics of the Virginian were sold after the merger. *N&W Photo, Author's Collection*

Class EL-2B

With the Virginian merger, the N&W inherited a partially electrified railroad with its electric locomotives. The N&W immediately retired the "squarehead" electrics in February 1960, but there were two classes of electrics that were as modern as could be. One of these classes was the Virginian designated Class EL-2B, which the N&W termed the same.

This class was composed of four locomotives of two units each. These 1,033,832-pound General Electric products of 1948 represented the epitome of electric motive power. The cab design was similar to that of the earlier diesel cabs, though the pantograph and four sets of two-axle trucks under each cab gave them a sleek, brutish look. Two cabs were permanently coupled together. The complete locomotive had sixteen traction motors, each axle with one. The horsepower rating at the rail was 6,800, while the continuous tractive effort was 162,000 at 15.75 miles per hour. They were considered the most powerful

continuously-rated motive power ever built. Likewise, on the "downhill" grades, the continuous braking horsepower was 7,800 to 7,900 between 18.5 and 50 miles per hour, enabling them to handle very heavy trains without the use of train air brakes.

The EL-2B were renumbered after the merger. The four two-cab units were numbered 125 through 128 for the Virginian. The cabs were serial numbered 37 through 44 with each successive group of twos being combined as the locomotive. The N&W renumbered each individual cab as follows: 37/221, 39/222, 41/223, 43/224, 38/225, 40/226, 42/227 and 44/228. The N&W number 221 was retired at Mullens in July 1961, while all the others were retired at Roanoke in June of 1962 with the demise of old Virginian (then N&W) electrification.

Class EL-C

The second Virginian electric class to be added to the N&W roster in December 1959 was the EL-Cs. Virginian numbers 130 through 141 became

N&W numbers 230 through 241 in that order. These "rectifiers" were practically new, having been built from October 1956 to February 1957 by General Electric. The term rectifier applies to this class since they used the high-voltage alternating-current from the catenary, and this current was then converted in a rectifier into direct current for the traction motors.

Each unit had two, three-axle trucks, with a traction motor on each axle. Its general outline somewhat resembled a road switcher diesel. The starting tractive effort was 99,420 pounds (twenty-five percent adhesion) while the continuous effort was 79,500 pounds (twenty percent adhesion). The horsepower rating was 3,300, and the maximum speed was set at sixty-five miles per hour. The EL-Cs were equipped for multiple-unit operation even with the EL-2Bs. They usually were worked in groups of two, which fulfilled most power requirements. Each unit weighed 394,000 pounds.

All remained in service until the scrapping of the old Virginian electric system, and all of the EL-Cs were retired in June 1962. All were subsequently sold to the former New York, New Haven and Hartford Railroad, which used only ten of these strong, silent workers in its own electric service.

Proposed and Experimental

"JAWN HENRY," LAST BID FOR A COAL-BURNING LOCOMOTIVE

The high continuous tractive effort of the electric drive was very attractive to N&W for mountain operations. Since a coal-burning locomotive was desired, the result was the coal-fired steam turbine electric as an experiment to succeed conventional steam. Testing revealed many attributes to "Jawn Henry," whose career was mostly in mountain service between Bluefield and Roanoke. Number 2300, with a muffled roar no louder than a diesel, is shown with a time freight near Arthur, Virginia, in March 1955. This photo accents "Jawn Henry's" clean lines and massiveness. *Courtesy N&W.*

The Norfolk and Western was passionately dedicated to the coal-burning locomotive. And why not? Here was a fleet of first-rate, coal-burning locomotives of the best design possible of the reciprocating steam engine. Furthermore, through modern servicing facilities and good engineering, these steam engines were competitive with other forms of power. "Competitive" here means they could equal or better efficiency indexes used in measuring a railroad's productivity. In these N&W equalled or bettered most roads of equal or greater size in the 1950s. And, too, the N&W was a coal hauling railroad that received seventy percent of its tonnage and roughly sixty-five percent of its revenue from coal! The railway wanted to keep the business and thereby promoted the coal industry.

What did the N&W "have up its sleeve" that would perpetuate the coal-burning locomotive? Four different types of locomotives, each employing a completely different approach to getting power at the rail were considered. Actually, only two of these were ever seriously contemplated to compete with the diesel: "Jawn Henry," a steam turbine electric-drive type, and the coal-fired gas turbine electric-drive. The other two never got off the drawing board. One, the steam turbine direct-drive, just would not function, as tests conducted on another road had shown. The second was a proposed 2-8-8-2 four cylinder, single expansion articulated to boost the output higher than could be obtained from the Y6s. The proposed engine died under bizarre circumstances.

Proposed Class Y7

No moss was growing under the keel of the N&W motive power design personnel in the mid-thirties. At this time, the totally new Class A 2-6-6-4 was first constructed for test as a high speed dual service articulated. Furthermore, the compound Mallet had been refined still further to be ushered in as the epitome of the Mallet, whose role was heavy mountain freight work. At this time, it was thought, a more powerful locomotive than even the A or Y6 was needed to increase the speed of the heavy freight. So what evolved was a locomotive that was to be as big as clearances would allow, and work back from there.

From early 1936 to July 1937, a 2-8-8-2 single expansion articulated was being designed. Some of the known specifications are the 112-inch maximum outside diameter boiler, the 26-by-30 inch cylinders, drivers sixty-three inches, tractive effort 153,000 pounds, grate area 130 square feet, twenty-three feet over the tubes, the firebox plus combustion chamber in front of the grate 128 inches, and the evaporative heating surface estimated at 7,100 plus square feet and superheater surface estimated around 2,900 square feet. Specialties included Baker valve gear, multibearing crossheads, roller bearings on all axles, bed castings, smokebox-mounted feedwater heater, American multiple front-in throttle and needle roller bearings on the valve rods and valve gear.

The engine would have had a look something like an "A" with sixteen drivers, except that the air and feedwater pumps were to be mounted on the smokebox front to meet clearances. It is unfortunate that this locomotive was not erected, for this engine would have been one of the most powerful locomotives ever built by any railroad. If the "A" could wheel 18,000-ton trains at speed, then maybe the Y7 could have hauled a heavier consist. We will never know, because in July 1937, federal legislation was introduced to limit train length to seventy cars, so the Y7 died on the spot. Unfortunately, the whole project was cancelled in February 1943.

Probably the proposed Y7 was not as attractive after the tests with the Class Y6 in 1937. (See chapter concerning "Improvements on the Compound Mallet.") With very significant jumps in power at higher speeds with the more economical Mallet, the single expansion Y7 would not have been a better engine for heavy mountain freight work. And the new Class A, 2-6-6-4, was more than up to the task for heavy coal trains on the flat lands. The seventy-car train limit was not imposed, but by the time that was resolved, the N&W had "off-the-shelf" steam power that was more than able to carry it to dieselization some twenty years later.

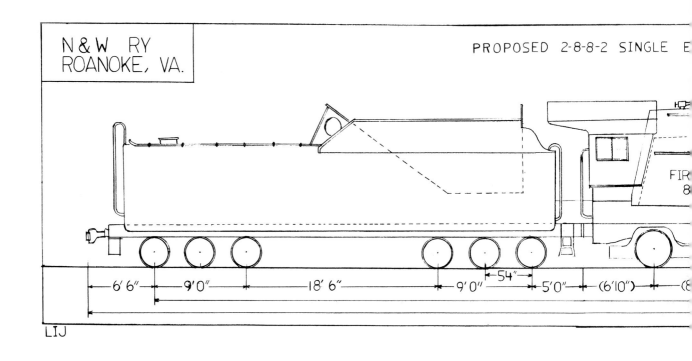

6′ 6″ 9′0″ 18′ 6″ 9′0″ 54″ 5′0″ (6′10″)

LIJ

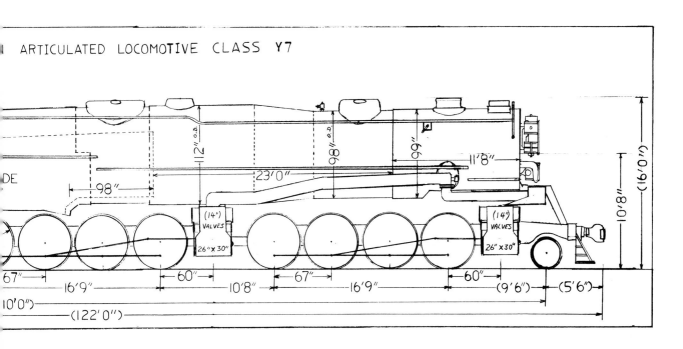

ARTICULATED LOCOMOTIVE CLASS Y7

Proposed Class Y7 2-8-8-2 single expansion articulated diagram compiled from available, detailed shop drawings. Estimated or measured dimensions are in parentheses, while all other dimensions were obtained from the design drawings. Tender is the same used on early class A and Y6s, although no information was available on the Y7's tender. *Author's Drawing.*

Proposed Steam Turbine Direct Drive

The Pennsylvania Railroad became interested in the turbine direct-drive type of locomotive as a possible competitor of the diesel. In April 1944 the "Pennsy" proposed that a locomotive be constructed by that railroad and Westinghouse that would incorporate a main frame carrying a coal bunker, operating cab and boiler; this main frame was to be carried on two four-axle driving trucks. Each truck would be driven by direct drive from a steam turbine, but the truck would be as free swinging as on a passenger car. A water tender would be attached behind the locomotive. With the two turbines, it was expected that the drawbar horsepower would be 8,100.

The N&W followed the proposed design with some interest, but the PRR scrapped the whole project probably after the failure of that road's Class S2, 6-8-6 turbine, constructed in late 1944. The 6-8-6 turbine could not match the diesel in operating economy. The N&W did not consider the direct-drive further.

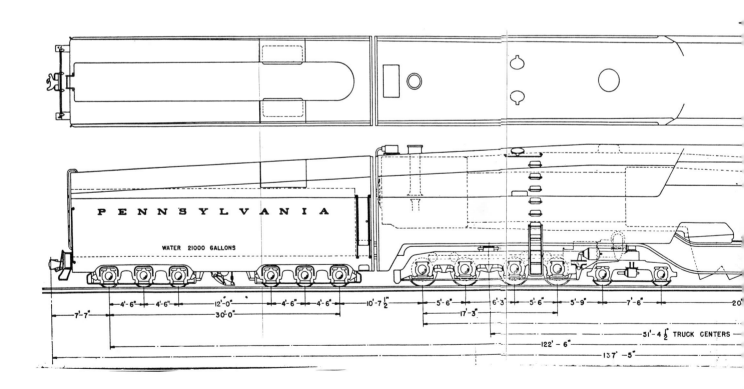

Proposed coal-fired steam turbine direct drive. *Courtesy Robert M. Pilcher Collection.*

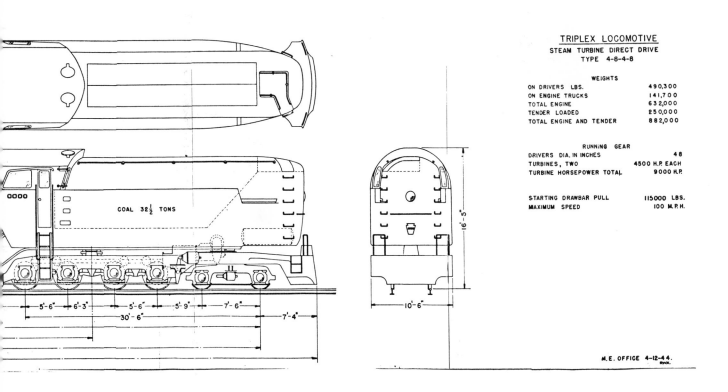

TRIPLEX LOCOMOTIVE
STEAM TURBINE DIRECT DRIVE
TYPE 4-8-4-8

WEIGHTS

ON DRIVERS LBS.	490,300
ON ENGINE TRUCKS	141,700
TOTAL ENGINE	632,000
TENDER LOADED	250,000
TOTAL ENGINE AND TENDER	882,000

RUNNING GEAR

DRIVERS DIA. IN INCHES	48
TURBINES, TWO	4500 H.P. EACH
TURBINE HORSEPOWER TOTAL	9000 H.P.
STARTING DRAWBAR PULL	115000 LBS.
MAXIMUM SPEED	100 M.P.H.

M.E. OFFICE 4-12-44.

Proposed Coal-Fired Gas Turbine

The N&W, in cooperation with five other railroads, three major coal companies and Bituminous Coal Research, worked to develop the coal-fired gas turbine, electric drive locomotive. The principle behind the gas turbine was that coal was to be fed into a crusher that would reduce the coal particles to the size of percolator-grind coffee. Next, to reduce the particles further, the percolator-size coal is blown at high pressure through a nozzle where the air pressure is suddenly released. The air trapped in the pores of coal tries to escape rapidly, thus blowing the coal particles into very small bits no larger than grains of talcum powder. This finely powdered coal is then blown into a combustion chamber where the coal ignites instantaneously, creating a large volume of hot air and gases that rotate the turbine when directed against the turbine blades.

Advantages? Experiments indicated the gas turbine had a thermal efficiency of twenty-four percent—three times that of the Y6. This new proposed locomotive would have no boiler, no water as a medium to use and few moving parts. Furthermore, it was so compact that a gas turbine locomotive half the length of a diesel of the mid-forties would deliver an equal amount of power.

In September 1946, the N&W announced that the work was proceeding well enough that orders were placed for two gas turbine locomotive plants, including generators, from two different manufacturers. The chassis and running gear orders were to be placed later. But there was one major problem with the coal-fired turbine. The fly ash from the talcum-like coal were very abrasive on the rotating turbine blades. Later, a 4,000 horsepower, coal-fired gas turbine installation was tested at the Bituminous Coal Research station at Dunkirk, New York. In the spring of 1956, the N&W was still interested in this new concept, and it was estimated that a locomotive would be built "within the next two years." The gas turbine never got further, for it is reported that the fly ash action on the blades was never remedied.

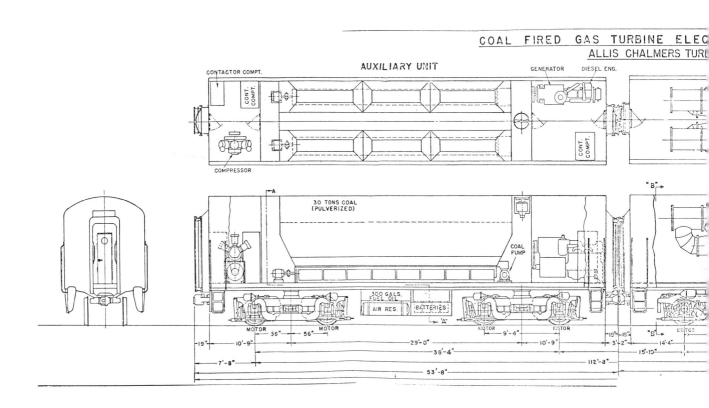

Proposed coal-fired gas turbine electric drive using Allis Chalmers turbine. General Electric also developed a turbine similar in appearance employing the same cab and chassis. *Courtesy Robert M. Pilcher Collection.*

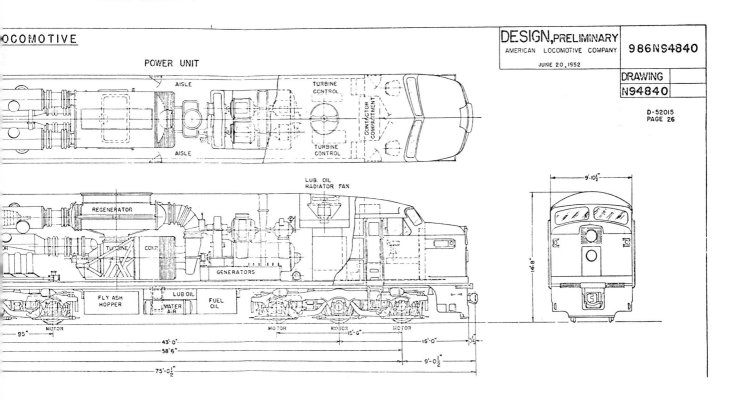

Experimental Steam Turbine Electric

The N&W announced, in its company magazine in September 1949, that it was to build a coal-burning steam turbine electric locomotive. The project was undertaken jointly by the N&W, Baldwin-Lima-Hamilton Corporation, Babcock and Wilcox Company and Westinghouse Electric Corporation. This locomotive was the N&Ws last bid to retain the coal-burning locomotive for U.S. railroad usage.

In May 1954 the new form of steam power was completed at the old Baldwin plant at Eddystone and delivered to the railway for testing. The engine had a look of its own and was unique in almost every way mechanically. The number 2300 was named "Jawn Henry," and in many ways it lived up to its name. Jawn Henry had a 6-6-6-6 wheel arrangement and was rated at 4,500 horsepower and a starting tractive effort of 175,000 pounds. The locomotive contained a watertube natural circulation boiler, the generator and turbine assembly, the twenty-ton coal bunker and the operator's cab. Behind the engine was the 22,000 gallon tender with a water softener mounted within the tank walls. The locomotive was almost 112 feet over the couplers and weighed 818,000 pounds, with each of its twelve axles having a traction motor and roller bearings.

When designing the Jawn Henry, every effort was made to use only proven equipment. The marine type watertube boiler was the biggest question mark because the fire tube boiler had proven most satisfactory for railroad use. The turbine and generator were considered the easier components to install and to meet the specification aimed for in efficiency. And to achieve the desired increase in efficiency over the conventional steam locomotive, the boiler would supply steam to the turbine at 600 pounds per square inch and at 900° F. The used steam was exhausted into the atmosphere. Shortcomings of the conventional steam engine that were discussed in the chapter on "Locomotive Engineering," were to be minimized in the new experimental locomotive by using the high pressure and high superheated steam to run the desired electric-drive.

In essence, the attempt was to combine the best of steam and electric drive characteristics. In actual work, Jawn Henry's boiler proved most successful. Even when working at full capacity it operated with a near clear stack. The generator and turbine did not meet the desired efficiency; consequently, the overall efficiency was lowered to about 11.5 percent instead of the approximate 12.1 percent expected.

What was the outcome of the Jawn Henry's tests? This great coal-burning monster had many attributes in its favor. In the mountain regions, it could perform better than the formidable Y6b. This resulted from the good characteristics of electric drive—high tractive effort at low speeds plus a wide speed range of high horsepower output. Thus, the steam turbine had a significantly higher tonnage rating than the Y6b on the tough Radford Division. The Jawn Henry once took 13,073 tons of eastbound coal over the Alleghenies with a pusher. The established rating for that run was 11,500 tons with the steam turbine, while the Y6b was rated at 10,300 gross tons.

Even though the Jawn Henry was slower from terminal to terminal, he could move more tonnage on about twenty percent less coal. The exhaust was a continuous one that was quieter than a diesel locomotive. But all of the economy gained from the boiler was lost due to the down time resulting from the feedwater pump's short life. This centrifugal pump had to be operated at a higher-than-designed-for speed to obtain the feedwater

Experimental 6-6-6-6 2300 "Jawn Henry" built by Baldwin-Lima-Hamilton Corporation in 1954. *Courtesy N&W.*

"Jawn Henry" combined the best of the coal-fired and electric-drive principles. Unfortuntely, the experiment was initiated too late to be perfected before the final rush of dieselization. New 2300 is shown at Bluefield in August 1954. *Courtesy C. W. Jernstrom.*

Much data was collected in dynamometer car tests about "Jawn Henry's" performance. Although having high tractive effort and good fuel economy, N&W's steam turbine electric lost out in the shops. It is unfortunate that its shortcomings could not be overcome because coal, the fuel for 2300, is America's most abundant source of energy. *Courtesy N&W.*

N&W was prepared to buy 20 of the impressive looking turbine electrics if other roads had bought any, thus reducing initial costs. But this was not forthcoming, and one reason for 2300's demise was the cost penalty of operating one locomotive requiring separate service, maintenance, and handling. "Jawn Henry" is pulling a coal drag eastbound past Christiansburg station on the way to Roanoke. *Courtesy C. W. Jernstrom.*

rates necessary. Since it required a shopping to replace the pump, it was necessary to use the pump until it destroyed itself before the shopping.

The steam turbine electric was automatic in every respect on the boiler controls. Steam flow, steam pressure, air flow and drum water levels were controlled by a device that had been a similar controller on the *USS Nautilus,* America's first atomic submarine. All the fireman had to do was to turn one little knob to select the pressure wanted. The controls then maintained that pressure regardless of the load demand. However, this complex control equipment required constant maintenance and repair. When this equipment malfunctioned, it was extremely difficult for the engineer to operate the boiler at peak efficiency.

N&W publicized the Jawn Henry extensively to encourage other railroads to purchase similar types of locomotives. The initial cost was in the range of $800,000, but it was hoped that unit production costs would be $600,000 or less. Had the costs been under $600,000, the new form of power would have been comparable to the conventional steam locomotive in economy gained. Furthermore, the N&W was prepared to buy a total of twenty such locomotives if the unit cost had been lower. Other railroads did not purchase any, and so Jawn Henry died at the end of 1957 as an experiment.

What killed this steam turbine electric? High initial costs, lack of significant increase in thermal efficiency, the feedwater pump and complexity of controls and the cost penalty of operating and maintaining one unit. If Jawn Henry had been built twenty years earlier, these shortcomings could have been overcome. Basically, the performance was good, but just too late for the diesel competition. It is too bad, for coal is America's most abundant fuel.

Diesels

THE DIESEL DECISION

N&W made a difficult decision to begin dieselization in 1955, which meant a major change in motive power policy. With an outstanding reservoir of personnel and extensive facilities to design, build, and maintain steam power, this decision was not easy. By January 1960, the final diesels were purchased and N&W's fleet of 466 "second-generation" diesels was hailed as the most modern roster in U.S. railroading. This foursome of modern GP-9/18s are returning empties to the coalfields in August 1960 along New River near Narrows, Virginia. *Courtesy N&W.*

ALCO RS-3 307 built in 1956. Original numbers of RS-3 300-307 were 99-92, respectively. Renumbered in 1956. *Courtesy N&W.*

ALCO RS-11 322 built in 1956. *Courtesy N&W.*

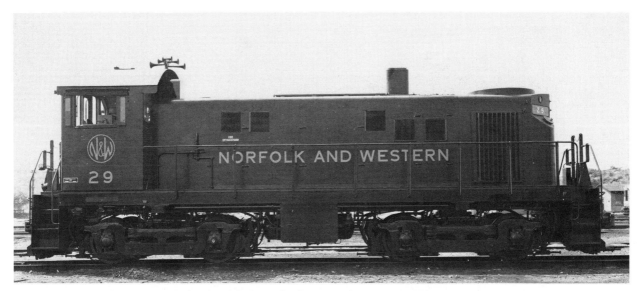

ALCO T-6 29 built in 1959. *Courtesy N&W.*

EMD GP-9 713 built in 1955. Original numbers of 710-713 were 10-13, respectively. Renumbered in 1956. *Courtesy N&W.*

EMD GP-9 for passenger service, built in 1958. *Courtesy N&W.*

EMD GP-18 922 built in 1959. *Courtesy N&W.*

EMD GP-30 528 built in 1962. *Courtesy N&W.*

EMD GP-35 204 built in 1963. *Courtesy N&W.*

Fairbanks Morse H16-44 126, former VGN 26, built in 1954. *Courtesy N&W.*

Fairbanks Morse H24-66 174, former VGN 74, built in 1957. *Courtesy N&W.*

The Changing N&W

Most are very aware of the changing motive power policy that took place in the N&W Railway during the mid-fifties. Some evidences of this change were clear-cut and easily seen. The N&W was about to emerge from a big, little railroad into a super railroad of increased dimensions and manifold capacities.

What started this change? Basically, moving more coal east than west! Before 1956 the railway's greatest revenue commodity, coal, was mostly westbound through the Columbus, Ohio, gateway to Great Lakes and western U.S. markets. In 1956-1957, a rising demand in Western Europe for metallurgical coal found the N&W hauling more tonnage to the east coast than the western destinations.

On eastbound hauls the Norfolk and Western freights had to cross three mountains on very heavy grades. With the increased tonnage, operating expenses rose significantly. The resulting higher operating costs forced the railway to do everything possible to hold down coal hauling rates in order to retain this very desirable coal traffic. For the Norfolk and Western, these circumstances required: dieselization, easier eastbound ruling gradients, and more merchandise revenues.

The N&W bought four EMD GP-9s and four ALCO RS-3s in the fall of 1955 to get a feel for what type of power to buy in large quantities when dieselization occurred. In the spring of 1956 the railway announced that it had ordered or bought a total of eighty-three diesels to eliminate essentially the Durham, Cincinnati and Shenandoah districts' steam operations.

Purchases of GP-9s and a switch to ALCO's RS-11s continued at a steady pace until 198 units were on hand or on order in April 1958. The diesel test of 1952 and the experiment with Jawn Henry had shown the electric drive locomotives to be superior to conventional steam power in mountain operations. Likewise, spread-out N&W steam terminals were a very costly operation. Thus, the aforementioned districts with their many steep ruling grades and the farflung steam terminals at Durham, Clare, Hagerstown, and Winston-Salem, necessitated early dieselization

N&W achieved very high utilization of its diesels, especially after the Virginian merger. These one year old GP-9s are rolling up gross ton-miles near Sargents, Ohio, in May 1960. *Courtesy N&W.*

N&W's first unit coal train from Roanoke to South Amboy, New Jersey, was in August 1962. These five GPs are shown pulling that first train on the hilly Shenandoah Valley line as the fully loaded train crosses James River at Natural Bridge Station. *Courtesy N&W.*

Five diesel "workhorses" with time freight 85 west of Roanoke near Singer, Virginia. Five B-B diesel units were the maximum worked together since that was the maximum safe load for the 300,000 pound capacity couplers. *Courtesy N&W.*

in these areas. Furthermore, the diesel made heavy inroads into the Radford Division and on the Elkhorn grade by 1958. The coming of the diesel was inevitable because of its economy, its desirable traits on heavy grades and the expensive steam terminals remote from the concentration of steam power.

In early summer 1958, N&W president Stuart T. Saunders announced that total dieselization was to be accomplished in 1960. By January 1960 the final 268 diesels were purchased, and this fleet of 466 "second-generation" diesels was

hailed as the most modern roster in U.S. railroading. And particularly noteworthy, the N&W operated its diesel fleet just as professionally as it had the railway's legendary steam locomotives.

All of the road units were B-B wheel arrangement equipped for multi-unit operation with dynamic braking and dual cab controls. The four-axle unit was bought and used exclusively right up to the time of the big merger in 1964, except for twenty-five Fairbanks-Morse H24-66 Trainmasters acquired through the Virginian merger in 1959. By buying only four-axle diesels, one type of locomotive could be used in heavy switching, passenger and freight service.

Since the N&W dieselized faster than any other major U.S. railroad (just over four years), it essentially had one type of locomotive, built by two builders, suitable for all operations. And these locomotives did have the highest potential availability factor possible—a factor the railway employed to the maximum. Especially after the Virginian merger, the N&W achieved an amazing utilization record even for the diesel.

The N&W acquired sixty-three Virginian diesels that were retained for service. Its 529 total units performed all the duties of the expanded system until additional units were added because of increased traffic and the scrapping of the old Virginian electrification. At the time of the 1964 merger, the N&W had on hand some 643 diesel units.

With the dieselization program going full tilt in the late fifties, the N&W next sought a way to ease eastbound ruling grades. Bear in mind that the Virginian Railway had been constructed in

the early 1900s for the sole purpose of transporting coal from West Virginia mines to the port of Norfolk. Smallest of the Pocahontas coal haulers, the Virginian was not as interested in merchandise and passenger traffic, so the routing of the railroad through the major communities was foregone except for engine terminals.

The Virginian's goal was to haul coal to port as cheaply as possible, and that was by using the easiest grades possible. Coursing east over the Alleghenies, the Virginian route was 0.6 percent as opposed to the N&Ws one percent. East of Roanoke, the Virginian tracks followed the near level Roanoke River through the Blue Ridge Mountains, whereas the N&W had to fight a steady 1.2 percent. The N&Ws Allegheny and Blue Ridge grades both required pushers. What did the Virginian have to gain from an N&W merger? The Virginian's coal reserves would last only about seventy years more, since the N&W, C&O and NYC blocked any expansion hopes.

After approval by the stockholders of both companies and by the ICC, the two railways were

New passenger power for "Santa Claus Special" at Roanoke Station on December 6, 1958. Hotel Roanoke is at far left, while stack of Roanoke Shops is seen beyond. *Courtesy N&W.*

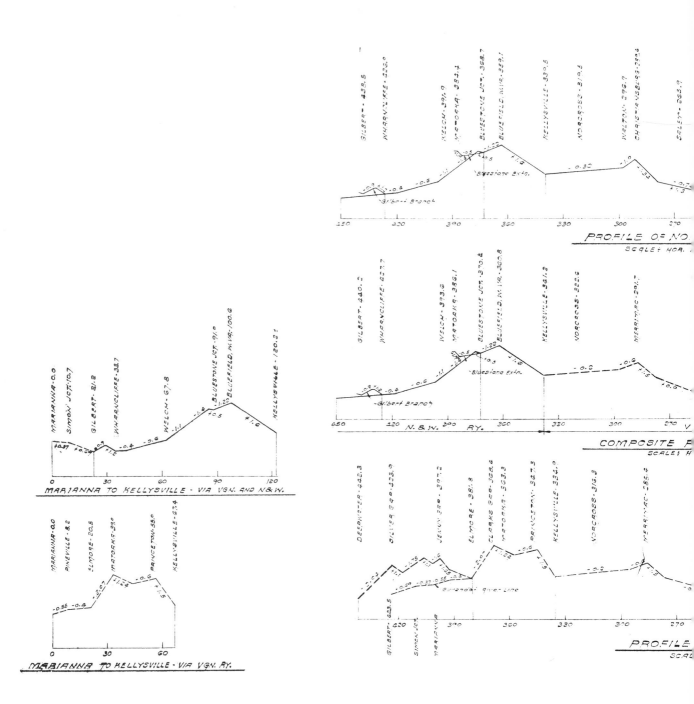

Composite profile of N&W and Virginian railways. Compare this profile with those of the premerger N&W and VGN. *Courtesy N&W.*

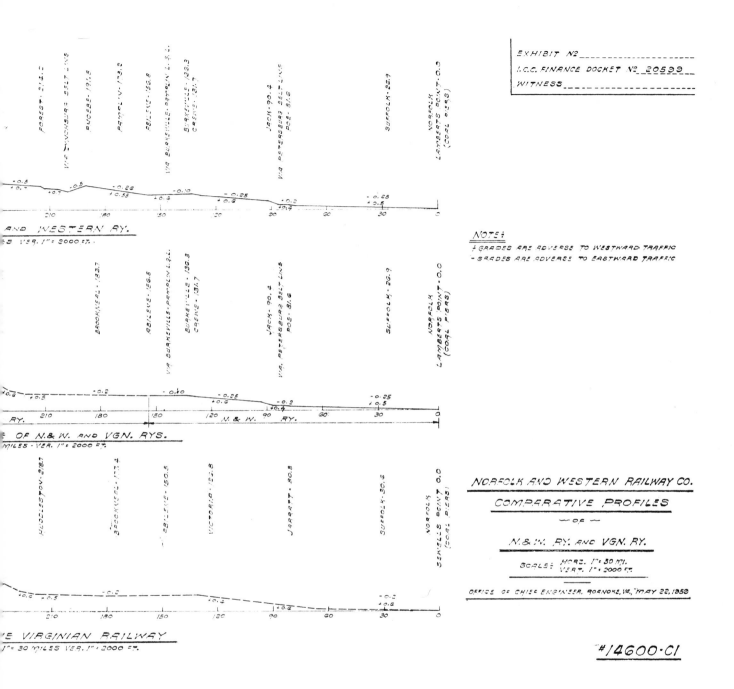

NOTE:
+ GRADES ARE ADVERSE TO WESTWARD TRAFFIC
- GRADES ARE ADVERSE TO EASTWARD TRAFFIC

NORFOLK AND WESTERN RAILWAY CO.

COMPARATIVE PROFILES

— OF —

N.&W. RY. AND VGN. RY.

SCALE: HORZ. 1"=30 MI.
VERT. 1"=2000 FT.

OFFICE OF CHIEF ENGINEER, ROANOKE, VA., MAY 22, 1958

#14600-CI

297

Before the Virginian merger, diesel era eastbound coal trains (with pusher) moved over the Blue Ridge to the eastern slope where more loads were added for the continuing trip east to tidewater. GP-9s 710-713, N&W's first four EMD diesels, are wrestling a coal drag upgrade on the Blue Ridge east of Bonsack, Virginia, in May 1958. *Courtesy N&W.*

merged on December 1, 1959, into one—the Norfolk and Western Railway Company. The new railway, to make the merger work and effect the desired savings, constructed six connections between the two former main lines. The two most important of these were at Kellysville, West Virginia, and at Abilene, Virginia. The former enabled eastbound coal trains from Bluefield to switch over to the old Virginian main for the easier grade eastward, while the latter allowed the coal trains to return to the old N&W main for the final run to Norfolk.

To effect greater efficiency from the merger, the former Virginian coal pier at Sewalls Point was closed and a new coal pier constructed at Lamberts Point; centralized traffic control was expanded to encompass a total of 1,534 track miles, 46.7 percent of the system; and 264 miles of track including 106 miles of former N&W double-tracked main line was removed. The only remaining double-track main east of Bluefield is

Walton through Roanoke to Montvale east of the Blue Ridge, and between Abilene and Norfolk. The former N&W helper grade from Walton to Christiansburg on the Allegheny climb had once been triple-tracked.

Although the merger produced many savings, the former Virginian electrification created a motive power bottleneck on the old Virginian line west from Roanoke. The electrics were a superior breed, but they were tied to the catenary. The electric motors hauled coal east, but it was necessary to pull empties west with them also. After considering extending electrification into Bluefield and to the old N&W yard in Roanoke from the Virginian, a management study indicated that diesels would be the more profitable operation.

In June 1962 the old Virginian catenary was inactivated. The Virginian line from Kellysville to Abilene became one of the most efficient, heavy duty lines in the world. That appraisal rests not on the number of trains but in number of loads and gross ton-miles per freight train-hour (one of the most basic of all railroad efficiency indexes). Empty cars for the mines returned westward over the former N&W main line. One of the most compelling reasons for the N&W and VGN merger had been the economy to be gained with 200-car coal trains moving east on the old Virginian. With the catenary pulled down, the maximum operating efficiency could be gained from the merger. And it was! For the mountain operations, five diesel units were worked as one locomotive, five units being the maximum safe load for the 300,000 pounds capacity couplers.

How could a predominantly coal road such as the N&W gain a larger portion of its revenues from merchandise freight? By decreasing running time of the merchandise hotshots, and promoting industry to move to the N&W region. The Norfolk and Western believed that anything moving more than 100 miles could be moved for less by rail, if given rate-making freedom. Piggybacking was started between the PRR at Hagerstown and the SR at Bristol, an attempt to compete with the truck. The N&W also hired a firm to survey for desirable industrial sites in the railway's region, and the research soon paid for itself. In the early sixties, the movement of automobile rack cars in large numbers began. But all of these undertakings were within the N&W and VGN area primarily between the Ohio River Valley and the eastern seaboard.

As a long range plan to expand the merchandise revenue base, in the early sixties the Norfolk and Western completed arrangements to merge with the Nickel Plate Road, to lease the Wabash and to buy the PRR's Sandusky line as a connecting link. This move would open up the midwestern market to the N&W in a predominately merchandise-hauling region. Thus, the railway would be more stable and more diversified. In October 1964 the proposed merger went through, and the

Four new GP-30s have a long string of hoppers in tow on December 17, 1962. The 44 2,250 horsepower GP-30s were acquired in mid-1962 to replace the retired Virginian electrification and to meet increased traffic demands. *Courtesy N&W.*

Crossing Blackwater River bridge on the Shenandoah Division south of Roanoke in August 1963. This Winston Salem line has a saw-tooth profile that required the power of a Y6 in the days of steam. This freight is not lacking power, with four diesels totaling some 7,000 horsepower. *Courtesy N&W.*

N&W was no longer just a regional coal hauler but a diversified road with a large volume of merchandise traffic. King Coal still wore the crown, however, as the road's largest single source of revenue.

The N&W changed far more than merely locomotives from 1955 onward. The changes were necessary due to the times, and the N&W, being a progressive carrier, forged ahead with innovations. The Virginian merger was the first merger of two major U.S. railroads in this century. Changes made in quest of more merchandise traffic could but strengthen the railway further to compete with other modes of transportation.

ALCO Freight Diesels

The N&W bought eight diesels initially, four of which were ALCO RS-3s. The railway wanted to try out ALCO products and one other maker's road units to get a feel for what type and make to buy in quantity. The ALCO RS-3s, numbers 99 through 96, were acquired in October and November 1955 and put to work on the Durham line. These B-B units were rated at 1,600 horsepower, weighed 247,000 pounds and could develop 60,000 pounds starting tractive effort. Like all road diesels bought by the N&W, they had dual cab controls, were equipped for multi-unit operation and dynamic braking. After the first four were broken in, four more RS-3s, identical to the first four, were purchased, numbered 95 through 92, and delivered in February 1956. The RS-3s had a twelve-cylinder, four-cycle 244-series diesel engine. Gear ratio from the traction motors to the forty-inch wheels was 74:18. The 99 through 92 were renumbered 300 through 307 in the spring of 1956.

Fairbanks Morse Trainmasters rolling through West Virginia in 1958. These Virginian 2,400 horse-power units were bought for mountain work, and befittingly they spent most of their careers in "hill" settings such as this. *Courtesy N&W.*

Brand new passenger GP-9s are whisking train 4 "Pocahontas" over the road at Montvale, Virginia, in December 1958. In late 1958, 16 new tuscan red GP-9s, along with six older passenger diesels, took over all steam passenger operations. All streamlined K2s were retired, and those beautiful Js were relegated to freight work to run out serviceable miles. *Courtesy N&W.*

ALCO introduced the RS-11 with its 1,800 horsepower rating as a replacement for the RS-3 line. The N&W began receiving the RS-11s in March 1956. This type was to be the standard ALCO diesel from then until just before the 1964 merger. The RS-11s had a new 251-series diesel engine of twelve cylinders. Wheels, tractive effort, weight and gear ratio were the same as the RS-3s. But the wheel base was one foot longer than the earlier model (forty feet, four inches), the hood higher and with a new look.

During the era of the change to dieselization, the N&W bought a large number of the RS-11s. Numbers 308 through 324 were acquired in 1956, 325 through 364 arrived on the property in 1957, and 365 through 400 were obtained between November 1958 and June 1959 in the final push to dieselize fully. With a slight upswing in traffic in the early sixties, numbers 401 through 406, RS-11s, were acquired in June 1961, and numbers 407 through 412, RS-36s, were added to the roster in March 1962. The RS-36s were a newer 1,800 horsepower version of the ALCO road switcher line, and these represented the last purchase of ALCO power prior to the 1964 merger.

Numbers 301, 302 and 304 were retired at Roanoke on July 17, 1964. All of the 110 remaining ALCO diesels were on hand and were rolling up ton-miles at the time of the merger. All were used interchangeably with other makes of diesel freight power.

EMD Freight Diesels

When the first eight diesels were bought in the fall of 1955, the first four were EMD GP-9s delivered in September. These new diesels were assigned to work on the Durham line along with the other four newcomers (all ALCO's). This quartet of GP-9s, numbered 10 through 13, headed a long parade of diesel workhorses, the end of which is not now in sight. The GP-9s had a sixteen-cylinder, two-cycle, 1,750 horsepower diesel engine of the 567-series. The weight of each locomotive unit in working order was 247,000 pounds. Its starting tractive effort was 60,000 pounds with a gear ratio of 62:15. As with all road diesels, these GP-9s were equipped with dual cab controls and dynamic brakes and were capable of multiple-unit operation. These first four GP-9s were renumbered 710 through 713 in late spring 1956.

N&W operated its diesel fleet just as professionally as it had the road's legendary steam locomotives. All diesel road units had B-B wheel arrangements, equipped for MU operation with dynamic braking and dual cab controls. Number 638 leads a time freight along New River near Narrows, Virginia, in April 1959. *Courtesy N&W.*

After the initial testing and evaluation of the four EMDs, the first large order for such new power went to ALCO. But starting in July 1956, one order after another was placed with EMD for more and more of the GP-9s. The La Grange products were delivered so fast over the next three years it appeared that EMD was stamping out each unit. Numbers 714 through 746 were acquired in 1956, then 747 through 812 rolled on the N&W property during 1957. In February 1957

the 762 through 767 arrived. Sporting steam generators, high speed trucks, and a tuscan red color scheme, they were pressed into passenger service.

The passenger GP-9s were identical mechanically to all other GP-9s except for the 60:17 gear ratio. One hundred and three GP-9s were on hand when the final decision to dieselize was made. From March 1958 through October 1959, numbers 813 through 914 and 620 through 699 were

Perhaps the greatest single plus for diesels was its electric drive. On the Elkhorn in the 1952 steam vs diesel test, diesels were very attractive because of high tractive effort at low speed and high horsepower output over a wide speed range. Five ALCO's moving heavy tonnage on the Elkhorn west of the new tunnel in February 1959. *Courtesy N&W.*

added to the N&W roster, which spelled doom to the remaining modern steam power. More passenger GP-9s were acquired in November and December 1958. This new passenger power was numbered 506 through 521, and they were just like the six earlier engines. The numbers 762 through 767, the earlier passenger power, were renumbered 500 through 505 between February 1959 and January 1960.

EMD switched to the GP-18, an upgraded GP-9 with 1,800 horsepower, as the general purpose road switcher. The N&W took delivery of twenty-four of the new GP-18s in December 1959 and January 1960. They were numbered 915 through 938, and bore the distinction of being the last die-

sel power purchased to replace all steam power then in existence on the N&W.

With the upturn of the economy in the early sixties, the N&W felt it needed yet more power, and bought twenty-four more GP-18s from June to September 1961, numbered 939 through 962. The 2,250 horsepower GP-30s soon replaced the GP-18 in the EMD line of general purpose road locomotives. The N&W received forty-four new GP-30s numbered 522 through 565 in July and August 1962. These GP-30s were bought to meet the demands from increased traffic and to replace the Virginian electrics that had been retired in June 1962.

This latest diesel power permitted the N&W to

Virginian was a big user of Fairbanks Morse Trainmasters—one of the first high horsepower diesels on the market. Trainmasters, like 174 and 169, rolled up ton-miles for years for its new owners. Christiansburg, July 1961. *Courtesy Harold K. Vollrath.*

Along with GP-9s, ALCO RS-11s were part of the diesel fleet mainstay that replaced steam. RS-11 396 was delivered in May 1959 and was among the last ALCO's received in the rapid push to dieselize all N&W operations. *Courtesy Harold K. Vollrath.*

When N&W announced in 1958 it was dieselizing all remaining steam operations, the largest single diesel order ever with EMD to that date was placed. The last diesel unit received from that 192-unit order was GP-18 938 in January 1960, thus signalling the end of the steam era N&W. Here 938 is beside the former modern steam servicing facility at Radford, Virginia, one month after delivery. *Courtesy Harold K. Vollrath.*

take full advantage of the recent Virginian merger and the easier Virginian eastbound grades for the 200-car coal trains. Again EMD changed its line and this time the N&W acquired the new GP-35, rated at 2,500 horsepower. Forty new GP-35s rolled onto the N&W property between December 1963 and April 1964, and were numbered 200 through 239. This was the last EMD diesel power purchased by the N&W prior to the 1964 merger. At the time of the merger, there were 411 EMD products busily at work in freight service.

EMD freight diesels are very popular with N&W crews and officials alike. From a mechanical point, they were very well engineered locomotives with the two-cycle V-16 engines. The crews speak well of them and also have most favorable comments for the old GP-9s of the pre-1964 years.

EMD Passenger Diesels

For passenger work, the railway used the standard freight diesel, modified with a steam generator, and high speed trucks. Mechanically, there were no other changes except for the 60:17 gear ratio. The color scheme was tuscan red with yellow lettering and numbering.

The first set of six passenger GP-9s were numbers 762 through 767 and were delivered in February 1957. These six soon took over the passenger runs that the streamlined 4-8-2 steam greyhounds had been the masters of—such runs as the Shenandoah Valley line's passenger service. In late 1958, sixteen more passenger GP-9s, numbered 506 through 521, were bought. They were identical to the first six. The 762 through 767 were renumbered 500 through 505, respectively, from February 1959 to January 1960. All twenty-two passenger GP-9s, with steam generator added, were numbered 500 through 521, inclusively. All were engaged in passenger service in 1964.

ALCO Yard Diesels

With the decision to dieselize the entire N&W motive power roster in 1958, the B-B road switcher was THE locomotive of versatility. It could be used in heavy yard work, freight and passenger operations. The large road switcher units were too expensive to buy and to operate for the lighter yard duties. Consequently, the railway

bought forty ALCO yard switchers for this purpose, designated T-6s, which were delivered between February and October 1959. The T-6 is rated at 1,000 horsepower; the railway numbered them 10 through 49. These yard engines bumped most of the 0-8-0 steam yard engines onto the rip track, except for a few diehards retained on the yards in the coalfields.

Two of this class, numbers 40 and 41, were sold to the Chesapeake Western Railroad, one in July 1963, the other in October 1964. The remaining thirty-eight were pushing and pulling mightily about the various yards at the time of the 1964 merger.

Two GP-9s are coming off the main line from Bluefield onto the Bristol line at Walton with a train heading for Radford. In the days of steam, trains between Radford and Bluefield were called the "Short Run." *Courtesy Earl Palmer.*

These diesel "growlers" have just descended the west Alleghany slope and are turning onto the Bristol line at Walton. The tracks curving left behind BH Tower are the main line to Bluefield. *Courtesy Earl Palmer.*

Fairbanks-Morse Freight Diesels

When the Virginian merged into the N&W system, the N&W acquired a new, relatively large fleet of freight diesels. These had been used on the Virginian's nonelectrified portions and mine runs. That railroad had dieselized most of its steam operations during 1954-55, though it was not until 1957 that the final diesel orders signaled the farewell of Virginian steam.

The first Virginian diesels were Fairbanks-Morse H24-66 Trainmasters. These six-axle locomotives were rated at 2,400 horsepower and 98,625 pounds starting tractive effort. Trainmasters were used to replace the aging Mallets in the coalfields for mine runs. The new power, nineteen in all, was numbered 50 through 68 and was delivered between March and May 1954.

During May and June 1957, six more Trainmasters were bought and were numbered 69 through 74. The six were practically identical to the first group, except for 525 pounds more tractive effort, and 2,100 pounds more weight. In 1960, the N&W renumbered the old Virginian 50 through 74 to 150 through 174. N&W 150 through 174 Trainmasters were all intact as a class at the time of the big expansion in 1964. The Virginian classed the Trainmasters as DE-RS, while the N&W used the F-M designation of H24-66.

In dieselizing its road operations between Roanoke and Norfolk, the Virginian again chose Fairbanks-Morse, but this time it went with the four-axle H16-44, rated at 1,600 horsepower. Units numbered 10 through 39 rolled onto the Virginian rails from June 1954 through October 1955. The final ten, numbered 40 through 49, were built in November-December 1956 and October 1957. The DE-Ss, the Virginian classification for the four-axle F-Ms, weighed about 262,200 pounds and developed roughly 65,500 pounds tractive effort. Weights and tractive effort varied slightly between the various locomotives. The Virginian normally used two units for the coal drags out of Roanoke, although occasionally it used more.

Locomotives 23 and 28 were retired in April 1957 as a result of a wreck. Two units, numbers 48 and 49, were delivered by the builder in October 1957, to replace the two retired locomotives. After the N&W and VGN merger, the Virginian 10 through 22, 24 through 27 and 29 through 49 were renumbered to become N&W numbers 110 through 122, 124 through 127 and 129 through 149. The N&W designated the old DE-Ss as the H16-44. Number 124 was retired in October 1962 after a wreck and was never rebuilt. The remaining thirty-seven H16-44s were hard at work at the 1964 merger. The N&W never did look upon the Fairbanks-Morse diesels with great favor from a maintenance standpoint, because the opposed-piston engine had two crankshafts that required more maintenance than the single-shaft diesels from other builders.

One other Virginian diesel made it to the N&W. This was a forty-four-ton ALCO-GE model of 380 horsepower, and rated at 22,100 pounds starting tractive effort. This 88,400 pound engine, number six, had been built in 1941 by GE, and the Virginian had bought it second-hand in 1954 for light switching duties at Suffolk. The N&W had no need for the little switcher, and it was retired and sold at Lamberts Point, Norfolk, in May 1960.

Epilogue

When one delves into the past, a longing for the "good ole days back when" takes hold. As for this author, he invariably reminisces about those days when the mighty N&W steam locomotives were hard at work. What a thrill it would be to return to the steep grades of Christiansburg Mountain for the sight and sounds of a Y6 in heavy freight service, or to see again one of those beautiful Js accelerating through the mountains. These are, regrettably, wishes that probably will never come true. To the author this is a misfortune. It is not that the new technology has not created something better, for it definitely has, but that the superior N&W steam power might someday fade from memory.

The appealing, even romantic, aspects of steam railroading gave to each railroad its own individual mark and characteristics, which created a certain pride within each company. During the steam era the Norfolk and Western employees had a pride in their railroad that many of them were certain was second to none. This pride was generated not simply by having great steam locomotives, but also because the N&W built its power according to its own superior designs, and built them in quantity for many years.

In addition, these steam locomotives' productivity and performance were such that the railway surpassed the average performance of U.S. railroads even during the decade of change to dieselization. In fact, the entire N&W Railway was operated in a manner consistent with its then motto, "Precision Transportation." To live in N&W "territory" and be associated with the railway personnel fostered a strong pride within the railway family and an even sharper pride in the railway's operating performance.

What contribution did the N&Ws modern steam locomotives make toward this superior operating performance? The real proof that their contribution was great was in the day-to-day operation. Of all that has been said so far about these superb machines, it was in this area that they were probably the most outstanding. Steam locomotive maintenance and servicing was a constant necessity, of course, but the modern N&W locomotives were so designed that these tasks could be accomplished very efficiently, consider-

ing the technology of that era. Each of the enginemen who operated this steam power had his own prime favorite class or type, yet every one of them were enthusiastic about N&W power. These locomotives, like any machine, were not infallible, for they had their peculiarities and idiosyncracies, yet the locomotive engineers and firemen could coax every possible pound of work from them. To the enginemen, these locomotives were "the finest steam engines ever built!" These men were convinced of this and were quick to say so. Certainly N&W steam power contributed much to the operating pride and efficiency of the "Precision Transportation" system.

The N&W was the last major U.S. railroad to employ steam power in quantity. When the last steam giant dropped its fire in Williamson, West Virginia, in May 1960, it completed a 122-year era of steam on the Norfolk and Western. But this was the start of a new era on this mighty railroad. This new era began with the Virginian merger in late 1959 that made the N&W a super coal hauler. Less than five years later, in 1964, the Norfolk and Western was expanded many fold, becoming one of the major railway systems of the East, both in size and in tonnage hauled.

This new system was the result of the consolidation of six railroads on October 16, 1964. These railroads were the Norfolk and Western (which included the former Virginian Railway), the former Nickel Plate, Wabash, the Akron, Canton and Youngstown (operated as a subsidiary), the Pittsburgh and West Virginia, and purchase of the Sandusky line of the former Pennsylvania Railroad. The eastern terminus was still the port of Norfolk while this new east-west route terminated at the cities of Omaha, Nebraska, and Kansas City, Missouri, in the West. Very importantly, the port of Norfolk was now linked by one railroad system to St. Louis, Chicago, Cleveland, Buffalo, Toledo and Pittsburgh in addition to those cities served by the old N&W.

Like the Norfolk and Western, the Wabash and the Nickel Plate were each formed from a series of mergers during the formative years of the American rail industry. A forerunner of the former Wabash got its start in 1838 in Illinois. By 1870 the basic route was established between Toledo

What a thrill it would be to see again one of those beautiful Js accelerating through the mountains. This is, regrettably, a wish that probably will never come true. *Courtesy Earl Palmer.*

The appealing, even romantic, aspects of steam railroading created a certain pride within each company. During the steam era, Norfolk and Western employees had a pride in their railroading that many of them were certain was second to none. *Courtesy Earl Palmer.*

and the state of Iowa. By 1881, Chicago and Detroit were included in that rail route. The late-comer Nickel Plate was organized in 1881 as the New York, Chicago, and St. Louis. Initially, the road operated between Buffalo and Chicago. It never served New York, its name notwithstanding, and only reached St. Louis in 1922 through the absorption of two other railroads. After undergoing a series of changes in ownership, the Nickel Plate became an independent company in 1947 when it was relinquished from the control of the C&O.

Today the Norfolk and Western system provides rail service to communities and shippers in fifteen states and one Canadian province over 7,500 route miles of track. Furthermore, the N&W is still one of the largest originators of

bituminous coal in the United States and now moves as much as sixty-five to seventy-five million tons a year. Steel and electric utility companies are the principal domestic users of this coal, while Japan and Western Europe receive most of the export coal. These foreign buyers get primarily high quality metallurgical coal, which totalled about twenty-five million tons in 1975, via N&W rails. Likewise, the Norfolk and Western handles a wide variety of commodities. In addition to coal, the principal revenue items are autos, automotive parts, primary steel products, grain, furniture, chemicals, forest products, and glass, stone and clay products. Movement of this torrent of tonnage entailed some 1,469 diesel electric locomotives and about 92,863 freight cars of all types in 1978.

The dynamic Norfolk and Western Railway Company has changed with the times to provide a better transportation system. Its once home-built steam locomotives were recognized as unsurpassed in quality and performance. The men who worked with these engines swore that they were "the finest steam engines ever built" and could cite ample reasons why. The N&W is now powered by a modern fleet of all-purpose diesels that are both efficient and dependable. Furthermore, the expanded N&W has even shortened its abbreviation to simply "NW." These physical changes are quite obvious.

Yet some things never change or else change only very slowly. A lasting attribute that has not changed on the new NW is the pride and spirit that has perpetuated itself over the years. Memories of a glorious past fade slowly. A winning attitude tempered by necessary changes for the better goes a long way in maintaining a successful enterprise.

May U.S. railroading forever be wed to free enterprise, the system under which railroad men of vision can continue to accomplish their dreams! As long as private railroads exist, the NW spirit seems certain to be here.

N&W locomotives, like any machines, were not infallible, for they had their peculiarities and idiosyncracies; yet, engineers and firemen could coax every possible pound of work from them. To N&W enginemen, these locomotives were the "finest steam engines ever built!" *Courtesy N&W.*

The rough counterpart to the steam era A and Y6 is this modern EMD SD 40-2. These big, dependable six-axle diesels are the mainstay for coal train operations in the mountains and the flat country. Rated at 3,000 horsepower, the SD 40-2 weighs 390,000 pounds and develops 90,500 pounds continuous tractive effort. *Courtesy N&W.*

Appendix

Locomotive Class Statistical Data

			2-8-0 DATA		
Class	G1	B	W1	W2	W6 *
Road Numbers	See Text	61-70	See Text	See Text	See Text
Builder	Baldwin	Baldwin	See Text	See Text	See Text
Built	1897	See Text	1898-1901	See Text	See Text
Cylinders	20"x24"	See Text	21"x30"	21"x30"	21"x30"
Boiler Pressure	180	200	200	200	200
Tractive Effort	29,376	See Text	40,163	40,163	40,163
Grate Area, sq.ft.	31	35	32.6	50.2	32.6
Heating Surface	1812	2796	2415	2300	2429
Superheater Surface	-	-	-	-	-
Valve Gear	Stephenson	See Text	Stephenson	See Text	Stephenson
Superheater		None all classes			
Feedwater Heater		" " "			
Stoker		" " "			
Tender Capacity:					
Coal, tons	13.8	8.5	9.6	14	2
Water, gals	6,000	4,000	5,000	9,000	2,000
Drivers	50"	56"	56"	56"	56"
Rigid Wheel Base	14'0"	15'6"	15'6"	15'6"	15'6"
Total Wheel Base	48'6"	51'8"	50'4"	55'11"	15'6"
Length over Couplers	57'0"	60'4"	59'0"	64'10"	42'0"
Weights: lbs.					
On Driving Wheels	107,000	165,585	147,300	158,600	186,900
On Front Truck	13,785	20,100	18,200	17,250	-
Total Engine	120,785	185,685	165,500	175,850	186,900
Engine & Tender	237,415	270,365	263,800	343,350	-

*0-8-0T

4-8-0 DATA

	M	M2,M2c	Switcher #
Class	M	M2,M2c	Switcher #
Road Numbers	375-499	1100-1160	1100
Builder	See Text	See Text	Roanoke
Built	1906-07	1910-12	1947
Cylinders	21"x30"	24"x30"	24"x30"
Boiler Pressure	200	200	200
Tractive Effort	40,163	52,457	52,457
Grate Area, sq.ft.	45	45	45
Heating Surface	2797	3586	3215
Superheater Surface	-	765	-
Valve Gear	Baker *	See Text	Walschaert
Superheater	See Text	Type A	None
Feedwater Heater	None	See Text	None
Stoker	None	Various	Stand.HT-1
Tender Capacity:			
Coal, tons	20	20	20
Water, gals	12,000	15,000	11,000
Drivers	56"	56"	56"
Rigid Wheel Base	15'6"	16'0"	16'0"
Total Wheel Base	65'10"	73'9"	70'0"
Length over Couplers	75'0"	83'4"	81'3"
Weights: lbs.			
On Driving Wheels	169,800	239,530	239,530
On Front Truck	36,400	40,000	40,000
Total Engine	206,200	279,530	279,530
Engine & Tender	431,700	550,730	491,530

*Originally Stephenson v.g.

#Experimental switcher rebuilt from M2 1100. All data as rebuilt.

```
                         4-6-0 DATA


Class                        V1                  A
Road Numbers             950-966 *             86-90
Builder                  See Text             Baldwin
Built                    1900-02              1902-04

Cylinders                19½"x28"             20"x28"
Boiler Pressure            200                  200
Tractive Effort          29,193               28,000
Grate Area, sq.ft.         32.6                 32.6
Heating Surface           2403                 2559
Superheater Surface         -                    -

Valve Gear               Baker            Stephenson #
Superheater              None                 None
Feedwater Heater         None                 None
Stoker                   None                 None
Tender Capacity:
    Coal, tons             14                   9.7
    Water, gals          9,000                5,000

Drivers                    62"                  68"
Rigid Wheel Base         12'6"               13'1½"
Total Wheel Base         54'11"               50'1"
Length over Couplers     63'5"                58'8"
Weights: lbs.
    On Driving Wheels   128,025              134,300
    On Front Truck       34,325               32,000
    Total Engine        162,350              166,300
    Engine & Tender     329,850              264,600

         *Nos 950-961      #Later Baker v.g.
          originally V1
```

```
                    4-4-2 DATA


Class                           J
Road Numbers            600-606
Builder                 Baldwin
Built                   1903-04

Cylinders               19"x28"
Boiler Pressure             200
Tractive Effort          21,750
Grate Area, sq,ft.           45
Heating Surface            2889
Superheater Surface           -

Valve Gear            Stephenson *
Superheater                None
Feedwater Heater           None
Stoker                     None
Tender Capacity:
    Coal, tons             13.8
    Water, gals           6,000

Drivers                     79"
Rigid Wheel Base          6'10"
Total Wheel Base         53'10"
Length over Couplers      63'0"
Weights: lbs.
    On Driving Wheels    85,340
    On Front Truck       39,480
    On Back Truck        42,880
    Total Engine        167,700
    Engine & Tender     284,300

        * Later Baker v.g.
```

```
                          4-6-2 DATA


Class                       E,E1         E2a,E2b             E3
Road Numbers              580-599        543-579         500-504
Builder                  See Text       See Text         Baldwin
Built                     1905-07        1910-14            1913

Cylinders                20"x28"        22½"x28"         26"x26"
Boiler Pressure              200            200              205
Tractive Effort           28,000         34,425           38,283
Grate Area, sq.ft.            45             45             55.3
Heating Surface             3463           3320             3691
Superheater Surface            -            730              791

Valve Gear               See Text          Baker       Walschaert
Superheater                 None         Type A           Type A
Feedwater Heater            None           None             None
Stoker                      None       Stand. HT        Stand. HT
Tender Capacity:
    Coal, tons              13.8             20               20
    Water, gals            6,000         15,000           15,000

Drivers                      68"            70"              80"
Rigid Wheel Base          12'0"          12'6"           13'10"
Total Wheel Base         57'10"          76'7"           78'11"
Length over Couplers      66'6"          86'2"            88'5"
Weights: lbs.
    On Driving Wheels    130,618        168,200          199,100
    On Front Truck        31,329         39,600           41,400
    On Back Truck         34,306         49,150           57,500
    Total Engine         196,253        256,950          298,000
    Engine & Tender      312,853        528,150          569,200
```

319

4-8-2 DATA

Class	K1	K2,K2a *	K3
Road Numbers	100-115	116-137	200-209
Builder	Roanoke	See Text	Roanoke
Built	1916-17	1919-23	1926
Cylinders	29"x28"	28"x30"	28"x30"
Boiler Pressure	220	220	225
Tractive Effort	62,920	63,800	68,880
Grate Area, sq.ft.	80.3	76.3	84.1
Heating Surface	3857	4439	4834
Superheater Surface	882	1085	1380
Valve Gear	Baker	Baker	Baker
Superheater	Type A	Type A	Type A
Feedwater Heater	Worth. 4BL	Worth. 4BL	Worth. 4BL
Stoker	Various	Stand. HT	Duplex
Tender Capacity:			
Coal, tons	26	30	23
Water, gals	18,000	22,000	16,000
Drivers	70	70	63
Rigid Wheel Base	18'9"	18'3"	16'9"
Total Wheel Base	84'2"	87'11"	83'5"
Length over Couplers	94'3"	100'11"	93'1"
Weights: lbs.			
On Driving Wheels	240,700	248,150	275,400
On Front Truck	53,030	52,620	56,917
On Back Truck	60,170	58,690	69,583
Total Engine	353,900	359,460	401,900
Engine & Tender	668,240	738,060	688,433

*Streamlined

```
                        2-6-6-2 DATA


Class                    Z1,Z1a            Z1b *           Z2 *
Road Numbers            1300-1489         Various          1399
Builder                 See Text          See Text        Roanoke
Built                   1912-18           1927-31          1928

Cylinders              22"&35"x32"       22"&35"x32"     (4)22"x32"
Boiler Pressure             200 #             225            225
T.E. Simple              86,250            90,996         93,342
T.E. Compound            71,875            75,830             -
Grate Area, sq.ft.         72.2              72.2           72.2
Heating Surface           4629              4629           5048
Superheater Surface        971               971            971

Valve Gear              See Text           Baker          Baker
Superheater             Type A            Type A         Type A
Feedwater Heater          None         Worth. 4¼BL     Worth. 4¼BL
Stoker                  Various           Various         Street
Tender Capacity:
    Coal, tons             20                26             23
    Water, gals         15,000            18,000         16,000

Drivers                  56½" #             57"            56½"
Rigid Wheel Bases        10'0"             10'0"          10'0"
Total Wheel Base         90'10"            94'7"          90'10"
Length over Couplers    100'5"            104'6"         100'5"
Weights: lbs.
    On Driving Wheels   354,500           376,581        377,825
    On Front Truck       23,000            20,298         20,780
    On Back Truck        49,500            43,121         42,395
    Total Engine        427,000           440,000        441,000
    Engine & Tender     698,200           752,700        727,500

        *Built from Z1a's.      # BP,TE & Drivers same
                                  as Z1b's later.
```

	2-8-8-2 DATA			
Class	X1 *	Y1	Y2a	Y3,Y3a
Road Numbers	990-994	995-999	1700-1730	2000-2079
Builder	Schenectady	Baldwin	See Text	See Text
Built	1910	1910	1918-24	1919-23
Cylinders	24½"&39"x30"	24½"&39"x30"	25"&39"x32"	25"&39"x32"
Boiler Pressure	200 **	200	270	270
T.E. Simple	83,615	83,615	139,454	136,985
T.E. Compound	66,892	66,892	116,212	114,154
Grate Area, sq.ft.	75	75	96	96.3
Heating Surface	5388	5894	6349	5753
Superheater	-	-	1510	1582
Valve Gear	Walschaert	Walschaert	Baker	Baker
Superheater	See Text	None	Type A	Type A
Feedwater Heater	None	See Text	None	Worth. 4½BL
Stoker	None	None	Duplex	Duplex
Tender Capacity:				
Coal, tons	14	14	23	26
Water, gals	9,000	9,000	16,000	18,000
Drivers	56"	56"	57"	58"
Rigid Wheel Bases	15'6"	15'6"	15'6"	15'9"
Total Wheel Base	72'10"	83'3"	97'3"	102'1"
Length over Couplers	89'0"	92'8"	106'11"	111'8"
Weights: lbs.				
On Driving Wheels	376,800	370,000	472,000	485,200
On Front Truck	-	15,000	26,500	28,400
On Back Truck	-	15,000	27,500	25,400
Total Engine	376,800	400,000	526,000	539,000
Engine & Tender	544,300	567,500	812,533	851,700

*0-8-8-0   **Later BP 230# with T.E.   #Y5 as built
                    S-108,211 & C-90,176

	Y4	Y5 #
	2080-2089	2090-2109
	Richmond	Roanoke
	1927	1930-32
	25"&39"x32"	25"&39"x32"
	270	300
	136,985	152,206
	114,154	126,838
	96.3	106.2
	5866	5843 ##
	1582	1582 ##
	Baker	Baker
	Type A	Type A ##
	Worth. 4½BL	Worth. 4½BL
	Stand. HT	Stand. Mod B
	27	26
	24,000	22,000
	58"	58"
	15'9"	15'9"
	104'3"	102'9"
	114'11"	114'0"
	508,500	522,850
	31,500	32,200
	27,000	27,850
	567,000	582,900
	1,002,500	961,500

##Heating surfaces varied.
2094 had Type E heater.

```
                    2-6-6-4 DATA


Class                          A  *              A
Road Numbers            1200-1209          1210-1242
Builder                    Roanoke            Roanoke
Built                      1936-37            1943-50

Cylinders              (4)24"x30"         (4)24"x30"
Boiler Pressure              275                300
Tractive Effort          104,500            114,000
Grate Area, sq.ft.           122                122
Heating Surface             6650               6639
Superheater                 2703               2703

Valve Gear                 Baker              Baker
Superheater               Type E             Type E
Feedwater Heater     Worth. 6-SA        Worth. 6-SA
Stoker             Stand. Mod B        Stand. HT
Tender Capacity:
    Coal, tons               26                 30
    Water, gals          22,000             22,000

Drivers                      70"                70"
Rigid Wheel Bases          12'4"              12'4"
Total Wheel Base          108'4"             108'4"
Length over Couplers      120'8"             121'10"
Weights: lbs.
    On Driving Wheels    430,100            432,350
    On Front Truck        30,300             30,480
    On Back Truck        109,600            110,170
    Total Engine         570,000            573,000
    Engine & Tender      948,600            951,600

Roller Bearings:  All engine & tender axles

        *As built. Later 1200-1209 data same
         as 1210-1242 except stoker and
         heating surface remained same
```

```
                        MODERN 2-8-8-2 DATA


Class                        Y5 *          Y6            Y6a           Y6b
Road Numbers           2101-2119     2120-2154     2155-2170     2171-2200
Builder                   Roanoke       Roanoke       Roanoke       Roanoke
Built                     1940-41 *     1936-40          1942       1948-52

Cylinders                            25"&39"x32"  all   classes
Boiler Pressure                        300 psi     "       "
T.E. Simple                            152,206     "       "
T.E. Compound                          126,838     "       "
Grate Area, sq.ft.                     106.2       "       "
Heating Surface            5822 **       5647         5647          4915
Superheater Surface        1582 ##       1775         1775          1478

Valve Gear                              Baker    all   classes
Superheater                             Type A      "       "
Feedwater Heater       Worth. 4½BL   Worth. 4½BL  Worth.4½BL-2   Worth. 6-SA
Stoker                 Stand. HT     Various      Stand. HT     Stand. HT
Tender Capacity:
   Coal, tons                          30 tons   all   classes
   Water, gals                       22,000 gals    "       "

Drivers                                 58"      all   classes
Rigid Wheel Bases                       15'9"       "       "
Total Wheel Base       102'9"          103'9"       103'9"        103'9"
Length over Couplers   114'0"          114'11"      114'11"       114'11"
Weights: lbs.     #
   On Driving Wheels   522,850         522,850      522,850       548,500
   On Front Truck       32,200          32,200       32,200        34,640
   On Back Truck        27,850          27,850       27,850        28,380
   Total Engine        582,900         582,900      582,900       611,520
   Engine & Tender     961,500         961,500      961,500       990,100
Roller Bearings:
   Engine Axles            Yes            Yes           Yes          Yes
   Tender Axles             No            Yes            No          Yes

     *Modernized       **5252 for 2110; 5021 for 2114     #Later Y5,Y6,Y6a Wt
                       ##1731 for 2110; 1320 for 2114      similar to Y6b
```

```
                    4-8-4 DATA


Class                             J
Road Numbers                600-613
Builder                     Roanoke
Built                       1941-50

Cylinders                   27"x32"
Boiler Pressure                 300
Tractive Effort              80,000
Grate Area, sq.ft.            107.7
Heating Surface                5271
Superheater                    2177

Valve Gear                    Baker
Superheater                  Type E
Feedwater Heater       Worth. 6-SA
Stoker                   Stand. HT
Tender Capacity:
    Coal, tons                   35
    Water, gals              20,000

Drivers                         70"
Rigid Wheel Base             18'9"
Total Wheel Base             95'5"
Length over Couplers        109'3"
Weights: lbs.
    On Driving Wheels       288,000
    On Front Truck          101,600
    On Back Truck           104,400
    Total Engine            494,000
    Engine & Tender         872,600

Roller Bearings:  All engine &
                  tender axles
```

```
                      0-8-0 DATA


Class                           S1              S1a
Road Numbers                 255-284          200-244
Builder                      Baldwin          Roanoke
Built                           1948          1951-53

Cylinders                    25"x28"          25"x28"
Boiler Pressure                  220              220
Tractive Effort               62,932           62,932
Grate Area, sq.ft.              46.9             46.9
Heating Surface               2600 *            2570
Superheater Surface              637              637

Valve Gear                     Baker            Baker
Superheater                   Type A           Type A
Feedwater Heater                None             None
Stoker                          None             None
Tender Capacity:
    Coal, tons                    15               15
    Water, gals                9,100           13,000

Drivers                          52"              52"
Rigid Wheel Base              15'0"            15'0"
Total Wheel Base              54'1"            59'11"
Length over Couplers         71'2"            77'1"
Weights: lbs.
    On Driving Wheels        247,000          247,000
    Total Engine             247,000          247,000
    Engine & Tender          421,566          459,270

                   *270-284 had same heating
                    surface area as S1a
```

```
                            ELECTRICS DATA


Class                                 LC1              LC2         EL-2B          EL-C
Road Numbers                     2500-2511        2512-2515       221-228        230-241
Builder                         BLW+W'house      ALCO+W'house          GE             GE
Built                              1914-15          1924-25          1948        1956-57

Type                   2-4-4-2+2-4-4-2      2-8-2+2-8-2    2(B-B+B-B)            C-C
Motors                           8-3 Phase        4-3 Phase           16              6
Gear Ratio                          85:18           100:21        70:17          74:18
Max Speed, mph                         28               28           50             65
Starting Tractive Effort          132,000          185,000      260,000         99,420
Continuous T.E.                    66,000           90,000      162,000         79,500
    @ __ mph                           14               14        15.75          15.75
Ratio of Adhesion                   24.4%            30.8%        25.1%            25%

Traction Wheels                       62"              62"          42"            40"
Rigid Wheel Bases                  11'0"            16'6"         9'0"          13'0"
Total Wheel Base                  94'10"            83'0"      133'10"         52'10"
Length over Couplers             105'8"            97'2"      150'8"          69'6"
Weights, lbs.
    On Traction Wheels            540,000          600,000    1,033,832        394,000
    Total Engine                  600,000          832,000    1,033,832        394,000
Roller Bearings:                     None             None          Yes            Yes

                                           VGN Numbers:     See Text        130-141
```

```
                        6-6-6-6 DATA


Class                    Steam Turbine Electric
Road Number                               2300
Builder            Baldwin-Lima-Hamilton Corp
Built                                     1954

Starting Tractive Effort               175,000
Continuous T.E. @ 9 mph                144,000
Rated HP @ Turbine Shaft                 4,500
Motors                        (12)Westinghouse
Gear Ratio                               63:15
Max Speed, mph                              60

Boiler          Babcock & Wilcox Water Tube Type
Steam Pressure                         600 psi
Steam Temperature                       900°F
Grate Area, sq.ft.                          67
Stoker                       Standard Type BK
Turbine, 2 Generators           Westinghouse
Boiler Controls                       Bailey
Feedwater Pump      Ingersoll-Rand & Coffin

Coal Capacity                        20 tons
Water Capacity              22,000 gallons
Water Softener                      Zeolite

Wheels                                  42"
Roller Bearings                   All Axles
Rigid Wheel Bases                   13'0"
Total Wheel Base                   147'4"
Length over Couplers               161'2"
Weights: lbs.
    Locomotive (All on drivers)      818,000
    Locomotive & Tender            1,182,000
```

```
                            DIESELS DATA

Class                        GP-9          GP-9  *      GP-18         GP-30
Road Numbers        620-699,710-914        500-521      915-962       522-565
Builder                       EMD           EMD          EMD           EMD
Built                        1955-59       1957-58      1959-61       1962

Horsepower                    1750          1750         1800          2250
Gear Ratio                   62:15         60:17        62:15         62:15
Max Speed, mph                 65            78           65            71
Max Tractive Effort          61,750        64,180       61,750        65,000
Max Continuous               44,800        38,200       46,000        50,000
     T.E. @ __ mph             12            14           12            12
Ratio of Adhesion Cont.      18.15%        14.9%        18.61%        19.2%

Cab Controls                  Dual          Dual         Dual          Dual
MU Control                    Yes           Yes          Yes           Yes
Hump Control                  No          3 Units        No            No
Dynamic Braking            All Units     All Units    All Units     All Units
Diesel Engine
     Model                    567C          567C         567D1         567D3
     No. of Cylinders          16            16           16            16

Wheels                        40"           40"          40"           40"
Total Wheel Base             40'0"         40'0"        40'0"         41'0"
Length over Couplers         56'2"         56'2"        56'2"         56'2"
Weight: lbs.
     Fully Loaded            247,000       256,720      247,000       260,000
Roller Bearings:          Journal bearings applied to all classes

                          *GP-9's with steam generators    **407-412 RS-36 blt
                           for passenger service. Nos        1962. RS-11's blt
                           500-505 originally 762-767.       1956-61.
                           See text.
```

GP-35	RS-3	RS-11,RS-36 **	T-6	H16-44 #	H24-66
200-239	300-307	308-412	10-49	See Text	150-74
EMD	ALCO	ALCO	ALCO	F-M	F-M
1963-64	1955-56	1956-62	1959	1954-57	1954-57
2500	1600	1800	1000	1600	2400
62:15	74:18	74:18	74:18	74:18	74:18
71	65	65	60	66	66
63,000	61,750	61,700	60,000	65,550	98,625 ##
51,400	53,000	53,000	57,000	53,000	79,500
12	8	10	4½	8.8	8.6
19.8%	21.5%	21.5%	23.7%	20.2%	20.15% ##
Dual	Dual	Dual	Dual	Single	Single
Yes	Yes	Yes	Yes	Yes	Yes
No	No	No	Yes	Yes	Yes
All Units	All Units	All Units	None	17 Units	All Units
567D3A	244	251	251	38D8 1/8	38D8 1/8
16	12	12	6	8	12
40"	40"	40"	40"	40"	40"
41'0"	39'4"	40'4"	30'0"	40'4"	49'4"
56'2"	57'0"	57'0"	45'8"	55'0"	66'0"
260,000	247,000	247,000	239,950	262,200	394,500 ##
			VGN Numbers:	See Text	50-74

#Minor variations between
H16-44 locomotives.
##Nos 169-174 Wt. 396,000#,TE 99,150#
with Cont. Ratio of Adhesion 20.05%

A Selective List of
Sources Consulted

1. Data compiled by Arthur M. Bixby, Sr.
2. Interview with George P. Bowman.
3. Interview with Walter Budwell.
4. Interview with John A. Gearhart.
5. Interview with Paul C. Housman.
6. Interview with George H. Kelch.
7. Interview with Gurdon P. McGavock.
8. Interview with and records of Frank C. Noel.
9. Interview with Charles S. Patton.
10. Interview with and records of Robert M. Pilcher.
11. Interview with and records of Clarence E. Pond.
12. Interview with Francis D. "Bud" Ripley.
13. Interview with and records of William T. Ross.
14. Interview with and records of Hobart L. Scott, Jr.
15. Interview with Howard G. Stultz and N. H. "Hub" Tanner.
16. N&W Booklet, *Powered by People*, January 1958.
17. "Our Railroad in 1955," *N&W Magazine*, vol. 34, no. 4, April 1956, p. 179.
18. "Better Service Powerhouse," *N&W Magazine*, vol. 34, no. 4, April 1956, pp. 186-87, 197.
19. "Improvements Speed War Traffic," *N&W Magazine*, vol. 22, no. 1, January 1944, p. 2.
20. "Our Railroad in 1951," *N&W Magazine*, vol. 30, no. 5, May 1952, p. 278.
21. "The Morning After Steam," *Trains*, vol. 19, no. 9, September 1959, pp. 27-32.
22. "The Story of Our Shops," *N&W Magazine*s, vol. 21, no. 10 and vol. 22, nos. 1 & 2 (Oct. 1943, Jan. and Feb. 1944).
23. "J. A. Doornberger Passes," *N&W Magazine*, vol. 31, no. 9, September 1953, p. 503.
24. "New Facilities for Better Service," *N&W Magazine*, vol. 25, no. 10, October 1947, p. 540.
25. "Our Modern Workhorses . . . ," *N&W Magazine*, vol. 29, no. 9, September 1951, p. 530.
26. "Your Better Service Conference," *N&W Magazine*, vol. 29, no. 5, May 1951, p. 288.
27. *The Steam Locomotive in America*, A. W. Bruce, W. W. Norton & Co., 1952, pp. 77-78, 185.
28. "Railroaders Gather for Better Service," *N&W Magazine*, vol. 30, no. 4, April 1952, p. 196.
29. "Switcher Locomotive Improved," *N&W Magazine*, vol. 25, no. 5, May 1947, p. 232.
30. "Improved Switching Locomotive Completed," *N&W Magazine*, vol. 26, no. 10, October 1948, p. 550.
31. "Old Days on the Radford Division," *N&W Magazine*, vol. 22, no. 1, January 1944, p. 10.
32. *Norfolk and Western Steam (Last 25 Years)*, R. Rosenberg and E. H. Archer, Quadrant Press, Inc., 1973, p. 22.
33. *Model Railroader*, vol. 41, no. 11, November 1975, p. 53.

34. "Heavy Power and Larger Tenders Change Operating Conditions," *N&W Magazine*, vol. 2, no. 1, January 1924, p. 19.

35. "Mountain-type Locomotives are Modernized," *N&W Magazine*, vol. 23, no. 10, October 1945, p. 442.

36. "Development of Steam Locomotives on the N&W," Speech by C. E. Pond, prepared November 7, 1950.

37. *Steam Locomotive Diagrams of the Chesapeake & Ohio Railroad*, edited and published by Alvin F. Staufer, Standard Printing and Publishing Co., Carrolton, Ohio, p. 50.

38. *The American Steam Locomotive*, vol. 1, Evolution, F. M. Swengel, Midwest Rail Publications, Inc., 1967, p. 124.

39. "Our New Class Y2a Locomotives," *N&W Magazine*, vol. 2, no. 5, May 1924, pp. 16-17.

40. "N&W Locomotive has Unique Improvements," *N&W Magazine*, vol. 27, no. 12, December 1949, p. 721.

41. "New Passenger Locomotives," *N&W Magazine*, vol. 21, no. 11, November 1943, p. 547.

42. "1943 A Record of Service," *N&W Magazine*, vol. 22, no. 2, February 1944, p. 51.

43. *N&W Magazine*, vol. 27, no. 9, September 1949, p. 530.

44. *C&O Power;* Shuster, Huddleston and Staufer; Carrollton Standard Printing Co., 1965, p. 16.

45. "A Railroader's Story," *N&W Magazine*, vol. 23, no. 10, October 1945, p. 481.

46. *The Virginian Railway,* H. Reid, Kalmbach Publishing Co., 1961, pp. 110-12, 121-22, 128-29, 176-78, 196-97.

47. "Stuart Saunders and His Moneymaking Machine," *Trains,* vol. 23, no. 4, February 1963, pp. 27-32.

48. *Pennsy Power*, A. F. Staufer, author & publisher, 1962, p. 240.

49. "The Gas Turbine Locomotive," *N&W Magazine*, vol. 24, no. 20, October 1946, pp. 470-71.